SOCIOLOGY IN MEDICINE

SOCIOLOGY IN MEDICINE

**R. K. Jones
and P. A. Jones**

A HALSTED PRESS BOOK

JOHN WILEY & SONS
New York

Published in the U.S.A.
by Halsted Press, a Division of
John Wiley & Sons, Inc.
New York

Library of Congress Cataloging in Publication Data

Jones, R. Kenneth
Sociology in medicine

  'A Halsted Press Book'
  Bibliography: p.
  Includes index.
  1. Social medicine. 2. Sociology. I. Jones,
  Patricia A., joint author. II. Title. (DNLM:
  1. Social Medicine. WA30 J78s)

RA418.J66 1975   362.1   75-11723
ISBN 0-470-44936-5

Printed and bound in Great Britain.

EDITORS' FOREWORD

The scope of this series has increased since it was first established, and it now serves a wide range of medical, nursing and ancillary professions, in line with the present trend towards the belief that all who care for patients in a clinical context have an increasing amount in common.

The texts are carefully prepared and organized so that they may be readily kept up to date as the rapid developments of medical science demand. The series already includes many popular books on various aspects of medical and nursing care, and reflects the increased emphasis on community care.

The increasing specialization in the medical profession is fully appreciated and the books are often written by Physicians or Surgeons in conjunction with specialist nurses. For this reason, they will not only cover the syllabus of training of the General Nursing Council, but will be designed to meet the needs of those undertaking training controlled by the Joint Board of Clinical Studies set up in 1970.

INTRODUCTION

Sociology is the study of the formulation and perpetuation of human relationships, both ordered and disordered, and of social systems and institutions into which mankind is born and which exist after them.

Medical and para-medical fields in Britain are beginning to realize that sociology offers considerable insight into relationships with patients, and also gives some understanding of how they can operate more effectively in their respective tasks. Recent work in the social sciences suggests that some health disorders may be due to strain or breakdown in the actual social conditions from which the patient comes. Nurses in particular have always been concerned with more than the medical care of their patients, and have perhaps felt or thought many of the things to which sociology gives articulation.

The importance of sociological factors in the diagnosis of organic illness as well as in the treatment is recognized in the writing of this book, which is written in the firm belief that the quality of care and the depth of the nurse–patient relationship will be considerably enhanced by a basic introduction to the subject of sociology.

This book has been written for nurses in general training, and also for those in training for specialized nursing roles. It will also be of use to medical students as an introductory text, and for those enrolled on the new nursing degrees. Others whose work it is to care for people in some way, for example social workers, may find it of some use.

There is a glossary included of all essential concepts, and some suggestions for further reading.

Kenneth Jones
Patricia Jones

7

CONTENTS

I

SOCIOLOGY AND ITS RELEVANCE FOR MEDICINE

WHAT SOCIOLOGY IS

The origins of sociology can be traced even further back in time than to the French philosopher who gave the subject its name—Auguste Comte, usually known as the 'father of sociology', who lived and worked in the first half of the nineteenth century. Some have seen vestiges of the discipline in the Greek and Roman philosophers and also in the Schoolmen of the Middle Ages. Nevertheless it did not really gain respectability until the present century, when both American and European universities established departments. In Britain, following the pioneer work of Booth and Rowntree into the conditions of poverty at the turn of this century, sociology has developed a strongly empirical slant, coupled with a strong theoretical inheritance from social anthropology.

It is never easy, useful or wise to attempt a one-sentence definition of any complex subject. There are many such definitions in existence, most of them different, and although there is this difference, nevertheless reputable sociologists are in general agreement about the content of these definitions. In other words, requests for definitions of medical and para-medical fields might result in different verbal formulations, but for both these and sociology there would be quite wide general agreement as to the field of competence and expertise of these areas. As a subject, sociology is concerned with the study of human relationships, and more specifically the formulation and perpetuation of these relationships, and of the individuals who enact them, within the broad context of human society. Sociology seeks to explain how it is that human systems and organizations exist over time in a recognizable and ordered fashion. It also concerns itself with the apparent order of human relationships—and of the concomitant disorder when such occurs. Above all it realizes that even cognitive and affective behaviour, the way we know things and feel things about the world, is socially formed.

No subject can be happily compartmentalized, least of all those in the social sciences. Sociology is closely related to economics, political science, history, social geography, psychology and social anthropology; indeed in the last two subjects it is often very difficult to establish any clear demarcation.

WHAT SOCIOLOGY IS NOT

Sociology is not a kind of practical philanthropy which exists for the sake of helping people. It provides information equally for those who are misanthropic as for those who care deeply about others. Neither is sociology to be confused with either socialism or social work, although it is true to say that the major growth point of the subject was coincidental with the development of the great urban problems which heralded the rise of the latter. Sociology is not necessarily linked with any political stance, such as socialism, nor with a practice in society, but it is an attempt at understanding. Such understanding is available, certainly, to social workers, but it is also available to nurses, soldiers, politicians and advertising men. Sociologists usually regard themselves as value-free, which means not that they themselves have no values but that these values must be eliminated as much as possible from the work that they are doing. It follows that the sociologist is also neither a 'do-gooder' nor social reformer.

Another confusion arises when the sociologist is regarded as a head-counter or statistician; this has been referred to as earthworm sociology. It is true that some sociologists have devoted enormous energy to asking 'how much?' or 'how often?'. Works such as that of the sexologist Kinsey have not helped to eradicate this image. The gathering of data, including statistical data, can often be a vital part of the sociologist's task, but eventually it has to be fitted into a sociological framework and interpreted sociologically if it is to count as sociology.

A further confusion is to regard the sociologist as a scientific methodologist. A number of practitioners have been guilty of using what has been termed outlandish jargon, often obtuse and pseudo-scientific. Lewis Carroll wrote, 'It seems very pretty (Alice said), but it's rather hard to understand'. Because the subject was in its infancy, and in the beginning uncertain of its status, sociologists resorted to using a language that they thought was scientific, covering up the defects of the subject in verbosity. However, all subjects suffer from this to some extent. Sociology can also be extremely lucid. Terminology *is* important for the sociologist simply because his subject matter is familiar. As we shall see later, not only does the sociologist deal with everyday phenomena in a special way, but he also uses as part of his technical vocabulary terms borrowed from day-to-day speech and situations, such as *role, class, community, culture*, and *society*.

Finally, the sociologist is not a detached, aloof and superior being, anxious to gather data about his fellow men and feed such data into a computer system. Above all he is concerned with understanding society through the special 'spectacles' that his subject offers. In recent years some have argued that sociology is weighted, not towards the sciences, but towards the humanities, that it is not concerned with gathering facts nor with establishing causal reasons, but rather that it is a quality of mind that equips its practitioners to utilize information and reasons so that they may better understand themselves and the world around them. This has been called the *sociological imagination*. Through this self-consciousness they experience a revision of values. Others have placed it more in the area of philosophy and history than the sciences. The *verstehen*, or understanding method believes that sociology can make people conscious of facts and situations in the world simply by seeing how or what makes these facts and situations 'tick'.

SOCIOLOGY AS A SCIENCE

Before looking at the scientific nature of sociology we must look at the distinguishing characteristics that go towards calling a subject a science. The word *science* comes from the Latin *scientia*, meaning knowledge, and although science is a certain type of knowledge, a more profitable way of viewing it would be as a way of looking at the world, or a way of thinking. The main method of scientific activity is the *hypothetico-deductive* method, the requirements of which are (a) general expectation, (b) an observation, and (c) a valid deduction. Most scientific observations are made because of some interest or expectation, and often there is no fast line to be drawn between pre-scientific or commonsense expectations and hypothesis. Science is *progressive* in a sense that the arts and humanities are not, so that Greek plays and philosophers, for example, are of interest today in a way in which early Greek science is not of interest to the scientist but only to the scientific historian.

Scientific thinking is essentially *methodological*: it is an orderly arrangement or construction of facts that constitutes science. The scientist is concerned with fact that is observable through the senses and capable of being treated through or by a particular method. Many think that it is the method which determines whether a subject is scientific or not. Any proposition or hypothesis of the natural sciences is dependent on what happens to exist in the external world, and the truth of these depends on what there actually is in the world, and on the use of induction by empirical observation or simple enumeration.

Science, then, seems to be characterized by the following activities: (a) collection of facts following observation; (b) a hypothesis explaining the relationships of the facts to one another; (c) testing the hypothesis, attempting to disprove it; (d) new facts may mean altering the original hypothesis; (e) the emergence of a general rule or law which requires universal agreement. Sciences are sometimes divided into the *exact* (mathematics) and *descriptive* (botany, zoology).

The kinds of questions that science can answer varies from 'Why are tides constant?' to 'Why can we predict eclipses?'. Certain kinds of questions which are called *metaphysical*—for example 'Why is there evil in the world?'—science could not answer, and indeed would not claim to do so. This is partly because we cannot answer such questions by pointing to empirical, or observable, facts which would help us in reaching agreement.

In science we often claim to have discovered something, but the act of discovery itself escapes logical explanation and description. We cannot, in other words, pinpoint the actual process of drawing an inference, and neither are there any rules for discovering something. To have a recipe for discovery would be already to have discovered. Many great scientific discoveries have been inspired guesswork, luck, or pure accident, and intuition plays no small part.

We turn now to considering sociology as a science. Some sociologists would say that the above formal scientific method, that is the stating of the hypothesis, the testing, and the consequent systematic description and classification, ought to be followed by sociologists, although some sociologists—even the majority—would suggest that sociology not only cannot but should not ape the physical sciences. It is often assumed that the logic underlying the social sciences is identical to the one which underlies the natural sciences, and that wherever generalization is possible, so also is science.

However, sociology, because of the infinite variety of the factors involved, is by nature incapable of the exactness possessed by the natural sciences. The difference between human and physical action is not simply one of complexity, and the difference of degree may really be a difference in kind. Only a poet would describe a brick wall as being in pain. The field of human behaviour requires a different framework to that of the natural sciences, and neither can supply the other with its own peculiar conceptual apparatus.

OBJECTIVITY AND PREDICTION

Sociologists, unlike medical scientists or physicists, for example, are involved in the stream of life of the very phenomena that they are studying. They are personally orientated to families, political systems, religion, and so on. They themselves have been, or are, or know others who are, deeply involved in many of the areas they study. Sociologists are constantly confronted by 'instant experts' on delinquency, new towns, the decline of institutionalized religion and so on. Some areas, such as race relations and religious behaviour, are more prone to this than others. The sociologist must, therefore, leave aside his personal views and prejudices, inasmuch as they are likely to affect the outcome of his research, and refrain from making moral judgements other than in terms of the beliefs of a given society. In practice it is as difficult for a sociologist to stand apart from his subject matter as it is for a doctor or nurse to assume the role of complete objectivity in dealing with certain patients.

Finally, a word about prediction in sociology. We can with relative certainty predict events in the natural sciences. But by the very nature of the subject matter we are unable to predict events in the field of social behaviour. If one's prediction of someone's behaviour is not fulfilled, this does not mean necessarily that one predicted incorrectly (as it would in the natural science analogy, in terms of inadequate theory, etc.) but possibly that this someone whose behaviour was predicted acted otherwise than the way it was predicted. That is, human beings are complex and also to a large extent free in their choice of actions. In the sense in which we use the word in the natural sciences there is no prediction in social behaviour. Even using the term loosely, sociology has not had the same success with predictions as other subjects. This is partly because of the newness of the subject but also because of meaning. That is, individuals are not simply creatures of instinct but interpret their situations. This factor means that different individuals interpret a situation along totally different lines. For example, a Buddhist places a different meaning on a symbol of a cross than a Christian. There are many *variables* in human actions of which the sociologist may have incomplete knowledge, and to predict or forecast with accuracy entails a reasonably complete knowledge of such variables.

THE BIRTH OF SOCIOLOGY AND ITS CONTEXT

Some insight into the nature of sociology might be gained from looking at the context in which it first appeared as a scientific discipline. Comte thought of the subject as studying social phenomena in the same spirit as physical phenomena were studied. Others later felt that there were general laws of social action which were there to be discovered. The world at that time was in the grip of the Industrial Revolution which brought with it the appropriate advance in science and technology. It was not to be wondered that the early sociologists saw the subject as lying along the path of science for this was considered to be the ideal path, although this does not mean that they believed social behaviour followed laws as inexorably as did scientific phenomena.

SOME SUGGESTIONS AS TO WHY SOCIOLOGY IS NOT A SCIENCE

We have already mentioned that what the sociologist is expected to be objective about is by its nature more infinitely variable than the subject matter of the physical sciences. What predictability we have is *general* rather than *individual*; that is, we can say that people from a certain category tend to vote Conservative, but the individual is less predictable. Although sociology makes use of experimental method, a pure scientist would regard this as pseudo-experimental. Experiments in the social sciences, unlike those in the natural sciences, are very rarely repeated, or even capable of exact repetition.

There are two main differences between the subject matter of the physical sciences and the social world. We are within the social world and interpret it intelligently only because we project onto it our own experience. The physical world of chemical substances, brain tissues, neutrons, and protons do not affect us in the same way. The second main difference is that the movements of the physical world depend on a mechanical causality while movements of social phenomena are to be understood in terms of purpose and value and meaning. It is also to some extent true that human events are unique and incapable of repetitions.

Sociology becomes, therefore, something which is evaluative, critical and sympathetic. The practitioner becomes a professional pryer. It is in its methodology and in its intentions that sociology *can* claim to be scientific. In the former because it is concerned with objective empirical facts, and in the latter because it aims at exact description and explanation.

It is not a necessary part of the concept of sociology that it must be of use nor that it should be *for* something. Sociology is not to be defined in terms of uses. It is not social reform; it is not doing something for the community; it is not helping industry; it is not working for any one organization; it is not a body of fact; it is not a purely descriptive discipline. The concept of sociology involves the deliberate conveying of something of value in a manner which is lucid and coherent, and which conveys to the listener a need to strive towards understanding it. It undoubtedly has a practical use; but this is incidental to its real value in enabling the learner to understand the world in which he is an actor.

THE USE AND APPLICATION OF SOCIOLOGY

As an academic discipline, sociology, in common with a great number of other subjects, is of no use as such, being an attempt to understand rather than do. It is nevertheless the case that thousands of sociologists are applying their knowledge to some practical purpose, either in advertising, fighting crime, census studies, the planning of new towns, examining the social origins of disease, and so on. They are extensively used in government agencies and in areas of political decision making. For example, government plans to introduce changes into certain programmes concerning health, income and retirement benefits usually employ sociologists at the blue-print stage. Changes in our national education system are generally brought about after years of research by sociologists into areas such as ability, streaming, occupational choices for school-leavers. Problems in industry, both in its location and efficient functioning, are generally brought to the attention of social scientists.

Sociologists play a major part in providing information on which decisions are taken in areas such as health, the army, the police, regional growth points, the re-organization of local government, and so on. On a smaller scale, they contribute to marriage-guidance counselling, group therapy, the organization of mental hospitals, and to the provision of data on which decisions which affect human relationships are based. Industrial sociologists play a major part in detecting day-to-day weaknesses in the social relationships of large commercial concerns. Only gradually, in this country, has sociology crept into the curriculum of schools, but it is increasingly recognized that in many respects it forms a valuable part of an individual's education. Many occupational training schemes have some element of sociology in them: for example, the training of clergy, the police, the probation officer, health visitors, and management.

In America, sociology has been important in the training of medical and para-medical personnel for some time. In this country, the training of future medical practitioners, either in general practice or the hospital service, has not kept pace with the real requirements of such training, which would adequately reflect the demands of modern industrialized society. General practice is increasingly being called upon to fill the role that was formerly entertained by the Church or the local friendly squire, and indeed deals with 96% of all illness in Britain. But many of the problems with which the GP is confronted with he is completely ill-prepared to deal with, often giving bad advice, or at the best advice no better than that which could be offered by a layman. Often he is unaware of the real nature of voluntary services or of the way in which they could compliment the NHS. More and more patients are expecting a warmth of human relationship in their GP. Very important were the results of a recent survey conducted by the Office of Health Economics, in which doctors listed the following as areas that they felt they should give advice; contraception 93%; other marital problems 83%; upbringing of children 67%; employment problems 51%. This is a further indication that doctors not only regard themselves as authoritative in non-medical matters, but also presumably that it is a reflection of the sort of advice that they *are* in fact asked for. In the 1970s doctor–patient relationships *are* important, but the other major areas in which he gives advice are sexual relationships and marriage, loneliness and old age, and psycho-social disharmony. A sound body of knowledge of the behavioural sciences, built into his training programme, would help the prospective medical practitioner to cope adequately with problems in these areas.

When we turn to the field of nursing, the situation is somewhat different. Nurses are altogether thrown into a situation with patients which involves greater contact over time. They get to know their patients much better than most doctors, and they share the problems of patients in ways that doctors do not. Often patients are nursed constantly for several months on end, and often it is the nursing staff who are with a patient at the last moments of his life. In many ways, therefore, sociology, because it deals with human situations and relationships, can offer much in this area in the way of assistance. A basic grounding in a discipline which deals with the nuances of social class, the development of individuals, the eccentricities of political, religious, and moral beliefs, the peculiarities of sexual and social behaviour, the meanings attributed to illness and death, the differences between the town and country dweller, the behaviour of individuals in small-group (perhaps ward) situations, the division of occupations, the social structure of the modern hospital, combined with a broad picture of trends in the sociology of medicine, will inevitably lead to a better understanding of the patient and finally to a more adequate system of nursing.

It has been necessary in the first part of this chapter to discuss the question of the *kind* of subject and the sort of knowledge that sociology offers. This is because questions arise as to whether sociology is a humanity or science, whether its methodology is scientific, what individuals think they mean by the term, the nature of concepts and models; all this is an important part of sociology and must be broadly understood before tackling some of the main areas of the discipline. It is important that the tools of the trade are mastered before we begin to use them. And unlike practical or technical subjects, questions such as these are encouraged.

Finally in this chapter we will turn to the nature of sociological concepts and take a brief look at some examples.

THE NATURE OF SOCIOLOGICAL CONCEPTS

Concepts are terms of general reference that refer to classes of phenomena, persons and relationships, for example doctors. Sociology is concerned with analysing classes of these phenomena rather than individual instances. Like physicists, sociologists use models which help them to conceptualize in a systematic manner. We have already mentioned that part of the difficulty with sociological concepts is that they need to be handled with extreme care because, firstly, they are already familiar to the layman and, secondly, they are used by sociologists in a highly abstract manner. Sociology uses such terms as *culture, status, role, power, authority, group, function,* which are common words which the sociologist makes into concepts. Such concepts are an *abstraction* of certain features from the total phenomena, and they help us to seek for patterns of *uniformity* in the world around us. They are the general tools of sociological enquiry.

SOME EXAMPLES OF CONCEPTS

STATUS AND ROLE *Status* refers to a fixed position which we occupy in society. It is independent of any occupant or actor. All social *systems*, that is more than two individuals interacting together within a defined boundary, are composed of status positions such as widower, Christian, only child, nurse. The status which an individual occupies determines to a large degree his actions towards others and theirs towards him. A status or position in society, such as husband, may carry with it rights and obligations which are shared by all holders of that status in that society; some, on the other hand, such as the Archbishop of Canterbury, are virtually unique. The manner in which a person behaves, or puts into action the rights and obligations expected of him by a given society, becomes the dynamic aspect of the status position, or the *role*. Any one individual has a number or roles. There is a biological basis for many roles and statuses which we occupy, for example age, sex, race, and social class. These are known as *ascribed* statuses, because the individual has no choice over receiving them. *Achieved* statuses are those that require some positive action on the part of the individual concerned, for example teacher, married woman. The kinds of behaviour expected or associated with these statuses are known as *roles*.

CULTURE *Culture* is the sum total of human action which is neither instinctive nor genetically transmitted. This social transmission is no longer thought of as being common to man, and consequently it is now extended to certain primates. Some would hold culture to refer also to the products or artifacts of human action, such as types of architecture or eating implements. The distinguishing element in culture is that it is learned or socially transmitted. Culture is a collection of behaviour patterns or *norms*, that is standards of behaviour which exist in all societies. Material culture traits are such objects as lipstick, and non-material such things as the 'no-ball' rule in cricket. *Culture complexes* refer to a number of traits which are found together. *Sub-cultures* are smaller, virtually self-contained which exist within a larger culture, for example the Cockney way of life is a smaller part of the cultural life of London. *Cultural lag* and *survival* are often confused, although the former refers to the time which elapses between the introduction of an innovation and its general acceptance, and the latter to an element of culture which has survived long after it has ceased to exist in the general culture. An example is the existence of 'teddy boy' clothes worn by some working-class youths in rural Wales, or the existence of buttons on the sleeves of men's coats. Two final sub-systems of culture which we should mention are *culture shock*, which occurs when one culture is suddenly introduced into another, and *culture conflict*, which occurs when members of one culture conflict with another. An example of the first is when vast populations are forcibly moved to a different environment, such as occurred in parts of Western Europe or even nearer our own doorstep in the movement of inner urban slum dwellers to new towns. Examples of the second are provided by many of the wars that have been fought in Europe, especially religious wars.

SOCIETY *Society*, in sociology, does not refer to a member of the titled nobility but to the totality of social relationships between men, that is, to the group within which men are likely to share with others a life with certain common characteristics. Societies are large and exist over a long period of time, and consequently they are to be differentiated from smaller and more impermanent groups.

COMMUNITY A *community* is a human group living within a limited and defined geographical area in which they carry out most of their day-to-day activities. The basis of community are locality and community sentiment.

CONCLUSIONS

It is common practice in all sociology 'introductions' to begin with a general discussion as to the nature of sociology, and particularly whether, as a discipline, it falls into the humanities or the sciences niche. Various suggestions were aired as to the limitations of sociology as objectified knowledge and also to its predictive ability. A further brief discussion about sociological concepts, together with some examples, clears away the major difficulties associated with the subject, namely its apparent abstractness, and also the peculiar taken-for-grantedness that people associate with the technical vocabulary of the subject. Nevertheless, sociology as a subject has a very great deal to contribute to occupations which are concerned with human relationships to some degree, because it is concerned with understanding such relationships in human society. The basis for such understanding, and a firm grasp of the groundwork, can be achieved by (a) gaining some familiarity with the terminology which is used, (b) learning to think of human behaviour as *patterned*, (c) developing a detached view of phenomena, (d) thinking very often of large-scale enterprises, that is, not the family you have come from or might know, but *the family*—African, American, British, pre-industrial or post-industrial.

SUGGESTIONS FOR FURTHER READING

BERGER, P. (1966). *Invitation to Sociology*, Penguin Books, Harmondsworth.
BREDEMEIR, H. C. and STEPHENSON, R. M. (1962). *The Analysis of Social Systems*, Holt, Rinehart and Winston, New York.
CHINOY, E. (1967). *Society*, 2nd ed., Random House, New York.
COSER, L. A. (1963). *Sociology Through Literature*, Prentice-Hall, Englewood Cliffs, N.J.
COTGROVE, S. (1972). *The Science of Society*, George Allen and Unwin, London.
INKELES, A. (1964). *What is Sociology?*, Prentice-Hall, Englewood Cliffs, N.J.
LUNDBERG, G. A., SCHRAG, C. C. and LARSEN, O. N. (1963). *Sociology*, 3rd ed., Harper and Row, New York.
MILLS, C. W. (1970). *The Sociological Imagination*, Penguin Books, Harmondsworth.
MCKENZIE, J. (ed.) (1968). *The Consumer and the Health Service*, Office of Health Economics, London.

2

THE SOCIAL FORMATION
OF INDIVIDUALS

SOCIALIZATION

The distinguishing characteristic of humans is that their behaviour, apart from that which is instinctual, is learned during the lifetime of the individual. It is this learning which sociologists term *socialization*, the study of which brings together sociology, social anthropology and psychology. Individuals become socialized by interaction with others in society; that is, the sum total of what makes us human is learned from social interaction with others, with certain limits which might be set by heredity. Childhood or initial or primary socialization refers to the learning process which takes place in the earlier years of a person's development, usually the first ten years. Adult or *secondary* socialization refers to the learning through interaction which occurs *after* childhood.

An important part of this process is the physical handling which an individual experiences from his mother or mother surrogate, which is generally termed maternal love or affection. As we shall see later, children reared in institutions tend to be maladaptive both in childhood and in later life.

The distinguishing characteristic of learned behaviour itself is the acquisition of language, which begins with the child's crying. Once he realizes that this alters the behaviour of others towards him because they now give attention he receives a further impetus.

Part of the process of socialization is by imitation. We learn to imitate the behaviour of our parents, siblings, and peer group by adopting a real object for imitating or a symbolic model. The theories of Sigmund Freud suggested that we identify with our fathers, whom we see as rivals to our mothers' affection for us in order to overcome the disturbance we feel about this. By identifying with our fathers (in the case of girls, with their mothers) we can love our mothers with a clear conscience. Developmental identification is simply being dependent on a person, liking him, and developing a positive identification with that person.

Role learning is an attempt to determine how we can later play certain adult roles. The little girl learns to be like her mother, or to play the mother role, just as the little boy learns to be like his father by playing father roles. These roles consequently become part of our total behavioural repertoire.

THE FORMATION AND CHANGING OF ATTITUDES

Attitudes are learned by experience, both direct and indirect. They are states of readiness or predispositions to action, which means that to say that someone has an attitude means that there is a probability of a defined behaviour in a defined situation. In other words attitudes are enduring syndromes of a consistency of response to a given set of objects, animate or inanimate, for example, national flags, negroes or Christian symbols. To say that a man has an aggressive attitude towards negroes does not mean that he is at this moment displaying it, but that given a situation involving negroes he will be liable to display a pattern of behaviour which could be termed aggressive. Attitudes are favourable or unfavourable behaviour tendencies to objects, persons, situations or ideas. They are personal if possessed only by oneself; they are *social* if they are shared by a number of individuals or large groups of people.

Attitudes form an important part of both our everyday lives and our socialization process. The nurse has attitudes towards patients, the customers to the shopkeepers, and the teacher to her pupils. We also have attitudes towards capital punishment, birth control, pre-marital sex, immigration and the National Health Service, these concepts acting as stimuli that produce a variety of feeling that cause us to act and think in particular ways.

It is generally agreed that attitudes are formed and developed as follows: (a) in the first five years of life in the parent–child relationship and in the child-rearing programme; (b) in later life by influence by association between individuals, groups and institutions; (c) throughout life by individual and unique experiences.

Anthropology has brought us a wealth of instances of varying attitudes. Margaret Mead, the American anthropologist, has studied the mountain dwelling Arapesh, the river dwelling Mundugumor, and the lake dwelling Tchambuli, all of whom show an amazing diversity of attitude formation. The New Guinea Tchambuli, for example, have reversed the normally accepted male role in society. The women in this tribe are dominant and aggressive and industrious, while the men are effeminate, graceful and artistic. The women also dominated in both economic and sexual matters, and in the latter take the initiative. In other words, we learn both to be male and female and also the attitudes that go with these two roles. Sexual identity, as we will see later when we look at homosexuality, is not a biologically inevitable phenomenon, but one which we learn through the socialization process. We have built-in expectations of males being aggressive and females submissive.

Studies of working-class communities in Britain have shown the same evidence that our attitudes and frames of reference are firmly rooted in our early experience. One such study showed a matrilocal (living with or near the wife's family) mother-dominated culture. Attitudes were immature and modelled within the culture, which itself produced the response which was the norm of that particular society. Comparative studies of attitudes and personality formation dispel for good the concept of a universal *human nature*. Attitude and personality are dependent to a large extent on child-rearing patterns which are themselves dependent on the society's traditions or culture.

Apart from language, the child has to learn (a) feeding, (b) toilet training (c) sexual expression, (d) aggressive tendencies. Because these are biologically based drives the child has to learn how or what behaviour is expected from him in these situations. Many studies have shown that child-rearing patterns vary from one social class to another, and that working-class mothers bring up their children very differently from middle-class mothers.

With new-born children the personality and its concomitant attitudes become formed by a combination of factors such as human contact, innate genetic characteristics, intelligence, temperament, and innate drives. An important source of attitudes is the attraction to or repulsion from a particular factor. As we proceed from lower to higher animals, the greater is the variety of fear-producing objects. Chimpanzees are frightened by a large number of objects. Similarly, the higher we progress in the animal scale the greater the causes of hostility. Generally, the child learns his attitudes within the system of rewards and punishments.

The child later comes into contact with a society which is outside his immediate home background, and where he is under the influence of a *socio-cultural* process. Society is divided into *primary* and *secondary* groups the former being relatively small in size with <u>all members having face-to-face contact with other members</u>, while the latter are composed of people indirectly connected whose unity is brought about by symbolic means. In a sense, the secondary group is non-existent and entirely dependent for its being on the primary, face-to-face groups of which it is composed. Thus an example of a primary group is a discussion group, and of a secondary group a trade union or professional association. During the adult stage of our lives we are members of a number of primary groups at the same time, just as we are of many secondary groups, and it is in these groups that we acquire our attitudes.

The third way in which attitudes are formed and developed, which we mentioned earlier, is by experiencing an event that is unique and isolated. An unpleasant experience, sexual or social, may lead to an avoidance of similar situations or conditions likely to produce the same result.

We can also distinguish between opinions, attitudes and character traits. *Opinions* are held on narrow and specific points and are easily changed. They are likely to be reflections of contemporary social feelings. *Attitudes*, as we have suggested, are more enduring and do not change

23

easily. *Character traits* are observable manifestations of character structure, that is, the organization of behaviour tendencies, and some would say that they belong to the nuclear personality of the individual and are only alterable by special techniques (if at all). A trait of respect for authority may manifest itself in two not incompatible but complementary attitudes of dominating one's inferiors and subservience to one's superiors.

Attitudes display a significant correlation (relationship between events or objects) to social class or socio-economic status. For example, high-status persons in Britain favour the Conservative Party while low-status persons favour the Labour Party. Of course, this is by no means true of all. Attitudes also tend to go together in bundles. For example, people who are religious tend to be more conservative than people who are not religious. Surveys in Britain and America show that non-Catholics tend to vote Conservative more than Catholics and Non-Conformists. Jews tend to be left-wing party adherents.

THE CHANGING OF ATTITUDES

Attitudes can be further divided into *norm conforming* (going along with the popular consensus) and *ego-defensive* (more entrenched mental defence mechanisms). The latter are more resilient to attitude change by (a) new information, (b) group or social pressure. We infer an attitude from the behaviour of others, and conclude that the attitude we infer possesses one or more of the following three components. It is, firstly, *cognitive*, that is, based on the knowledge we have about a certain item or topic. Secondly, it is *affective*, because it is based on how we feel about an issue or topic. Thirdly, it has a *behavioural* component, because the person either does or says he will do something.

One of the ways of changing attitudes is by propaganda. The first device is by the use of weighted words. Some words are neutral, such as lamp or table, while others are emotive, such as democracy, freedom or totalitarian. Often attitudes can be affected by merely selecting the context, information and even figures. One study of arithmetic books in America showed that they unconsciously contained examples of capitalistic ideas. History books of the old type constantly emphasized the grandeur of the British Empire.

Advertisers and politicians rely on our accepting statements, with conviction, in the absence of any logical grounds for doing so. One of the ways of effecting suggestion is by the use of prestige, usually based on birth, occupation, education, income and power. Famous people are used to advertise commodities. Another means of changing attitudes is by social suggestion, where we are persuaded that everyone is buying a particular sort of commodity. An experiment by an American social psychologist in 1936 used the autokinetic effect of placing a small light in a completely darkened room. Because it could not be localized definitely, there being nothing to which to refer it, the light appeared to move. If a subject is told that the light moves he is more likely to say it moves than otherwise. Similarly, when shown ambiguous drawings, children tend to make a response similar to one suggested by a 'prompter', though seldom identical to it. A recent analysis of television programmes in America found that four out of five characters in drama were white. Europeans provided 10% of all heroes but 24% of all villains. Only 44% of Italian characters were law-abiding. People who worked with their hands were deprecated as against people in managerial capacity, and Anglo-Saxon names featured highly in prestige advertising.

RACIAL ATTITUDES

Research has shown that attitudes towards coloured people are determined mainly by contact with attitudes rather than with the coloured people themselves. If we are surrounded by prejudiced people we are more likely to adopt their attitudes through simple contact over time. If we have grown up in a prejudiced community we have learned the attitudes in almost the same way as learning to read. The mental defence mechanism theory would suggest that we adopt discrimination and prejudicial attitudes towards others from our own ego-inferiority. People who are physically different in some way easily become scapegoats. People who are discriminated against in time deteriorate because they have the worst in education and housing. Thus a self-fulfilling prophecy occurs because they develop these characteristics expected of them.

ATTITUDE MEASUREMENT

Because attitudes are important, there have been several attempts to measure them. The *Thurstone scale* consisted of grading on a 1 to 11 scale the favourable and unfavourable responses to some twenty questions, giving an approximation of the quality of attitude. The Likert scale attempted to gauge such issues as internationalism, morale, and so on. The subject is asked to underline one of the alternatives, strongly approve, approve, undecided, disapprove, strongly disapprove for each statement in the test. The pro-stand is valued as five, and the anti-stand as one. Other means of measuring attitudes are public opinion and market research studies made with samples of people representing a particular group, such as smokers or whisky drinkers. The questions must be brief and simple, usually eight to ten in number. Thus, in polling, one question must serve as an attitude gauge, whereas many questions can be used in an attitude scale. It is the constitution or composition of the sample which is important, not its size. The two main methods of sampling are quota and area sampling. In the former, interviewers are assigned a number of people with specified characteristics whom they are to interview, for example three over-fifty males, five under-thirty women. Although cheap, this method requires the interviewer to estimate variables such as age, social class, and so on, which are often difficult to gauge. Quota sampling consistently shows greater errors in prediction than can be accounted for in terms of the statistics of sampling theory. The area method is more accurate. Here the total area is divided into districts and these again into dwelling units. By a process of random selection, certain dwelling units are chosen and certain inhabitants of these units are specified, with no substitutes allowed if these inhabitants are absent.

COGNITIVE DISSONANCE THEORY

Dissonance in a cognitive system means lack of agreement between the parts of the system, and *consonance* means the opposite. Leon Festinger's theory assumes that dissonance in a cognitive system is uncomfortable for the individual, and he consequently tries to reduce dissonance and increase consonance by avoiding situations or information which would be likely to reduce consonance. The individual interprets information and situations in a subjective manner as being liable to produce dissonance. Sources of dissonance can include new information, cultural mores, and inconsistency with past experience, and dissonance can be changed by altering behaviour, changing the conditions of the environment, and by adding a new cognitive source of information. For example, one may 'rationalize' statistics that associate smoking with lung cancer by finding reports that criticize such statistics.

INTELLIGENCE

The biological approach to intelligence views it as stretched on a continuum ranging from the simple sensory motor to the complexity of thinking patterns. The statistical approach thinks in terms of the g-factor, or common factor, and the s-factor, or specific factor. The psychological approach views intelligence in terms of some kind of general mental energy. According to Piaget the intelligence of lower organisms and of infants is innately neural or biochemical activity in relation to external stimuli, and this in later life becomes a process of the central nervous system. Some think of mental development as being due to assemblies of neurones. Usually the word is confusingly referring to the innate potential of a person and the extent to which this potential is realized in later life. Strictly speaking we can only be aware of the realization of the sort of behaviour designated by intelligence.

It is now increasingly popular to define intelligence in purely empirical terms as being what intelligence tests measure, in that they are standardized tests on the basis of how large numbers of people perform them. Intelligence can also be looked at as an overlapping of abilities rather than as a faculty. Recent work has shown that there is a very strong connection between the socialization process and the level of intelligence. A person's intelligence or rather intellectual performance varies from one subject to another, and is also exposed to motivation and the effects of training. A man may be a professor of history and yet extremely poor at mathematics. The intelligence quotient (IQ) is not a stable factor as it changes by moving from an urban to a rural environment, and from one year to the next. A study of canal boat children in England, from very poor environmental backgrounds, showed a correspondingly low intellectual performance. Correlations between IQ and degree classes obtained among Cambridge University students were very low and work in California showed that only a relatively low level of IQ was necessary for quite high accomplishment. That is, many professors and people prominent in academic life had an IQ of only 120 (the mean being 100), which is that of an English grammar-school pupil.

The relation of heredity and environment to intelligence is a hotly debated point. Evidence from situations like those of the canal boat children and from isolated American Hill Billy communities, together with laboratory studies of animals reared in restricted environments, seem to indicate that intelligence is a matter of environment. However, other studies on rats genetically mated according to standards of intelligent behaviour resulted in the bright group making better scores than the dull group. It is a mistake for us to come down on heredity *or* environment. Intelligence is the combination of both these in combination with the physical and social environment. Very often we make the mistake of equating slowness of speech, or even ungrammatical speech, with a low intelligence. And a common mistake is to assume that all professional people have a high intelligence whereas all workers have a low one. On average this is true but other factors such as life-chances and motivation enter into this.

SOCIALLY DEPRIVED ENVIRONMENTS

This section is concerned with the broad process by which individuals are socially formed, a process which social scientists call socialization. What happens when this process either breaks down or is non-existent? Animals, we know, can be raised in isolation or even apart from their parents and yet still be recognizably animals. This is because they rely not so much on *language*, but on innate mechanisms which transmit the developmental messages. There are many examples of children reared in extreme isolation. A girl called Anna was discovered in 1937 who had been deprived of normal human contact and care for almost all of her first six years of life. She died in 1942, aged approximately ten and a half, of haemorrhagic jaundice. When found she could not walk, talk, or exhibit any intelligent behaviour. Two years after being discovered she had grasped the rudiments of social living, and could walk, although she was unable to talk. A comparable case was that of Isabelle discovered shortly after Anna and approximately six and a half years old. She was unable to speak and to all intents and purposes her actions where those of a six-month-old infant. By the age of fourteen she was almost normal. Obviously there are a number of questions we would have to ask before drawing any firm conclusions from these two instances. One thing we can say, with certainty, is that these children were unable to participate in society. We all learn social behaviour patterns, and this is what is meant by socialization. We learn to speak and to draw, to write and to paint. It has been estimated that individuals have a range of 200 000–600 000 words at their disposal. We also learn a very important unspoken language—that of gesture—sometimes called *non-verbal communication*. The interactive process can be divided into non-verbal (visual) and verbal. In the first category we include bodily contact, physical propinquity, bodily orientation, posture, physical appearance, facial expression, head and hand position and movement, and direction of gaze. In the second we include types of attention, praising or scolding, latent meanings and so on. An individual reared in a socially deprived environment is denied a situation in which he can learn any of these. Various descriptions of children reared by animals, especially wolves, are open to some doubt.

The above are obviously cases of extreme isolation or social deprivation where individuals were prevented from participating in effective socialization in order to acquire social behaviour. The central focus of socialization is the internalization by the individual of the culture in which he is born. If we want controlled situations we must turn to the strict scientific observations of the effects of deprived environments on animals and humans.

THE HARLOW EXPERIMENTS

Some very recent research has been carried out by the Harlows in Wisconsin in connection with socially deprived monkeys. Previous experiments have been done on social deprivation on sheep and goats, and puppies, but in this experiment monkeys were chosen because they are, when born, anatomically akin to a baby of one year.

The experiments achieved social isolation by not allowing individual monkeys any means of approach to monkey playmates. Monkeys reared in this way developed unusual and deviant behaviour such as (a) passive sitting and vacant staring, (b) repetitive stereotyped movements, (c) hands clasped on head and constant rocking backwards and forwards, a pattern also displayed by orphanage children.

From 6 to 12 months more severe social effects appear, and when placed with normal monkeys the deprived lack any noticeable demonstration of friendship. None of the deprived monkeys (male) developed adequate heterosexual behaviour, although for females the prognosis was 50%. Impregnated females rejected their offspring.

Next raised were monkeys without mothers but with access to infant monkeys. No sexual abnormality resulted because lack of normal mothering was compensated for by infant play and affection.

The next move was to compare monkeys raised by *dummy* or *surrogate* mothers and those raised by real mothers. Although the former were slow in developing patterns as time progressed, there were no noticeable differences.

Next, infants with their own mothers were prevented from contacting other infants. The mothers became over-solicitous, although they provided compensation for infant deprivation.

Finally, the effects of *total* deprivation were studied with the results shown in Table 2.1. Although these experiments are important, we must temper our conclusions by reminding ourselves that these are monkey communities, and that the direct analogy to human society may not be so simple.

TABLE 2.1

Duration	Result
After three months	Total shock and self-imposed starvation
After 6 months	Delay and repression of capacity for social interaction
After 12 months	Cessation of all play; incapable of survival.

HUMAN IMPAIRMENT

The work of Bowlby in England on orphanage and motherless children showed that certain experiences in the socialization process produced characters that were affectionless and delinquent. These experiences were (a) lack of opportunity for forming an attachment to a mother-figure during the first three years, (b) deprivation lasting from three to more than six months during the first three or four years, (c) changes from one mother-figure to another during the same period.

The adverse effects of the deprivation could last either during the period of separation, during the period immediately after restoration to maternal care, or permanently.

Bowlby stressed the necessity of having a psychic organizer, the mother-figure, during certain critical periods of a child's formation. These critical periods include that when the child is in the process of establishing a relationship with a clearly defined person, usually achieved by six months of age, and up to his third birthday, during which stage the child needs the almost constant presence of the mother-figure. The final critical period is when the child is becoming capable of maintaining a relationship with the mother in her absence. The work of the Harlows appears to substantiate any move away from too rigid a connection between mother and child. In monkey infants, at least, lack of a mother relationship can be adequately compensated for by allowing for periods of play with other monkeys of the same age.

SOCIAL FORMATION OF ABILITY IN INDIVIDUALS

A study of socially deprived environments is, however, not limited simply to large-scale psychological effects. Environmental deprivation exists to a lesser extent than in the studies of the Harlows and Bowlby, but is none the less important for any sociological study of society. The elements of an environment are usually thought of as being physical, social, and cultural. It is the social and cultural that we now want to deal with, particularly with reference to some of the factors concerned with the formation of ability.

Studies of canal boat and mill children have shown that a poor cultural environment has the correspondingly poor IQ result. Studies of orphanages have shown that when children are removed from an inferior background to an enriched nursery-school environment a considerable increase in IQ results, although little improvement is evident after the age of about seven.

If the effects of some circumstances are to be assessed by experiment, it is usual to observe two groups under conditions which are identical except that one group, called the *experimental* group, is subjected to that circumstance and the other, called the *control* group, is not. Such experiments have been carried out in the laboratory on rats, the control group being reared in the usual type of cage and the experimental group in enriched environments consisting of ladders, tunnels and mirrors. In later testing the latter group displayed much better ability in maze-learning and other situations involving problems. It seems that intelligence rises to the level of heredity or environment, whichever one of these is lower. A perfect environment is limited by an inherited factor, and the genius is limited by the environment.

Environment has an effect on verbal development. Verbally deprived children are handicapped in the manipulation of ideas, and verbal responses and patterns of a home that is culturally backward are poorer than those of a middle-class home. Ability at verbal manipulation enables a child to be more flexible even in apparently non-verbal problems.

BERNSTEIN'S SOCIO-LINGUISTIC THEORY

A recent important work in socio-linguistics (the sociological study of language origins and development) has been that of the English sociologist Basil Bernstein, who suggests that there are two types of language spoken in this country, that of the working class and that of the middle class. The latter is articulate, rich and flexible, and provides a vehicle for logical argument by its vocabulary and form. The former is limited in vocabulary, adjectives, conjunctions, adverbs, and often consists of stereotyped phraseology, one phrase having to do many functions. Much of his work is supported by test results in terms of social class, when middle- and working-class children score equally on numerical ability tests and yet the latter invariably scores lower on verbal reasoning and ability tests.

Bernstein distinguished two types of code, the *elaborated* and *restricted*. In the former, the speaker selects from a relatively wide range of alternatives; in the latter the range of alternatives is severely limited. In both codes the distinguishing characteristic is one of *predictability*, the restricted code possessing a high level of predictability and the elaborated code a low one. The middle class have the advantage because they are socialized into both codes, while lower working-class children are confined to only the restricted code. Ability tests and the academic school curriculum are heavily biased towards the elaborated code. Lower-working-class children appear relatively backward, but this may well be the result of a culture which has transmitted such backwardness through the linguistic process.

Children from the relatively deprived environment of the lower working class are also severely handicapped in terms of attitudes and aspirations, these being constantly lower than those of middle-class children with the same IQ. Studies of school leavers, for example, have shown that working-class children often aim at occupations well below their actual level of ability. Children do not choose from the whole range of occupations. Their mental ability, together with the social and educational *milieu* in which they grew up, have fixed the area of choice which they exercise. Other studies show that children from secondary modern schools ranked very low in the scale of ambitiousness irrespective of their IQ.

The education system itself can or cannot be used intelligently, and middle-class parents on the whole have a better 'know how' than working-class parents on the best type of school, which subjects to drop or maintain, and future career possibilities.

THE SCHOOLS

The school itself is a middle-class institution run on a middle-class ethic and staffed mainly by middle-class teachers. Many teachers discriminate, not in terms of ability but in terms of social class. Teachers' judgements of ability tend to be influenced more by the type of home the child comes from than by other factors. The selection procedure misfires when, given the *same* ability, the middle-class child finds himself placed in the upper-stream and the lower-class child in the lower stream. One study found 11% more middle-class children in the upper stream than would be expected from their measured ability at eight, and 26% fewer in the lower.

The dirty and badly clothed tend to be placed in a lower stream than their ability warrants. 29% of children in lower streams had a record of poor maternal care, although only 21% should have been there on their test ability.

Of the children of apparently equal ability, half of whom are streamed higher and half lower, the latter deteriorate in ability while the former show some improvement. The gap, therefore, negligible at the beginning, becomes artificially widened. Given equal ability, middle-class children always tend to do better in terms of classroom allocation than working-class children. This is the result of unconscious biases in selection procedure, and not necessarily a condemnation of selection itself.

CONTINUING SOCIALIZATION

All that we have discussed so far is part of the way in which individuals become social beings. Socialization, however, is a continuing process. We have, also, socialization into the peer group, into school, into adolescence, into courtship and dating, into marriage, into work, and into the secondary groups that form so much of an individual's adult life.

We acquire internal constraints during socialization that enables the infant to participate in social life. That is, we learn how to behave in particular circumstances. The prime agency is the family or kinship group. It is here that individuals are assigned, and encounter, roles to which they are expected to conform. The peer group offers the first break away from the family, and the child encounters role obligations on an equal footing with others of his own age. The school transmits both a formal knowledge, through the curriculum, and also informal knowledge and attitudes through the playground and extra-curricula activities. The mass media are also a socializing factor because they offer us models of behaviour and attitudes which we regard as desirable.

These agencies of socialization act as mechanisms, and we learn a whole complex pattern of behaviour appropriate to the culture in which we live which through repetition and reinforcement become part of our behaviour.

THE DEVELOPMENT OF THE SELF

The child is egocentric. By contact with others he learns that other people exist. His mother, for example, becomes a person with feelings and values not necessarily the same as his own. As he develops, these are applied outside the immediate family, to his peers, until he learns to see himself as an object. This view that he takes of himself, which he receives initially from his parents, becomes eventually that of the society in which he lives. This is called *the generalized other*. The imitation of this early behaviour includes vocal behaviour and non-verbal behaviour such as facial expressions and gestures. By using what he has imitated as a reference point he is now in a position to imagine how others are regarding him. This has been called the *looking-glass self*. From the beginning others are approving and disapproving of the child's behaviour by verbal and non-verbal means. These become reflections, or a series of mirrors, which enable the child to see himself as others see him.

What used to be called *human instincts* are, in fact, culturally acquired through socialization. The self is socially created by (a) a self-image, (b) an ideal self, (c) an ego (how we should behave even when not observed).

PERSONALITY

By *personality* we mean the sum total of a person's behaviour and characteristics, including his religion, colour of hair, and habits. A personality *trait* is one aspect of this total. The determinants of personality are of various types. (a) *Biological* influences include the anatomy, physiology and neural composition of individuals. *Discrete variation* is that which we find distinguishing the sexes, and *continuous* variation refers to weight and height, and so on. Biological differences often have values imputed to them by the particular culture (fat people are figures of fun) but they can also be culturally induced (bad eating habits and social stress can make people fat). Physical changes in the human body are referred to as *maturation*, and if these are in some way odd they can affect the socialization process. (b) the *physical* or *geographical environment* in which we live can influence behaviour by limiting the activities that can be performed. (c) The *cultural environment* differs very much from society to society and influences socialization and personality. (d) The *social environment* refers to the group experiences which an individual encounters, and while the cultural milieu may often be the same, this is not the case with the social environment.

SOCIAL INFLUENCES ON BEHAVIOUR

An individual is born into a cultural and social environment which already exists and which he must learn to accommodate to. It is this environment which shapes his experiences and his behaviour, and it is by the process of *internalization* that he adopts this environment as his own. Culture refers, as we have seen, to the traditions and customs of a people and to the attitudes and beliefs they have about numerous aspects of their life. It is the sum total of behaviour and belief transmitted by a particular society. Each member of a culture reflects the distinctive pattern of that culture in himself. The Zuni Indians live in the American south-west and are ceremonious and ritualistic. They are mild and inoffensive and have adopted the ceremony and ritual to avoid being thrown back onto their own resources. It is an endeavour to stop individualism and initiative. The Dobu are hostile and treacherous, and all life is antagonistic. The Kwakiutl are competitive and hierarchical and status conscious. The behaviour of the individuals of these three cultures reflects the social environment in which they live.

Human learning is a social process, and early in life an individual identifies himself with the cultural process going on around him. It is from the social milieu that an individual derives much of his personality and most of his behaviour patterns. It is from his environment that a child learns his attitudes, his interpretation of the world, and his patterns of behaviour. It is here that his perceptions are socially standardized, e.g. in sex, social class and age, and that he learns his reactions to situations.

CONCLUSIONS

This chapter on social formation of individuals has looked at socialization. How attitudes are formed and subsequently changed is an important part of this process. It appears that people strive to maintain an equilibrium and avoid situations and ideas which can cause unpleasantness. Intelligence is to a substantial degree socially formed by the individual's hereditary characteristics interacting with the social and physical environment, and socially impaired environments have the effect of damaging both personality and intelligence. The socialization process continues through life, during which time ability is processed by the educational system.

Socialization is viewed as a morphostatic process. That is, social structure (the network of social positions to which are assigned tasks and responsibilities) carries on in time, even though the occupants of social positions change. Society changes the raw biological man into a socialized being because individuals learn roles in an interactive situation. By taking the roles of others we adopt the perspectives of others in relation to ourselves. These others vary in significance, and the others become merged or generalized over time. Socialization is not restricted to the *primary* stage but is a continuing process (*secondary*). Some have argued that man is over-socialized, by which they mean that we must not forget that man is a biological as well as a social animal. Very often the transmission of culture can do violence to man's socialized bodily drives. This results in the repressed and frustrated man or woman whose actions often become manifested as *deviant*. When socialization is impaired in some way, we often produce individuals who are deviant.

Many people entertain expectations of our role performances, some of which are conflicting. We gradually build up a scale by which we rate some expectations as being more desirable or beneficial than others.

We must learn to resist some social influences. Some groups, which we call *reference groups*, become more important for us to relate to. Finally, non-voluntary secondary socialization processes such as the armed forces or prisons exercise power as a means of coercion.

SUGGESTIONS FOR FURTHER READING

BERNSTEIN, B. (1970). 'A Socio-linguistic Approach to Socialisation,' in Gumperz, J. and Hymes, D. (eds.) *Directions in Psycholinguistics*, Holt, Rinehart and Winston, New York.
BERTRAND, A. L. (1967). *Basic Sociology*, Appleton Century Crofts, New York.
BOWLBY, J. (1957). *Child Care and the Growth of Love*, Penguin Books, Harmondsworth.
HUDSON, L. (ed.) (1970). *The Ecology of Human Intelligence*, Penguin Books, Harmondsworth.
JAHODA, M., WARREN, N. (eds.) (1966). *Attitudes*, Penguin Books, Harmondsworth.
KELVIN, P. (1970). *The Bases of Social Behaviour*, Holt, Rinehart and Winston, London.
KLEIN, J. (1965). *Samples from English Cultures*, Routledge and Kegan Paul, London.
MEAD, M. (1935). *Sex and Temperament in Three Primitive Societies*, Routledge, London.
SWIFT, D. F. (1969). *The Sociology of Education*, Routledge and Kegan Paul, London.

3

THE FAMILY

DEFINITIONS OF MARRIAGE AND THE FAMILY

The family is a complex social institution which is universally found wherever there are human groups. Naturally there are many different forms in which it is organized and therefore we would expect to find these differences in the family structures of the Hopi, the wandering Bushmen of the Kalahari, and in English, European and American advanced technological societies. We can also find a rudimentary form of such a structure among other animals such as free-living chimpanzees and apes. Social groupings involving mating and a relationship between a mother and infant have been variously described in birds, rabbits, dogs, cats and rodents. The social organization of the family is based upon fundamental biological functions, but man's rich cultural nature results in a greater variation of his species.

MARRIAGE Marriage is to be distinguished from mating, and is to be regarded as social rather than biological. It implies primarily a relatively *stable* relationship between one or more men and one or more women. The form of family which we think predominates, the monogamous family (one wife to one husband), is in fact not found in 80% of societies throughout the world, and in these societies polygamy (the existence of more than one legal spouse at the same time) is common. In the 80% of societies where polygamy is the structure the most common type is polygyny (one man is legally contracted to more than one woman) although we can still find examples of polyandrous marriage (more than one husband to one woman) in certain parts of India.

An important element in defining marriage is the *principle of legitimacy* by which a relationship between a mother, father and child is socially approved or legitimated. Sexual relationships between various members of a society are given legitimate approval by some form of *incest taboo*, which prohibits sexual intercourse between designated members. The family has given rise to the social institution of marriage and not the other way round. Marriage is a contractual agreement based upon certain regulations and rules which govern the rights, duties and privileges of a wife to a husband and vice versa, and of both to their offspring, their relatives (extended family), and society at large. It would be incorrect to think of marriage as a way of regulating sexual intercourse. It is more helpful to think of it as a means for making the reproduction of offspring legitimate. It becomes obvious, also, that to become pregnant (or even give birth) before marriage is in some societies a signal of fertility and has full social approval. The variations in the structure of marriage we have mentioned means that sexual behaviour is not uniform but can vary enormously. Many societies allow 'privileged relationships' which can allow a man to have sexual relationships with the wife of his brother (some 34 societies), with his wife's sister (some 28 societies), and with his mother's brother's wife (6 societies). In the Old Testament the Hebrews had a form of marriage (*levirite*) which provided that a childless widow should be retained in the husband's clan by marrying his brother or kinsman. These 'extra-marital' relationships, although socially prescribed, may surprise some more used to the western form of marriage, yet in many ways they can be seen as providing a means of giving security to the woman, and also binding together various tribes and clans. Even in western society it is less shocking to think of a husband as being promiscuous than a wife, and in Japan sexual relationships are socially approved between a man and women other than his wife, although not the other way round. Marriage requires a husband and wife to live together in the same household and to cooperate economically for certain goods and services.

Romantic love between two members of the opposite sex is a comparatively new phenomenon, and was certainly unknown in Europe before the rise of the trouvères and troubadours in any general sense. The Samoans, when told the story of Romeo and Juliet, were reduced to laughter. Many societies have systems of marriage arranged without choice of any kind between the partners concerned but based rather on property or 'bride-price' between the parents.

THE FAMILY   The family is a social structure, or a sub-system, which commences when marriage has taken place or kinship ties have been established, and of which society approves. Generally, members of a family live together and interact socially according to roles, norms and status positions prescribed by the greater society. More clearly, we can think of it as a particular grouping of persons united by socially sanctioned kinship, marriage or adoption ties, who tend to live together and interact together according to well-defined social rules. It differs from other sub-systems in society in a number of different ways. Firstly, it is generally the group which the individual encounters from the outset and for an extended length of time. He is in the family for initial or primary socialization and usually has the family as a base for the period of secondary socialization, although emphasis here is on other groups with whom he mixes and by whom he is influenced. Because of this extended and intensive period during which the individual is living with the family we can expect the time to be one in which vitally important influences are brought to bear on the formation of the individual's behaviour and personality, and one which leaves a lasting pattern of loyalty and deep affection on all of us. Secondly, of all the groups of which we are or become members, the family is the smallest (or, in families composed of several marriages and their offspring, one of the smallest). This is certainly true of the *conjugal* family, which is the name given to the typical family structure found in industrial society. Thirdly, some of the other systems in society would find it difficult to function without the family. In modern industrial society functions of the family are gradually being eroded and taken over by specialist agencies. Lastly, the emotional intensity of family relationships and the control of members makes it particularly suitable to act as a vehicle for the exercise of constraint.

FORMS OF MARRIAGE AND TYPES OF FAMILY One of the questions that immediately spring to mind is why there are so many variations in the forms of marriage and the types of family, and indeed why there should be any variation at all. The answer cannot be framed in terms of individuals wishing or desiring a certain kind of form or type, but in the way in which cultural conditions pre-empt the entry of the individual into society and determine to a large extent the social patterning of his life.

Monogamous marriage is generally universal and found in societies which also practise a more dominant form. Usually in such instances the practitioners of monogamy are far too poor to afford more than one partner. Very often a form of marriage denotes the social status of an individual so that polygynous practices reflect wealth, status and power manifested in a number of wives belonging to a high-status chief. On the other hand polyandrous practices are nearly always a sign of poor social conditions because of which a number of men pool their labour in order to establish a household.

Differences also occur in the way in which marriage partners are selected. *Endogamy* requires a person to marry within a specified group of which he is a member. Such groups are usually based on religion, race and social class. *Exogamy* refers to the prohibition of marrying within certain groups of which an individual is a member. The incest taboos which we have mentioned deliberately exclude certain groups from being eligible, namely close blood relatives. The manner in which mates are selected varies enormously from society to society. In many areas of the world it is still the accepted practice to choose a spouse for one's own children of marriageable age. Thus the elders, in this case the parents, choose the marriage partners for their children because of the cultural belief that love, if these societies entertain such a notion, is something which is expected to develop after rather than before the marriage. Very often economic interests enter into mate selection and Goode has likened mate selection to a market system.

The children of marriages require a social placing in order to facilitate such matters as inheritance and status succession. One way of doing this is to relate offspring to already existing 'positions', namely the father's, mother's, or both. These lines of descent can be counted solely through the male line (*patrilineal*), the female line (*matrilineal*), or through either (*bilateral*). Generally speaking, quite broad patterns are to be seen in the places where those married take up residence. In a system favouring a *patrilocal residence* the newly married take up residence near or with the parents of the groom or husband, whereas in one favouring *matrilocal residence* they live near the wife's family. *Local residence* means that residence is socially sanctioned with either the bride or groom's family, usually on a permanent basis. A small number of societies have a pattern known as *avunulocal residence* where the newly weds live with the family of an uncle. The practice which we are most familiar with both in England and Europe is known as *neolocal* residence, in which a household is established separate from both parental families.

Some social anthropologists have attempted to relate residential practices with other, and especially economic, activities, for example matrilocal residence is claimed by some to be predominant with agricultural societies where women both tend and own the land. Very often, of course, two or more of these patterns which we have described exist side by side.

A further distinction occurs between the *extended* and *nuclear* family. The former includes a married pair and their offspring, and is a socially recognized kinship unit that in addition includes one or more others related to these who are defined as kin. The nuclear family is a kinship unit limited to a married pair and their children. A distinction is generally made between an individual's *family of orientation* (that into which he was adopted or born) and the *family of procreation* (his own family which he procreates through his marriage).

THE FUNCTIONS OF THE FAMILY

Although there are different variations in types of marriage and the form that families take, nevertheless the *functions* of the family are considered as essential for the fulfilment of certain social requirements. By 'function' (a term widely misused both by the general public and by sociologists) we will mean those that the family can be held to perform for other social institutions in society. It is generally agreed that there are six of these functions, as follows:

1. The family provides the setting for the socialization of the young by conveying values, modes of behaviour and social traditions on the one hand, and attitudes, and cognitive content on the other.

2. The family provides provision for and regulation of sexual and parental behaviour or requirements.

3. The family provides a basis upon which private property in the broadest sense can be passed on with the minimum of conflict.

4. The family provides a group of people who are expected to give affection and love.

5. The family provides care and training for the otherwise helpless young.

6. The family is the means by which society passes on its titles or statuses which are ascribed to the young.

This list could be extended indefinitely, but these six functions are general rather than specific, to enable a comparative approach to be made across societies. Some sociologists limit the functions to only four, namely the regulation of sexual behaviour and reproduction, the care and training of offspring, providing role models for the division of labour, and primary group satisfaction.

THE FAMILY IN INDUSTRIAL SOCIETY

If we take four functions usually held to be of central importance to society and to the maintenance of human life and culture, namely the sexual, the economic, the reproductive and the educational, we can examine them in relation to a popular thesis that in modern urban and industrial society such functions have been eroded.

THE SEXUAL FUNCTION Evidence to substantiate extra-marital or pre-marital intercourse and its frequency abounds, but by the nature of the material with which we are concerned error and misinterpretation are almost bound to be important factors. If we accept the evidence of Kinsey, there is some suggestion that pre-marital and extra-marital sexual behaviour has increased, but of course we are lacking in any real base figure from which to draw any conclusions as to how great the trend has been. Similarly, there is some evidence that men are not using prostitutes to the same extent as they were. Evidence from literature and social history does not indicate any remarkable change for the last century. Studies among teenagers have shown that they tend to marry those with whom they copulate, and those that get divorced marry again (over three-quarters) presumably in most cases those they have had extra-marital relations with.

THE ECONOMIC FUNCTION The industrial revolution has meant that the centre of production has moved from the home or 'cottage industries' to the factory system, necessitating a process in which only selected members of the family are employed. This process of industrialization away from the home is for consumption within the home, and the family as an economic unit has changed to one which consumes rather than produces. The family appears to be the chief unit of consumption in society, spending most of the wage on such needs or requirements as food, clothing, housing, and so on. The family is also of importance in the passing on of inherited property and a vehicle for legal arrangements to facilitate the inheritance of capital.

THE SOCIALIZATION FUNCTION In many ways this function is the most apparent. In the last century, the educational system has grown at an enormous rate with specialized institutions providing pre-school, school and post-school facilities. Thus many of the processes that previously were carried on inside the home are now catered for away from the family. Nevertheless, much of the work in the sociology of education is concerned with the way in which the home and family situation complement the educational system rather than existing independently of one another. It might be better to use the word 'interact' rather than 'complement', because many families, principally those of semi-skilled and unskilled manual workers, are at variance with the educational system and its values and consequently tend to perform more badly, or get less out of, the school and other institutions.

THE REPRODUCTIVE SYSTEM We mean by this not the biological reproductive function of the family but the way in which the family 'passes on' its social statuses and positions. If we consider for a moment the reproductive functions, we have a position in Great Britain alone where 1 out of every 4 children is illegitimate. In many cases the child is retained by the mother to form an incomplete nuclear family. In a greater number of instances the child is adopted by a nuclear family other than its own procreative one. A number of children become institutionalized, fostered and so on. All these cases of impairment of the family's reproductive function are examples of the way in which legitimate social statuses and positions, in other words social descent, is not carried out in the normal manner.

A number of state agencies have arisen to care for, or take over, the reproductive system, such as maternity hospitals and health visitors. Thousands of pounds are spent each year on maternity benefits, child allowances and family-planning clinics. In the last hundred years the mean ultimate family size has declined from 6·16 in 1861–9 to near the 2·5 mark today. Some might well see this as a deliberate attempt to limit the reproductive function of the family.

THE 'DECLINE' OF THE NUCLEAR FAMILY

One of the problems with which sociologists and social historians concern themselves is whether the emergence of the nuclear family facilitated the development of industrialization or whether it emerged as a consequence of the industrialization process. The first view sees the emergence of a mobile, untied, and 'rational' labour force as a pre-condition for industrialization. Such a force would be best provided by the nuclear family, with its stress on allocation by achievement rather than ascription. The second view sees the industrial process as rendering superfluous the extended family by a process of social evolution. In other words, because the industrial process required ease of mobility and lack of encumbrance, the extended family became less of a necessity. Difficulties of interpretation make it virtually impossible to attain any real agreement. Some studies by Laslett have shown that the family of the seventeenth and eighteenth centuries was not so very different from that of today, with an average size of between four and five, while contemporary empirical studies indicate a nuclear family within a network of kinship interaction.

Another way of looking at the problem is to realize that the nuclear family always contains elements of both the *consanguine* (related by blood to all members of the family of origin) and the *conjugal* (the parents in the nuclear family must *not* be related by blood). In other words the child of the family is related by blood to all the family of origin but he must not become further related by marrying any of them. Another way of describing these two types is that the consanguine family stresses the parent–child relationship based on blood-descent, whereas the conjugal family stresses both the parents as the 'conjugal pair'. In the former descent is through the male line with a strong system of authority, while in the latter the stress is on autonomy and responsibility. A certain amount of confusion between *nuclear* and *conjugal* exists, but despite this many sociologists of the family see the conjugal family, rather than the nuclear family, as being conducive to industrialization. The conjugal family is regarded as fitting rather well with the demands of industrialization; according to Goode, 'because of its emphasis on performance, such a system requires that a person be permitted to rise or fall, and to move about wherever the job market is best'. Because it is neolocal (each couple sets up its own household) the conjugal family has weak kinship networks which permit a greater flexibility and mobility. These neolocal, independent households themselves produce problems such as the ambiguity of the older people in society (nearly eight million pensioners in Great Britain), the denigration of 'wisdom' as opposed to specialized technical knowledge, and the inability to deal with disruptions such as the children left over from divorce or separation. The effect of women as forming a large part of the labour force of any industrialized country—and of that labour force a large number are married—produces problems in terms of coping with a household and with work. Industrial societies are striving, also, to produce some sort of balance between population and *fertility*, and nations undergoing industrialization are attempting to reduce the birth rate.

Several empirical studies have shown, in New York, Detroit and England, that so-called nuclear families saw their kin very often once a week (67%) and some more than once a week (20%). Similar results were given in a San Francisco study in 1957. Arguing against Parsons' view of the nuclear family pattern as predominant, some have emphasized that the nuclear family does maintain contact of various kinds with kin. Others have stressed the importance of family 'friends' and suggested that 'isolated families are largely a figment of the imagination'. Still another suggestion is that Parsons was thinking too much of the classical extended family, and did not pay sufficient attention to developing a new conception of extended family, in which the assistance sought and given by kinsmen is not occupational but social. Bell's work on the middle-class extended family in Britain showed it to be a functioning social entity. Some studies have shown this contact to be as high as three-quarters of children (married) who have contacted their parents within the period of one week. American data suggest that the higher the social class of the families involved, the higher the participation. The Firth studies in London and the Young and Wilmott research in Bethnal Green and in Woodford have shown that in these areas nuclear families in the usual sense simply do not exist, and the extended family is a safer tool of analysis.

The view that industrialization encourages the development of a non-extended type of family appears to be theoretically quite strong. It is in such a system that we have achievement-based criteria with universalism and specificity as opposed to ascription, diffuseness and particularism. That is, industrial society is likely to display a pattern whereby work is allocated on the criteria of achievement rather than ascription, people are emotionally uninvolved rather than involved, and where men and women tend to perform only the task in hand rather than any 'overflow' of such a task.

While industrial society can provide many requirements it fails, because it emphasizes the above pattern-variables, to provide for the emotional needs of individuals. Some would argue this was indicated by the lack of affection, the increase in divorce, and the rise in the ill-treatment of the young. However, it is also suggested by some that because many of the functions of the family in an industrial society are being eroded or taken over by the state machinery, this then leaves the family to cope with being the only agency capable of giving real warmth, in terms of human relationships, to its offspring.

The solution seems to lie with the suggestion that it is the conjugal family that has 'fitted' the industrial society of the last century, and not the classical extended family (or *paterfamilia* of the Roman world), nor the nuclear family.

DIVORCE: AN INSTITUTIONALIZED ARRANGEMENT FOR THE EROSION OF FAMILY GROUPINGS

Both male and females generally marry two years earlier in the early 1970s than they did in the early 1950s. Divorce, however, has not changed all that drastically, except during the two world wars and after the introduction of the legal aid for divorce in 1950. What does seem to be the case is that those who marry very young are more likely to have a divorce than those who marry later, but 60% of divorces are among those who have been married for more than 10 years. A third of divorces are between childless couples, another third having only one child. Despite these facts divorce exists in society as a socially sanctioned arrangement when the marriage contract can be terminated and the family dissolved. It occurs in nearly every society in some form, although in some pre-literate cultures it merely involves a return of the original dowry.

INCIDENCE AND TIMING OF MARITAL BREAKDOWN Many studies suggest that marrying early is an important factor in a later possible termination. The early years of a marriage are also crucial, because this is the period when many breakdowns occur. One of the reasons for this is that people's personality *does* change over time and often the person one has married is unable or seen to be unable to cope with new demands. Similarly with marriages that dissolve after the children have left the home. Here again, individuals thrown back upon themselves after a busy period of child-rearing often find it difficult to reorientate their lives to each other.

Traditionally individuals have tended to choose their partners from within a broadly similar socio-economic and religious background. Similarly, people on the whole have tended to marry within their own race or culture or colour. Other factors which enter into the choice of partner include one's parental image and one's personality needs. Sometimes this choice is inverted; that is, people will become attracted to those with an opposite or dissimilar personality, and who are opposite or dissimilar to one's parental image.

An undoubted contribution to marital breakdown is made by sexual difficulties, whether non-consummation, failure of coitus or sexual deviation. Nevertheless, even when breakdown appears inevitable, agencies exist whereby the married couple or even just one of them can be given guidance and advice from qualified personnel. Very often damage is done by well-meaning GPs consulted over problems with which they are expected to deal because they are forced into a situation with absolutely no training and which they know nothing about. The kind of agencies capable of dealing with marital breakdown include the probation service, voluntary grant-aided bodies such as the Marriage Guidance Council, family service units, and the psychiatric services within the NHS.

The fact that the divorce rate is higher now than it was a century ago (under 1 per 10 000 women of child-bearing age compared with over 33 per 1000 in the 1960s) may indicate a number of factors. For example, it may suggest that the rate of divorce is related to the ease with which it can be obtained. For a fuller picture, however, we would have to take into account such factors as we mentioned above, such as sexual and personality problems and incompatibilities. If the partners come from a happy home themselves, this further decreases the risk of divorce. Large social upheavals such as world wars certainly appear to place marital relationships in a very precarious position. The variation of rates of divorce in five countries places in ascending order Great Britain, Germany, Australia, France, Sweden and the USA. In fact the USA has three times the number of divorces per 1000 marriages than Great Britain.

In general we can list some main social factors, as follows: (a) greater *toleration* of the divorce action resulting in less stigmatization; (b) greater *alternatives* offer themselves to either partner, for example a divorced woman can either support herself or claim compensation (admittedly there is still difficulty experienced by many women but certainly not as much as 50 years ago); (c) there are correspondingly fewer social pressures to stay married.

Among the more specific factors which contribute towards divorce we can list the following: (a) a more tolerant religious climate due to secularization; (b) a more tolerant legal climate; (c) a high density of urban living with the accompanying anonymity of social behaviour; (d) the increase in birth control methods can perhaps be equated with childless couples being more prone to divorce; (e) the growth of industrialization has meant the minimization of the family as a productive unit and a stress on its consumption; (f) greater geographical mobility has decreased neighbourhood constraints; (g) high commercial 'romantic love' expectations through advertising and television may not be met in reality.

ADJUSTMENT TO DEATH AND DIVORCE   The processes of both death and of divorce erode or dissolve the family unit to roughly the same degree. Goode has listed six ways in which the life situation might be affected by death and divorce as follows: (a) sexual satisfaction will cease; (b) loss of security, love, friendship, etc.: (c) the children lose an adult role model: (d) the domestic work-role for the remaining spouse is increased, especially where young children are concerned: (e) increase in economic problems, especially if the husband has departed: (f) household task and responsibilities are redistributed. According to the type of society in which divorce occurs there are varying social arrangements to help cope with the social disorganization which follows. For example, in an extended-kinship system many of the above problems would not be nearly so important.

FAMILY DISSOLUTION AND CHILDREN   Probably one of the most important ways in which the dissolution of the family affects society is when the divorced parents leave behind children lacking one parent. For example, in the USA in 1956 343 000 minor children were involved in divorce cases and 350 000 children orphaned. In Britain a year later 30 765 children were involved in the dissolution or annulment of 23 785 marriages. In America in the mid-1950s there were some six million children classified as minors who were having to adjust to some form of marital disorganization. These figures are enormous, and the problem becomes even more serious when we relate them to such factors as delinquency, inadequate socialization, sexual deviancy, lack of success in later marriage, poor school performance, and so on. Some of these points are discussed elsewhere.

CHANGING FAMILY PATTERNS

In Britain there is a marked difference to be discerned between the pattern of the family 50 years ago and today.

1. Women have improved their status considerably both in the politico-legal field and economically. More and more are now released into the labour force, benefit from higher and further education, and so on.

2. A more egalitarian 'share-out' of household tasks occurs where the woman is herself employed on the labour market, and this tends to vary according to the socio-economic class of the spouses.

3. Children are increasingly viewed as not merely an economic asset but as humans in their own right, and this results in greater permissiveness in child-rearing techniques.

4. There is an increasing concern by people entering upon the marriage contract to 'make it work'. This is done by a variety of methods including preparatory classes.

5. There is a growing number of households (18·6 million in 1971 as compared with 14.9 million in 1951) which is not due simply to the increase in population. One of the reasons is that many women who have either survived their husbands, are divorced or are rearing children out of marriage are finding themselves playing the role of household (or family) head.

6. People are becoming increasingly aware that sexual intercourse is a technique which has to be learned. There is a greater interest in sexual variation and a general permissiveness towards techniques that will improve intercourse.

7. Individuals have a greater freedom in which to choose their 'mates' and a decline of certain restrictive norms now means that mates can be selected from other socio-economic classes, religions and races. Greater geographical mobility has also facilitated the increased flexibility in choice.

THE CONTEMPORARY BRITISH FAMILY

Fletcher describes the contemporary family as being established at an early age (and of long duration), small in its size (because of birth control), having separate households in an improved material environment, economically self-providing, founded on an equal relationship, democratically managed, centrally concerned with the procreation and maintenance of children, and aided by statutory and voluntary public bodies. However, there are many families who in their thousands receive supplementary benefits, unemployment benefits, who live in completely inadequate households, have large numbers of children, have a dominant father, and where children are neglected to a degree requiring hospitalization.

THE FAMILY IN A MEDICAL SETTING

The patients admitted to hospital or seen by a GP come from families of very different backgrounds. Some of the very rich families drawn from the upper-middle classes are, in fact, never seen by either the ordinary GP nor the NHS in general. More and more people are seeking private medical care not simply as a reaction to the deficiencies of the NHS but as a means of differentiating themselves from the middle and lower classes. Nearly eight million individuals received the state retirement pension in 1972, whereas in 1966 it was only just over five and a half million. Some 280 000 claim neither this pension nor a supplementary benefit (some presumably had private means), and nearly a million receiving a pension had not claimed for a supplementary benefit for which they are eligible. It is estimated that nearly 400 000 people (nearly 6% of all those over 65) are incapacitated and living alone or with no children near.

These are the kinds of situations which a modern industrialized society in a sense 'creates' and which the modern family is ill equipped to deal with. The modern welfare state contains numerous examples of the effects of the disorganization and malfunctioning of the family. Many of these examples reach the nurse and doctor in the hospital and the GP in his surgery. Many more at one stage or another enlist the aid of state medical services in one form or another. By understanding some of the ways in which the family is organized and some of the ways in which family membership can determine subsequent behaviour, especially among children who come from an eroded family unit, medical and para-medical personnel may see a little more clearly many of the complexities they face in the day-to-day exigencies of their task.

SUGGESTIONS FOR FURTHER READING

FLETCHER, R. (1966). *The Family and Marriage in Britain*, Penguin Books, Harmondsworth.

GOODE, W. J. (1964). *The Family*, Prentice-Hall, Englewood Cliffs, New Jersey.

DOMINIAN, J. (1968). *Marital Breakdown*, Penguin Books, Harmondsworth.

LASLETT, P. (1965). *The World We Have Lost*, Methuen, London.

YOUNG, M. and Willmott, P. (1962). *Family and Kinship in East London*, Penguin Books, Harmondsworth.

BERTRAND, A. L. (1967). *Basic Sociology*, Appleton Century Crofts, New York.

4

BELIEFS, VALUES AND NORMS

All individuals possess some kind of belief and some set of values about some other people, groups, objects or ideologies. Sometimes a patient holds quite specific beliefs about the nature of disease which might be in direct conflict to those held by medical professionals. At other times, and on a broader level, any meeting between two or more individuals involves, among other things, a confrontation between the beliefs and values that each individual holds dear to himself. It may be the case, also, that certain individuals hold beliefs and values that are not only bizarre but in addition may contain a possible threat to the well-being of the community in general. Doctors, for example, may entertain a belief that the prescription of antibiotics should be delayed as long as possible. Nurses may believe that patients should or should not be 'mollycoddled'. Again, patients entering a hospital come equipped with a vast repertoire of beliefs and values that need to be accommodated to the hospital organization. In this chapter we shall be concerned with values as they are learned through the process of socialization and to the extent that they affect behaviour, and with articulate value systems in the form of religion.

VALUES

The study of values has traditionally been the area of concern for philosophers; hence sociologists have studied *social values*. These are not necessarily the same as moral values. Whereas the former might be defined as an awareness that persists over time in relation to an object, the idea or person, and is also charged with emotion, the latter are not to be identified exactly (because of the criterion of *collective welfare*, which is part of the definition of social values). In a sense social values are abstractions, which are emotionally charged because they are important to the individual and relate to goals for any action that the individual might perform. Such values are not beliefs because the latter relate to the truth or falsity of certain facts in society, while the former are more like feelings about objects, ideas or persons. Table 4.1 shows some examples distinguishing between values and beliefs.

TABLE 4.1

Beliefs	Values
God exists	People should believe in God
Britain is morally declining	Immorality is wrong

Each of us possesses a set of abstract sentiments such as 'we are all the same, basically' or 'good will out in the end' which are shared by a great number of people in society. These abstract sentiments, however, change over time and are sometimes contradictory. Another type of social value is the moral norm, which is basically a standard of behaviour which we use as a frame of reference for social action. Sometimes, as we shall see with delinquent gangs, some groups entertain norms which are in conflict with a wider society and indeed actually turn such values inside-out.

We learn values during the process of primary and secondary socialization, and sometimes we learn them so deeply that they are said to be *internalized*, meaning that we carry out a course of action associated with them in a virtually automatic manner. Obviously not all values are held in equal esteem by the individual; hence sociologists talk of *dominant* and *subordinate* values. The strength with which values are held can be measured by testing how many of the population display them in their behaviour, for how long, with what intensity and so on. A study of American society revealed a number of core values that shaped the behaviour of the mass of the population, as follows:

1. achievement and success
2. activity and work
3. moral orientation
4. humanitarian mores
5. efficiency and practicality
6. progress
7. material comfort
8. equality
9. freedom
10. external conformity
11. science and secular rationality
12. nationalism-patriotism
13. democracy
14. individual personality
15. racism and related group-superiority.

America, for example, places a great stress on physical health and great value is placed on a mastery of the environment (rather than adjustment), a concern with practical rather than mystical activities, and the idea of progress towards a goal (rather than the attainment of it). Freidson shows how the rise of a social value such as health is impossible without the rise 'of a vehicle for the value—an organized body of workers who claim jurisdiction over the value'. He is arguing that because physicians may be willing to deal with an aspect of behaviour that is problematic, that does not mean that that behaviour is therefore an illness. Others could be more competent to deal with it.

RELIGION

We turn now to the elaborate organization of beliefs and values into systems which are termed *religions*. Religion may be described broadly as a system of beliefs and practices which are usually considered as being directed towards the 'ultimate concern' of a particular society. Perhaps a better sociological definition of religion (and there are many!) is as follows:

a system of symbols institutionally organized consisting of supra-empirical references that establish powerful and pervasive and long-lasting moods in men by formulating conceptions of a general order of existence, and which point beyond the domain of our 'natural' reality.

A number of people would claim that religion holds the key to the ultimate 'meaning' of the central values of a society and, furthermore, a 'power' of an ultimate nature which stands at the back of such values as some kind of sanction.

SOCIOLOGY OF RELIGION   The study of religion has been one of the important areas of concern of the great sociologists such as Durkheim and Weber. It is important to examine it from our point of view because it *is* so central but also because it gives one of the clearest examples of sociologists in action in an area which is both problematic and delicate.

Sir Edward Tylor attempted, in 1873, as a minimum definition of religion, to describe it as a belief in 'Spiritual Beings'. He felt that this belief could best be examined by looking at animism, which divides into two areas of dogma: (a) posthumous survival of souls; (b) the existence of other spirits up to the rank of deity. Tylor went on to develop an evolutionist theory which postulated four successive stages which arose out of the concept of the soul: animism, polydaemonism, polytheism and monotheism.

In contrast to Tylor's now defunct theory Father Wilhelm Schmidt postulated the idea of an *Urmonotheismus*—original worship centred on the High God—all other religious forms are corruptions of this. However, what Schmidt considered monotheism was in many instances monolatry (worship of one god) and in any case monotheism is rare among primitive peoples.

A more recent theory is that of Pettazzoni, who views the monotheistic religions of Yahwism, Zoroastrianism, Christianity and Islam as having arisen from a reformist protest against polytheism.

Emile Durkheim saw religion as arising in a collective form of experience based on the supposed relation between a human group and the supernatural society and its god. The latter is the totem and is the personification of the clan. His position is sometimes termed *angelicism*. To Durkheim religious phenomena consist of beliefs and practices which are relative to sacred 'things' which are set apart from men and forbidden. All the beliefs and practices join together to form a *moral community*, which is what he called a 'church'. His real contribution in this field was to stress the identification of society with God, and his concern, unlike that of his predecessors, was with seeing the role of religion as a vast symbolic system making social life possible by safeguarding the sentiments or values of society. The role of ritual and ceremony in society was to encourage and sustain discipline, integration, euphoria, and so on.

A number of sociologists have been concerned with the *function* of religion. Although their work is of considerable interest it is, however, misleading to talk of religion as exercising a 'function' because this suggests that it is somehow necessary or inevitable. It encourages us to think of society as consisting of a number of tailor-made slots into which certain phenomena must somehow fit. Malinowski was concerned with the function of religion and magic and held that they are to be found 'whenever man comes to an unbridgeable gap, a hiatus in his knowledge or in his powers of practical control, and yet has to continue in his pursuit'. Religion is born out of 'the real tragedies of human life, out of the conflict between human plans and realities'.

A modern *functionalist*, Talcott Parsons, postulates two main types of frustration arising out of the human situation that provide a focal point for the development of religious patterns. Firstly, men are 'hit' by events that they cannot predict, control or prepare for, such as premature death or severe illness. Secondly, there is a strong emotional investment in the success of human effort but uncontrollable factors intervene, for example the weather damages the crops. These situations pose problems of meaning.

The nature of religion as a modern institution contains a number of features elaborated by Parsons; (a) beliefs; (b) symbols; (c) activities; (d) moral community; (e) rules of conduct. Thus the institution of religion helps man to overcome the 'breaking points' which confront him from time to time, namely contingency, powerlessness and scarcity.

The functionalist would argue that religion (a) provides support, consolation and reconciliation, (b) offers a secure transcendental relationship, (c) makes sacred the norms and values of society, (d) has its own independent value system, (e) provides identity functions, (f) is correlated with maturation of the individual.

However, Bryan Wilson has argued that to accept the functionalist approach is to posit some kind of unchanging psychological nature inherent in man. It completely ignores, as a theory, the changing patterns of social organization, social experience and social opportunity 'which are constantly modifying man's emotional needs and responses. If religion exists to meet certain human needs which it purports are unchanged, functionalists are faced with the fact that nevertheless religion changes. Having derived the needs from religious phenomena, it now refers to the needs in order to assert that religious practices must exist to meet them'. He goes on to say that 'if a given form of religion disappears, then some other "religious" behaviour must be arising in its place. Thus mass-entertainment, mass-rallies, science, totalitarian political parties and ideologies, expensive consumer goods are variously accredited with fulfilling some of the functions once filled by religion'. There have been many criticisms of functionalism in religion. For one, it assumes that social systems are completely integrated and that all elements of such a system are functionable and indispensable.

DILEMMAS IN THE INSTITUTIONALIZATION OF RELIGION   Thomas O'Dea has shown how, looking at the early church from the writings of *Acts* and the *Epistles*, we can see the beginning of religious institutionalization developing into the *cult* and the emergence of *belief patterns*. At a later stage we see the rationalization of belief patterns and the emergence of religious organization. By 200 AD the church had its bishops, doctrine and service of worship. However, the institutionalization of religion poses a number of dilemmas which O'Dea categorizes as follows: (a) Dilemma of Mixed Motivation—the emergence of wide range of individual motives; (b) The Symbolic Dilemma—the objectification of ritualization means a great number of people lose the 'meaning'; (c) The Dilemma of the Administrative Order—the alienation of the 'office' from the rank-and-file; (d) The Dilemma of Delimitation—concrete definition versus substitution of the letter for the spirit; (e) The Dilemma of Power—conversion versus coercion.

RELIGIOUS ORGANIZATION   The *church* (ecclesia) and *sect* have the significant characteristics shown in Table 4.2 according to Troeltsch and others.

TABLE 4.2

Church	Sect
Membership by birth	Voluntary joining
Inclusive	Exclusive
High economic status of members	Low economic status of members
Compromising with existing society	Attitude of ethical austerity

The church is usually fully at one with the social and economic order prevailing in a given society at the time. The *denomination* can be viewed either as a sub-class of the church with a more restricted membership or as an institutionalized *sect*. Wilson sees sects as exclusive bodies who impose some test of merit on entrants. Members of such groups are kept under scrutiny and the pattern of their lives regulated in some way. Wilson offers a typology of sects:

(a) the *conversionist* sect (e.g. early Salvation Army)
(b) the *revolutionary* sect (e.g. Jehovah's Witnesses)
(c) the *introversionist* sect (e.g. various 'holiness' movements)
(d) the *manipulationist* sect (e.g. Scientologists)
(e) the *thaumaturgical* sect (e.g. Spiritualists)
(f) the *reformist* sect (e.g. Quakers)
(g) the *utopian* sect (e.g. various 'hippy' groups).

A typology such as this is based on the responses of the sect to the world. For example, the Jehovah's Witnesses are a revolutionary sect because they look forward to the passing of the present social order, whereas the Scientologists are manipulationists because they claim some special knowledge and techniques for reaching goals which are acceptable by society.

Such schemes as these by Troeltsch and Wilson are called *typologies*. They are useful for purposes of illustration and research but they do not exist 'out there'. Complex human behaviour just cannot be fitted or compartmentalized so neatly. Some sects, for example, are distinctly marginal to the categories and do in fact overlap with a number of them. Perhaps the most damning condemnation is that such schemes tend to try to reduce patterns of behaviour which are very complex to apparently simple social-psychological attitudes which are then seen in terms of motivations, goals and so on.

A final addition to categorizations of this sort is what is usually called *cult*, which consist of a short-lived group which is highly individualistic. There is some disagreement among sociologists as to whether *cult* should indeed be a separate category and some, such as Wilson, have obliterated the category altogether.

RELIGION AND SOCIAL DIFFERENTIATION

Types of religious organization are reflected in relation to the aspect of society to which they refer. For example, it was the political unity of the Church which appeared to give medieval Europe an apparent unity of *society*. Unity of *community*, on the other hand, would involve a different organization of religion. Pre-literate societies generally have religion as 'all pervading' and particularly centred around the rituals of puberty, marriage, birth and death. Pre-industrial society generally has a single religious organization which competes or joins with the state. Industrial–secular society produces a type of religious organization which is pluralistic and divided. Today, in Britain and America, very broadly speaking we can see how social differentiation leads to two very different modes of expression. On the one hand we have the intellectual and liturgical appeal of established organizations for the facilitation of 'middle-class' religious expression, and on the other hand we have the emergence of groupings stressing

53

prayer, emotionalism and piety, principally growing in areas, and catering for segments of the population who were not accommodated by the established religious organizations.

Sociologically it is important to realize that religion (and a lot of other activities) is not a personal and individual idiosyncrasy, but socially determined. In any society which we care to look at it is public, received, inherited, learned and transmitted. The visions of the wise are themselves culturally transmitted and determined and must conform to the expectations of the listeners. One of the important factors in determining the religious experience and belief of an individual is the position he or she occupies in the social strata simply because to a large extent this position determines the way in which one looks at the world and the manner in which we accrue meaning to the life-experiences we receive.

Karl Marx was not specifically concerned with religion as such but with the social phenomenon of *alienation* which results in *false consciousness*. The discovery that man is alienated by religion gives scope for the further discovery that there are other forms of alienation such as the economic structure of capitalism. Weber was later to synthesize these ideas in his thesis that the Protestant Ethic of Calvin was the main vehicle for the emergence of capitalism in Western Europe. Marx also suggested that the bourgeois capitalism of the nineteenth century found its best form of expression in Protestantism: 'For a society based upon the productions of commodities, in which the producers in general enter into social relations with one another by treating their products as commodities and values, whereby they reduce their individual private labour to the standard of homogeneous human labour—for such a society Christianity with its cult of the abstract individual, more especially in its bourgeois developments, Protestantism, Deism, etc. is the most appropriate form of religion.'

One of the main functions of religion, in Marx's view, was as a response to frustration. Man, in his struggle against the world, pits himself initially against the 'spiritual aroma' of the world, religion. But religious suffering is at one and the same time an 'expression of real suffering and a protest against real suffering'. The economic deprivation of the working class is alleviated by adherence to religion, though Marx maintained that this adherence masked the real cause of deprivation and unhappiness, that is, the capitalist system of economics. 'Religion is the sigh of the oppressed creature, the sentiment of a heartless world, the soul of soulless conditions. It is the opium of the people.'

However, it is extremely difficult to assess whether religious activity is a response to frustration, and it is also difficult to demarcate adequately between economic and social status deprivation and other forms of deprivation, for example, impairments such as illness, ageing, and so on. Certainly, the available evidence seems to suggest that religious involvement is strongest in the middle and upper classes than in the working classes, at least in its manifest forms. In a latent way, of course, it may well be that the ideological superstructure of society makes itself felt in other, more sophisticated ways than mere attendance and observance in religious organization. This highlights an important methodological approach to the sociology of religion, that is the difference between the *objective* and *subjective* dimensions of religiosity, on the one hand between actual church attendance and on the other the attitudes and beliefs of individuals.

WEBER AND RELIGION The German philosopher Nietzsche described religion as the means by which the repressed resentment of the powerless was expressed. The Christian religion in particular was the slave's revolt. Weber developed this correspondence in a more sophisticated manner and showed how the differentiation in the interpretation of salvation and suffering varied from social class to social class. Weber argued that religion provides different 'rewards' for different social strata.

1. The 'theodicy of good fortune' is expressed by those with high social and economic privileges who, rather than cultivate a theology of salvation, 'assign to religion the primary function of legitimizing their own life pattern and situation in the world'.

2. The 'theodicy of the dispossessed' or disprivileged, is concerned with release from suffering, misfortune, and so forth, and this group is particularly concerned with what it can *become* rather than with what it *is*, endeavouring to establish a principle of 'just compensation'.

Weber further elaborated the strata which he regarded as the special vehicles and interpreters of the world religions. For example, Christianity was carried by itinerant artisan journeyman, Hinduism by literati, and Buddhism by mendicant or beggar monks. This interpretation dispenses with the 'great man' theory of the origins of the world religions and instead stresses the influences of the particular strata which developed them. It is these strata which accommodated and articulated the ideology, and although the external symbols may bear resemblance to each other the interpretation is different. Weber goes on to state that even though the social situation may give rise to, and be reflected in, a religion, and economic, political and social influences shape a religious ethic, 'it receives its stamp primarily from religious sources'.

Or course, religious forms of expression do not arise in a social vacuum. Christianity's revolutionary origins were to a large extent to be expected in the context of a revolutionary age. Again, the rise of a large number of sects in the period immediately after 1800 and until the 1840s can be explained in terms of the socio-historical context of the times.

RELATIVE DEPRIVATION Various attempts have been made to describe religious satisfaction for particular segments of the social strata in terms of a typology of relative deprivation. Glock talks about five possible types of deprivation: economic, social, organismic, ethical and psychic. *Ethical* deprivation is the lack of needed legitimizing values, and *psychic* deprivation is concerned with the search for a 'meaning' to life. *Economic* deprivation is the lack of prestige and wealth, and *social* deprivation is particularly deprivation of status. *Organismic* deprivation is deprivation of physical and mental well-being. Glock and Stark relate these 'felt' deprivations to appropriate types of religious groups, as follows.

sect (economic deprivation)
church (social deprivation)
healing movements (organismic deprivation)
reform movements (ethical deprivation)
cult (psychic deprivation)

The problem with this sort of scheme is that it is too ambitious. It tries to establish a one-one correlation between deprivation and religious groups, and one of which incorporates a multiplicity of beliefs and value systems. More important, schemes such as this ignore two important aspects of religious organization. First, religious groups have their own *dynamism* and often arise from 'internal' conflict or schisms and not from a postulated need of a number of individuals who have been deprived of some aspect of social experience. Second, one must be wary of theories which try to suggest a succession of universal needs which either are attached to people like arms or legs or which at best are unchanging.

MILLENARIAN MOVEMENTS Messianic and millenarian movements flourished particularly in the Middle Ages as a response to deprivation, mostly social, although on the whole they were essentially religious and not political protests. Cohn shows how such movements as the People's Crusades, the Flagellant Movement, the Taborites of Bohemia and many more arose among the uprooted and disoriented peasantry. As Cohn says, 'Between the close of the 11th Century and the first half of the sixteenth it repeatedly happened in Europe that the desire of the poor to improve the material conditions of their lives became transfused with religious fantasies. Briefly it would seem that when the existing order or structure of a society is undermined or devalued, this process is a cumulative one; and if it has gone at all, or some major catastrophe strikes the lower and more exposed strata of the population, the way to revolutionary chiliasm is open.' With the breakdown of the supporting agencies for the Feudalistic structuring of society and the emergence of a new economic and labour pattern, Cohn sees these great movements as originating through a combination of circumstances such as the following: messianic cultural elements already *in* the culture, such as the Book of Revelation (a favourite source for such groups); surplus population; no institutionalized means for expressing grievances; weakening of the authority framework in society; and the opening of new horizons and possibilities.

In more recent times the impact of European culture upon the small, simpler societies of the world has frequently inspired what are now called *nativistic* movements (variously known as millenarian, chiliasm, nativistic, messianic and revitalizing movements). Analysable in terms of culture shock, these movements have given us considerable insight into the dynamism of religion. Two examples of such movements among the modern American Indians are the Paiute Ghost Dance religion and the Peyote Cult. The former occurred at the end of the nineteenth century, in the

1870s. The buffalo had disappeared from the Great Plains, the Indians had been herded into reservations, and the Indian culture had collapsed. The originators of the movement promised a re-establishment of Indian values and life, with the proviso that recruits underwent a period of prolonged dancing. The movement led directly to the catastrophic Sioux uprisings. The rapid spread of the movement can be accounted for by the relative amounts of deprivation among the tribes. The Navaho did not succumb to the movement because, (a) they possessed a stable culture pattern; (b) ingrained in their culture was a fear of the dead and ghosts; (c) their economy was not centred on the vanishing buffalo but on sheep and goats.

The second movement provided an alternative response to deprivation because its approach was essentially peaceful. The violence of the Ghost Dance led to its being forcibly exterminated, and therefore the Peyote Cult was able to survive in areas the Ghost Dance had been forced to evacuate. In its present form it is the largest native movement and is organized as the Native American Church, embodying a compromise between Christianity and nativism.

Worsley and others have described the emergence of Melanesian cults which have as part of their object the acquisition, for their members, of the European manufactured goods known as *cargo*. Worsley has shown a political element underlying some of these cargo cults, and in the case of the Sanusi of Cyrenaica how the movement's leaders represent a *political* response by the islanders to foreign mobilization of wealth and control. The revitalization elements are suggested by the emphasis on the magical modelling of the White Man's goods in the hope that success equal to that of the European will be forthcoming. It is difficult to discern a pattern in these diverse movements—the New Guinea Cargo Cults arose without their ever having seen a white man, whereas the Ghost Dance arose in direct response to white–Indian contact. Again, the medieval movements are not nativistic, although the others are, and so on. Again, similar culture clashes among the Xhosa of South Africa and the Christians of Porto Nova have given way to a reasonable fusion process without the consequences which have arisen out of similar culture clashes.

RELIGION AS AN ALTERNATIVE RESPONSE   Alternative courses of action to the 'meanings of life' are socially structured in the sense that the particular response an individual or group takes is somehow embedded in the society around him. Liston Pope in his analysis of a strike in a cotton mill in Castonia, North Carolina, in 1929, gives a graphic example of this. The religious section of the community came out unreservedly against the strike organizers and justified the practices of the management. The point he is making is that when the strikers joined the Holiness sects they might just as effortlessly have joined a political protest movement—a religious response is only one response among many. One of the reasons for an essentially *religious* response in this particular instance was the *availability* of the Holiness sects. Another was the underlying theme which a number of students of sects favour, that of *transversibility*: 'Because they have no jewelry to wear, they make refusal to wear jewelry, including wedding rings, a religious requirement. They transmute poverty into a symptom of grace.' In other words, they substitute high (religious) status for low (economic) status.

Stark has made the point that 'if reform is possible a political party rather than a religious sect will appear on the scene; if reform is a distinct *impossibility*, a religious sect rather than a political party will appear'. Stark sees sects very much as protest movements which express their economic and political discontents in religious terms. Generally, he says, sects have arisen among individuals or groups which are of low social status and he attempts to substantiate his thesis by a description of the role of textile workers in the history of European sectarianism. It is true, of course, that the working class predominate in certain sectarian movements such as Christadelphianism, Jehovah's Witnesses, and that movements such as the Elim Foursquare Gospel Church flourishes in market and seaside towns where there is often a culturally deprived population. Wilson has said that 'intense religious experience is one way of adding depth to lives otherwise shallow, insecure and difficult'. This is by no means the whole story, of course, because some sects are in fact middle class, such as the Catholic Apostolic Church and the Christian Scientists.

THE PROTESTANT ETHIC AND THE RISE OF CAPITALISM   As we have mentioned Weber suggested a link between the 'rational' capitalist enterprise and a set of fundamental beliefs because he noticed that high-status occupations, especially the leaders of big business, were overwhelmingly filled by Protestants. This led him to suggest that there was a *congruence* between the two 'meaning systems', that of the spirit of capitalism and that of the ascetic ethic, or what he termed an *elective affinity*. Although not the sole cause of capitalism, Weber nevertheless regarded Protestantism as one cause. His thesis has been criticized on a number of grounds. There is not sufficient evidence for postulating a *causal* link between the two meaning systems; there was nothing very peculiar about the spirit of capitalism and therefore he need not have singled it out; Calvin's ideas were not those of Puritanism, and neither was the latter a consistent body of thought. However, Weber did highlight the *transformative* aspect of Protestantism, that is, the capacity of religion or secular ideologies to legitimize, either in secular or religious ideological terms, the emergence of new social institutions and individual motivations.

Some empirical work on the Weberian thesis has been done in America. Mayer and Sharp found that both white and negro Catholics had the least economic success. Jews, followed closely by Episcopalians and Calvinists, have achieved the greatest worldly success. Lenski, in his study of Detroit, found the same evidence for Catholics ranking low on the economic motivation scale. 'The Jews and white Protestants have identified themselves with the individualistic, competitive patterns of thought and action linked with the middle class ... By contrast Catholics and negro Protestants have more often been associated with the collectivistic, security oriented, working class patterns of thought and action.'

Lenski's findings have been directly challenged by Father Andrew Greeley, who found little difference in the degree of assimilation to American society of the Detroit Catholics, that Catholics increasingly approximated the American average in their values, and that once assimilated any distinctiveness disappears. In his sample, Greely found Catholics more interested than Protestants in making money, more than likely to choose business as a career, and fully achievement oriented. We must bear in mind, however, that perhaps Greeley took his sample, a particular age-group/educational group, from those who are more likely to be achievement oriented and anxious to get on in the world.

Will Herberg, in order to find out the reason why so many Americans attend church, discovered that being a Protestant, a Catholic or a Jew are three expressible ways of accepting American identity, and that being religious has become, in fact, evidence of adherence to national values. The many sects in America are, in fact, simply versions of the three main positions.

SECULARIZATION   The rise of a modern pluralistic society has meant the increase of rationalization in all the spheres of life. Ironically, Christianity, particularly in its Protestant form, has accelerated the process. Some of the factors which have contributed to the decreasing embrace of religion on most areas of human life are the rise of positivism and science, the emergence of linguistic philosophy, the rise of Protestant biblical criticism, and modern behavioural psychology. Sociologists have long recognized that the process of secularization, 'a process whereby religious thinking, practice and institutions lose social significance', has not affected different strata of the population uniformly. Berger states, 'Thus it has been found that the impact of secularisation has tended to be stronger on men than on women, on people in the middle range than on the very young and very old, in the cities than in the country, on classes directly concerned with modern industrial production (particularly the working class) than on those of more traditional occupations (such as artisans or small shopkeepers), on Protestants and Jews than on Catholics, and the like. At least as far as Europe is concerned, it is possible to say with some confidence, on the basis of these data, that church-related religiosity is strongest (and thus, at any rate, social-structural secularisation least) on the margins of modern industrial society, both in terms of marginal classes (such as the remnants of the old petty bourgeoisies) and marginal individuals (such as those eliminated from the work process).'

SECULAR ALTERNATIVES   Recent work in the sociology of religion has tended to suggest that perhaps many of the characteristics to be found in religious groups can be seen in secular groups as well. Religious groups are legitimizing systems, but there are other legitimizing systems which are not overtly religious. Such groups are sometimes called para-, surrogate, or pseudo-religions and might include Marxism, Positivism or Freudianism, Alcoholics Anonymous or certain groups for former mental patients such as Recovery, Inc. or Neurotics Nomine. Often such groups have a similar organization and structure but they are ordered systems in society, also, governed by or possessing discernible rules or relationships of systems. Fringe politics, for example, often resembles fringe religion, and indeed is sometimes described in terms of sects. Black Nationalism displays both political and religious strands. Humanist societies display some of the characteristics of sects. It has been pointed out that Marxism and Christadelphianism have analogies to each other. Again, conversion to both types of belief system displays much the same patterns.

RELIGION AND THE SOCIAL CONSTRUCTION OF REALITY   As we mentioned earlier, Durkheim saw society as though it was the *sui generis* out of which religion was made, and which both produces the fears that make men turn to religion and in turn the religion that offers some a solution. Berger is concerned to show how man is concerned with imposing 'meaning' upon 'reality'. When the legitimization for our actions is greater than the *nomos* (the meaning of the humanly constructed social order) this becomes the *cosmos* (or religion). In a pluralistic modern technological society there may, indeed, be competing systems that can legitimize our actions and provide 'man's ultimate shield against the terror of anomie'.

RELIGION AND MEDICAL ORGANIZATION

In the beginning religion provided the only explanation of disease and death in society and even now, in some simple societies, a magical or religious account predominates. Freidson draws attention to the remarkable similarity between Zande witchcraft and modern medical practice, both occupations having 'gained the command of the exclusive competence to determine the proper content and effective method of performing some task'. Further, 'the occupational group, then, must be the prime source of the criteria that qualify a man to work in an acceptable fashion'. Gradually we witness the general 'public belief in the consulting occupation's competence, in the value of its professed knowledge and skill'. Similarly, Silman has described the process whereby the priesthood (doctor) becomes separated from the believer (patient).

Glaser locates Judaism, Western and Eastern Christianity and Islam as factors affecting the rise of the modern hospital. Buddhism and Hinduism have mixed implications but neither appears to have initiated a programme for mass care of the sick or for a sustained welfare service. Religions of taboo are inimical to Western medicine and clients prefer 'instant' cure to a prolonged period of hospitalization. Glaser suggests that Christianity is the only major religion which has so many functionaries employed in hospital care. He says that the novices of religious orders 'tend to come from large, closely-knit and religious families, from the lower middle and lower classes in towns and rural areas, and that novices have depended heavily upon their parish priests for advice'. There is no evidence that recruits to nursing are any more religious than the average in the population, although the religious nurse from, for example, the Community of the Daughters of Charity of St Vincent de Paul, may be expected to regard nursing itself as a *means* and 'her professional activity is the framework in which she exercises her mission'. Glaser quotes a Spanish doctor accusing nurses from a religious order (and he was not alone) of being 'usually less exact in measuring doses. They are less exact in accounting for time, that is, they are less careful in giving injections exactly on time'. In their practice of nursing nuns appear to be more strict, to avoid catheterizing patients or bathing patients, to be more hesitant to unlock doors in psychiatric hospitals and so forth. Nuns, however, regard 'worldly' nurses as being less dedicated, less total in their commitment, and more likely to try to avoid very unpleasant tasks. The work of McClelland on *n Ach* or achievement saw it as a function of the situation and the enduring strength of the motivation in the individual personality. He supposed that Protestant-reared children would be high achievers, although Catholic children would be high on affiliation. It is 'not surprising that medicine gains many recruits among Protestants while nursing is particularly attractive to Catholics'.

Religion is also of some importance in determining medical policy in relation to such important events as birth, death and food, so that a policy of birth control can produce severe conflicts in religious personnel whose particular beliefs prohibit such a practice, post-mortems are anathema to Arabs and often end up with a riot or occasional assassination of the dissectors, and various food taboos can arouse difficulties in preparation.

CONCLUSIONS

The relationship between social status and belief systems has been graphically illustrated by when Katherine and Charles George's analysis of 2490 saints who had been canonized in the twenty centuries of the Christian era. Over 70% came from the upper and 17% from the middle classes. Only 5% came from the working class. Even after death differential practices in funeral rites and decisions vary according to social class and religious affiliation, the rites of the middle class being essentially prestigious while those of the economically depressed offer facilities for the equalization of injustice incurred in this world.

Measurement of the relationship between social status and religious practice can be tackled at two levels of analysis: (a) overt religious involvement, for example church attendances; (b) covert religious involvement, for example private prayer. It need not necessarily be the case that the two coincide to any extent, and thus high attendance is only *part* of the way in which people can be religiously involved. Again, attendance at religious meeting places in America is more secularized than it would seem to be here. Generally it appears that the middle and upper classes are the most active in church attendance although there is some evidence that the lower classes are more *religiously* involved, tending to have a higher incidence of personal prayer and more creedal and devotional activities. Some have made the point that a large number of the lower class have no religious commitment whatsoever, and may well have found functional alternatives to religion via political extremism.

Patients and staff who exhibit various values and attitudes at variance with the general tenor of the hospital community are doing so not because of any personal or private reason but because for one thing or another they have opted for that interpretation, and to impose that meaning system on the world around them.

SUGGESTIONS FOR FURTHER READING

BERTRAND, A. L. (1967). *Basic Sociology*, Appleton Century Crofts, New York.
COHN, N. (1961). *The Pursuit of the Millennium* (2nd edn.), Harper and Row, New York.
FREIDSON, E. (1972). *Profession of Medicine*, Dodd, Mead and Company, New York.
GLASER, W. A. (1970). *Social Settings and Medical Organisation*, Atherton Press, New York.
GREEN, R. W. (ed.) (1959). *Protestantism and Capitalism*, D. C. Heath and Company, Boston.
HILL, M. (1973). *A Sociology of Religion*, Heinemann, London.
O'DEA, T. (1966). *The Sociology of Religion*, Prentice-Hall, Englewood Cliffs, New Jersey.
THOMPSON, K. and Jones, R. K. (1972). 'Religion, Stratification and Deprivation', in *Beliefs and Religion*, Open University Press, Bletchley.
SILMAN, R. (1972). 'Teaching the Medical Student to Become a Doctor', in *Counter Course*, edited by Pateman, T., Penguin Books, Harmondsworth.
WALLIS, R. (ed.) (1975). *Sectarianism: Analyses of Religious and Non-Religious Sects*, Peter Own, London.
WILSON, B. R. (1970). *Religious Sects*, Weidenfeld and Nicolson, London; (1966) *Religion in Secular Society*, C. A. Watts, London.

5

SOCIAL DIFFERENCES

There have already been indications that people differ from one another in a number of important ways, some of which may include differences in income but also such things as power and prestige. Every society allocates these and other things according to their own distinctive criteria, and during the course of history both the criteria and the system of social stratification might change. By social stratification, we will mean the way in which people are *ranked* on a scale of inferiority/superiority, which results in differences between them of privileges, rewards, obligations and restrictions. The term itself is taken from geology, where it refers to successive layers of rock, but when we talk of people as being socially stratified the problem becomes much more difficult because people think, feel and sometimes act about the way they are stratified and about their social position. Moreover, each stratum interacts with every other, producing a conflict of interests.

The patients that are seen by nurses and doctors obviously differ in a number of ways. They are fathers, mothers, brothers, sisters, male, female, tall, short, old, young, good-looking, ugly, and so on. Most of these differences are determined in a way that it would be almost impossible to alter, but social stratification is not concerned with these kinds of criteria (although they may enter into it) but more with the problem of *scarcity*, and more particular the scarcity of positions in society which individuals desire.

STRATIFICATION IN SUBHUMAN AND SIMPLE SOCIETIES

It is well known that animals try to exert social dominance over each other. Among birds this is commonly referred to as the pecking order. When a new bird is introduced into a cage or pen full of other birds he has to fight at least one of the birds in order to establish which one will become dominant. Once such dominance has been established the defeated bird, on subsequent meeting, retreats from the victor. Research suggests that social dominance is established by a number of such factors as strength, size, degree of fear, familiarity with the territory, and the general state of health. As far as chickens are concerned, to be at the top of a pecking order establishes a number of privileges such as the first choice of a partner or the best food. Observations of rodents, dogs and primates revealed very different patterns of social domination according to such measurements as intensity, duration, and so on. In insect societies there exists a very rigid structure of stratification.

Many simple societies operate a system of stratification based on age sets. The Australian aborigines have such a system, and it is one in which the social status (the relative degree of honour or prestige which individuals accord to other individuals who occupy a social position) of any one aborigine is the same as that of another of his own age. Contrary to what we might think such a society is *open* because no individual is able to remain in the same position all his life, all have a chance of working through each position, all do the same type of work associated with each position, and so on. This stands in marked contrast to a *closed* stratification system such as caste (a stratification system where individuals are accorded a permanent rank at birth and in which contact between categories is severely restricted).

MAJOR SYSTEMS OF SOCIAL STRATIFICATION

Generally, sociologists have isolated three major systems of social stratification: caste, estate, and class systems. In one sense these are what are known as ideal types (constructs or models of the real world) because they do not exist in a pure form in any society and are used rather as ways of comparing any actual system of social stratification both with other systems and with the pure form itself.

CASTE The caste system is composed of a number of horizontal strata each responsible for a number of functions within a society. Every caste or sub-caste has specific functions it can perform and others that it cannot. Thus a member of a high caste cannot become 'contaminated' by performing a function or an occupation reserved for one from a lower caste. The ranking order of such a society is usually the result of some struggle of powerful groups in the society at some time in history, or the result of military conquest by an outside power.

The best known example of such a system is the Hindu caste system in India, which is usually divided into four main categories (although there are an estimated 10 000 caste groups) of *Brahmins* or priests, *Kshatriya* or warriors, *Vaisya* or merchants, and *Sudra* or workers and peasants. In addition to these four main groups there exist the *Untouchables* or *outcastes* who have been expelled from their caste (either themselves or through some action of their ancestors which violated the rigorous caste rules). It is estimated that 6% of the Hindu population of India are Brahmins, and 20% untouchables. These four traditional *Varnas* (the term originally meant *colour*) are held by some to be very similar to the next major system we shall discuss, the estate. There is evidence that passage between castes was always possible either by intermarriage or some other means and that they were not as closed as is popularly thought. Today caste lines are being considerably weakened in the big cities and by government legislation.

Theoretically caste is ascribed and fixed for life and marriage is endogamous. Social interaction between members of different castes is rigidly fixed by a series of rules meant to consolidate the purity of the Brahmin and the impurity of the Untouchable. Some of these rules prohibit the entry of the lowest class into the city walls between 3 p.m. and 6 p.m. for fear that their shadows, lengthened by the afternoon sun, would contaminate a member of a superior caste. Untouchables were not permitted within 124 feet of a Brahmin, and for them to even glance at a cooking pot necessitated the destruction of the contents. This was particular attention paid to a set of complicated rules governing eating behaviour of Untouchables (Harijans) and Brahmins.

Generally, the caste system appears to be closely tied to occupation with the Harijans occupying the very low-status jobs such as road-sweepers and basketmakers and the Brahmins or priests at the top followed by warriors, herdmen, fishermen and so on. Many Harijans have made fortunes, and by the process of *Sanskritization* or the spread of Hindu influence on tribal ritualized beliefs, whole groups have bettered their caste position. Caste is, however, not just an occupational group but an example of a closed status group because individuals who perform the occupations are designated inferior/superior by others. Social mobility (the extent to which an individual or group moves up or down the social stratification system) is usually achieved by a group or collectivity rather than by individuals.

There are two ways that are frequently used to explain the caste system. Firstly, the historical explanation for the existence and persistence of caste refers to the original Aryan invaders who brought their system of ranks into a highly tribalized society through the introduction of food taboos, subsequently consolidating their social distance by these food taboos. A religious and magical system later consolidated their maintenance of social distance from the conquered people. The second explanation lies in the relationship between *Jati* (the social reality of caste life for Hindus) and *Varna*, the former being the actual division of the local community, endogamous, and often having the same occupation, and being able to 'fit' into the Varna system. The system of division is supported by the *Karma* (which teaches that membership of a particular caste is deserved) and *Dharma* (the rules or code of duty). Some have seen the caste system as being fundamentally indebted to the rules and regulations governing pollution while others have tried to distinguish between Hindu religion and Hindu law, seeing the latter as the main factor behind the caste system.

What does seem to be the case is that the dominant castes sustain their superior position, both social and economic, by also controlling the religious system of the country. In a country where the majority of the population are still desperately poor and illiterate this has been comparatively easy for a period of some three hundred years. Recent social change following the departure of the British had led to some erosion of the caste system, although some sociologists would argue that there is evidence that caste-consciousness and organization have *increased* in modern India, and point to the proliferation of caste shops, banks, papers, and so on, in support of this.

SLAVERY Very brief mention must be made of slavery which, although not a major system of social stratification, is nevertheless treated by some sociologists, notably Bottomore, as being able to contribute to the approach as a whole. Slavery is a system whereby an individual and his labour are regarded as capital. These systems can vary from one of extremity in which the slave has no rights to one in which he is protected to some extent by laws. The basis of slavery is economic, and the individuals concerned are subjected to a system of social inequality in which he is compelled to work as the property of an aristocratic group.

MODERN EXAMPLES OF CASTE AND SLAVERY In modern times the caste system has been introduced into countries other than India, such as South Africa and the Southern States of America. Similarly with the Jews under Nazi Germany. In all these examples a certain group of people are categorized as inferior in relation to superior groups on the basis of some criterion.

Slavery was introduced on a large scale into the plantations of the Southern States of America and some of the British colonies. This is usually known as *commercial* slavery and associated with plantation agriculture in areas of the world with a labour shortage. The nineteenth century saw the introduction of *domestic* slavery into industrial nations, basically a large group of people providing domestic or household services in addition to personal service for a small privileged section of the population. The rise of Nazi Germany saw the introduction of large-scale slavery in Europe, although it has always persisted in Moslem countries to some extent.

ESTATE Another closed system is the estate system, similar to the caste system but less rigid. It was at its most prominent during feudal times in Europe and, like the caste system, consisted of ranking various positions according to a classification based on functionalism. It was a less rigid system because the different estates, orders or categories were held to be of equal or near equal importance. The estate system comprised a horizontal group or orders, namely politics, military, religious, economic and peasant. Each horizontal division also contained a hierarchical stratification; for example, in the peasant order the yeomen were at the highest position and the serfs at the lowest.

There was legitimate interaction between the orders such as when the religious order, due to celibacy, sought recruits from the peasant order.

Girls, also could transfer from one estate to another through marriage. The serf, at the bottom of the vertical order of an estate, had no right of appeal to the king over his chattels, and so on. Some social historians would argue that there were only two estates in classical feudalism, the nobility and the clergy, while others would recognize that the burghers formed a group before they finally took over the entire system.

Like the caste system the estate system was supported by a religious ideology and a legal system, and the church was an essential force in maintaining the feudal society of the middle ages.

CLASS Class systems are usually found in advanced, market-oriented societies and are generally described as groups possessing the same economic position in society. A section of the general population sees itself, and is seen by others, as differing from other sections of the population in value orientations, prestige, possessions, occupation, education and life style. Compared with caste and estate systems this kind of system is relatively open and allows individuals to transfer from one section to another.

THE IMPORTANCE OF SOCIAL CLASS

Class is one of the terms used by sociologists which has a different meaning to the non-sociologist or man in the street. It is important to the sociologist because it helps to bring out a number of theoretical issues. It is also important because it concerns all of us and affects many other social processes such as behaviour, political habits, religion, ability and educational opportunity, manner of dress, accent, and so on. It is not, however, simply an intellectual concept, but embraces our eating habits, our thinking, our way of copulating, our choice of marriage partners— in fact all our behaviour as humans. Very often people from one social class find it very difficult to communicate or understand a person from a different social class. Upper class people may be regarded as 'cissies' by working-class men who in turn might be regarded as uncouth and barbaric by the upper or middle classes. Middle-class psychiatrists, for example, have less success in the treatment of working-class patients than in that of middle-class ones, and middle-class teachers are not the most successful in coping adequately with working-class children.

In terms of health, individuals who belong to the middle class are likely to live longer, be generally healthier, suffer from fewer crippling diseases, and have a secure pension in their old age. In more general terms social class is now known to be associated with mortality rates, the educational level reached by individuals, one's likelihood of becoming physically or mentally ill, juvenile delinquency, one's occupational level, and crime and divorce rates. Social class factors are also seen to be important in the degree to which any one individual seeks to *achieve* something, and levels of achievement are seen to vary with social class.

Different strata of the population seek to 'get on' more than others (although even in the same class there are differences in the stress on achievement).

Social class also enters into religious affiliation and behaviour, and into the values and attitudes held by people in society in relation to politics, education, thrift, and so on. It also enters into the degree and type of social participation so that leisure patterns vary enormously in relation to the different social classes, as do reading habits and viewing habits.

THEORIES OF SOCIAL CLASS

Karl Marx (1818–83), a German sociologist and social theorist who laid the foundations of the Communist movement, was very concerned with social class, and because he was also interested in economics he came to the conclusion that members of a society who have in common the same relationship to the means of production belong to the same class. He argued that to produce something affected social relationships and that an individual's class position depended on his position in the economic system. Marx saw capitalist society as ultimately composed of two opposing groups possessing different interests:

1. bourgeoisie or owners—who owned and controlled the industrial and commercial means of production;
2. proletariat or non-owners—who owned nothing but their labour, which they sold to the bourgeoisie for wages.

Marx was not describing an actual society here but offering an analytical tool for examining what he termed capitalist societies. Endemic to such societies is the notion of *conflict*. The two main classes are constantly at war because 'the interests of capital and the interests of wage labour are diametrically opposed'.

Max Weber (1864–1920), a German sociologist and politician, built upon Marx's work and distinguished between three dimensions of social class:

1. Class—the amount and source of individual income in so far as these affect the chances of obtaining other valued things, mainly property and services;
2. Status—the unequal distribution in society of social honour, and particular styles of life and the consumption of commodities. Status is obviously tied to class, particularly occupations. Thus a second-hand car salesman may have a higher income than a nurse or schoolteacher and therefore in Weber's sense a higher class, but his status is lower;
3. Power or parties—the ability to influence the actions of others. This includes trade unions, political parties, professional associations, and so on.

Any individual can be rated along each of these three dimensions, but generally speaking a high position in one of the dimensions usually brings with it a high position in the other dimensions, for example a consultant surgeon may have high status and high class. However, incongruities can occur, such as the example of the member of the aristocracy who has lost his material wealth and possessions (low class), his ability to enforce decisions in society (low power), but is still regarded as having a 'good standing' in society (high prestige or status).

Talcott Parsons, the American sociologist, sees social stratification as being potentially conflicting, but in reality it integrates society and makes it cohesive. What we have is not two great conflicting classes but a series of gradations in which social honour is given to members of society by other members of society. This view, of integration and cohesion, is known as the *functionalist* theory of society, which sees society as relatively stable, and its individual members as being in consensus or agreement about certain values which they hold in common. The stress is on the inter-relationships in society.

Some others of the functionalist school have suggested that social stratification is important for the maintenance of society, especially in the way in which occupations vary in their degree of importance, and that such importance is attached, generally, to those occupations which occupy a *scarce* position in society and where recruits to such positions need to undergo a prolonged course of training. Differential rewards are important in order to induce people to undergo such a training.

THE NUMBER AND DETERMINANTS OF SOCIAL CLASS RANK

Until now we have been discussing theoretical models of social class. A great amount of work is undertaken, however, on distinguishing the social classes in society from one another and deciding how wide or how narrow they are going to regard each category of social class.

DETERMINANTS In terms of specific examples of the kinds of behaviour, accomplishments, possessions, and so on, that we normally use to decide a person's social class, we look at his education, income, occupation, type of housing and so on. A second, and more theoretical way of looking at the problem, is to try to gauge the relative power which an individual is accorded by others in society.

NUMBER The *continuum* theory states that social classes are not sharply distinguished from one another, but overlap. While a number of sociologists might agree with this they feel that in terms of analysis it is not much help. The *three-class* theory sees society as composed of an upper, middle and lower class. Others who felt that such a theory was too simple and did not distinguish strata sufficiently suggested a *six-class* theory in which the upper class becomes divided into upper-upper and lower-upper, the middle into upper-middle and lower-middle, and the lower into upper-lower and lower-lower.

More recent studies of social stratification and *social mobility* between different strata have been carried out largely in terms of occupational-prestige scales. In this country scales of occupational status are usually based on some modification of the Registrar General's Classification (Table 5.1).

TABLE 5.1

I–II	Professional and managerial
III	White collar
III (Man)	Skilled manual
IV	Semi-skilled
V	Unskilled

Although occupation as a measure of an individual's class position is a fairly accurate measure in itself, we must still be wary of equating occupation exactly with class status. Also certain confusion can easily arise, for example in placing a musician in class III—whether he is a member of the Royal Liverpool Philharmonic Orchestra or a member of an insignificant pop group.

Moser and Hall attempted to rectify some of the confusion in the Registrar General's scale as in Table 5.2, with percentages of the working population in each class shown on the left. The percentages are based on

TABLE 5.2

3·0%	I	Professional and high administrative
4·5%	II	Managerial and executive
10·0%	III	Inspectional, supervisory, and other non-manual (high grade)
13·0%	IV	Inspectional, supervisory, and other non-manual (low grade)
41·0%	V	Skilled Manual, and routine grades of non-manual
16·5%	VI	Semi-skilled manual
12·0%	VII	Unskilled manual

the Hall and Jones study in 1950, but it gives some idea of the relative *spread* of individuals into the different categories. Another way of doing this is to compare the occupational categories with the percentage of the male population and in terms of social class, as on Table 5.3.

This gives 30·5% of the population (male) as being middle class and 69·5% as being working class.

OTHER MEASUREMENTS Other ways of measuring class position in the

TABLE 5·3

Occupational categories	% of male population	Social class
I	3·0	Upper middle class
II	4·5	Middle middle class
III and IV	23·0	Lower middle class
V	41·0	Skilled working class
VI and VII	28·5	Semi-skilled and unskilled working class

relatively open societies with which we are most familiar are the *life-style* approach, the *subjective* approach, and the *reputational* approach. The life-style approach uses the criteria of who a person mixes with, what he owns and what he wears and eats, and so on. This approach assumes that people tend to mix 'like-to-like' and also that their social behaviour or the way they live tends to distinguish them. The reputational approach usually entails people with a knowledge of a society acting as judges and placing individuals into social-class categories. The subjective approach is merely to ask an individual what category he would classify himself. There are, in fact, various faults in each of these approaches and researchers tend to use a *multiple-index approach* (two or more of the above approaches) when working on data.

SUBJECTIVE ASPECTS OF STRATIFICATION

As opposed to the *objective* aspects of class—how individuals relate to the means of production and how this affects their lives—sociologists also show interest in the *subjective* aspects—how people see their society as being socially stratified, whether they agree with this, and so on. One well-known example of this subjective element is derived from Marx and involves the notion of *class consciousness* (the realization that a number of individuals share the same interests but that these interests are in opposition to other groups in society).

Individuals who share this class consciousness have an image or picture of the way society is run, ordered and held together. For example, some might see virtually everything in society as being dominated by evil and wicked capitalists who manipulate and control the destinies of everyone and everything. Elizabeth Bott, writing about the family and social networks some twelve years ago, gave a vivid picture of complementary and independent family activities with 'close-knit' and 'loose-knit' networks. Although she was arguing about the degree of segregation in the relationship of roles between spouses and how this varies directly in relation to the degree of connectedness of the social network of the family, she also, in addition, gave a graphic picture of the way in which the people she was studying 'saw' society. Various studies of communities in rural Wales, England, and working-class communities in Britain as a whole often give quite clear descriptions of the way the people 'see', through their ideologies and so on, the way *they* or their group view the construction of society. David Lockwood described three types of workers, each with their different images of society. The proletarian worker adopts the power model of society, the deferential worker adopts the status hierarchy as his perception of social inequality, and the privatized worker adopts the pecuniary model of society. These images are determined by the work situation and the way it is organized, how the work is related to the community in which the worker lives, and the way in which status is allocated. CLASS AND VALUES To belong to one social class rather than another can imply a number of different life-styles, different types of social relationship, and different values and norms. For example, the degree to which one uses the educational system and succeeds in it depends to a very large measure on social-class influences. Florence Kluckholn suggested a model of the different ways in which different social strata answered different fundamental questions about the environment. These fundamental answers, which are accepted and unchallenged by the strata, she termed *life orientations*. For example, the lower classes tend to live in the immediate period of time and think not of the future but of the present and its problems. The middle classes think constantly of the future, and hence *defer* their gratification, while the working class requires *immediate* gratification. The middle class, also, sees nature as capable of manipulation, while the lower class sees itself as being manipulated by nature. We therefore can expect the working class to be relatively fatalistic and to use such expressions as 'it had to be' and to invoke the concept of 'luck' a little more often. Sociologists have subsequently applied these *models* to the achievement of children from different classes in terms of a 'getting on' ideology (middle class) and a 'getting by' ideology (working class).

TABLE 5.4

Orientations or problems	Range of variations		or possible solutions
1. Relationship between man and nature	Subjugation to nature	Harmony with nature	Mastery over nature
2. Time	Emphasis on the past	Emphasis on present time	Emphasis on future time
3. Activity	Emphasis on being	Emphasis on being in, or becoming, or development	Doing accomplishment of tasks
4. Significant relationships	Individualistic	Collectivity	
5. Human nature	Evil	A mixture of good and evil	Good
	Lower class	Lower-middle class	Middle class

Some sociologists have argued that class cultural differences may involve differences in language and intellectual approaches to problems. Basil Bernstein, following a long tradition among anthropologists, has argued that working- and middle-class people use linguistic codes that are different both in their grammar and in their words. Working-class people use what he terms a *restricted code* (for example, a limited and restricted use of adjectives and adverbs, frequent use of personal pronouns rather than impersonal ones (we, you, rather than one, it), small use of conjunctions, poor grammatical sentences, and so on.) Middle-class people use an *extended code*. He points out that middle-class people sometimes also use a restricted code (at church services, cocktail parties, etc.) but they can alternate and switch to an extended code. He is not suggesting that the working class have not got a richly expressive syntax, but in a society in which middle-class extended codes are dominant (especially in the educational system) then they are obviously at a distinct disadvantage. Experimental work has tended to support his general theory. Work with English mothers of small children has shown that different social classes use their speech for different ends and in varying degrees of effectiveness (even when the intelligence of the participants was held constant). What these studies mean is that middle-class children have an ability to control verbalized behaviour which can help in producing a high achievement and success in planning for long-term goals. Some experimental work by Bernstein himself gives further support for his theory because he found that middle-class mothers verbalize with their children far more and that such extensive 'talking to' children helps in a number of ways.

GESTURE. One implication of Bernstein's theory of the two codes may be that the working-class restricted code is more effective as speech (rather than written form) and that the working-class support their speech through the use of elaborate gesture. Working-class people may be expected to have different speech structures and accents than middle-class people but they also have different facial and gestural movements. One example is the manner in which a working-class man holds a cigarette in a cupped hand, usually behind his back, while a middle-class man probably holds it well in front of him between his index and middle finger. An elaborate analysis of facial expression, hand movements, body posture, head position, the distance a speaker positions himself from the person he is speaking to, and so on, has been carried out by Michael Argyle and others.

SOCIAL STABILITY We would expect the working class to be anxious to overthrow the upper strata of society if what the sociologists described was true, that is that the latter dominated and in terms of wealth and income controlled the destinies of the former. On the whole, however, they tend to support the present order of society and its institutions such as the monarchy and turn out in thousands to support royal weddings and funerals. Several theories have been suggested to account for why the deprived of a society don't become more radical. One answer is known as the *relative-deprivation* theory and suggests that men compare their condition not with society as a whole, or the very wealthy, but with their nearest reference group. For example, an old car may not occasion envy, jealousy or rage when seen alongside a number of other old 'bangers', but surround it with limousines and it is more likely that frustration and enmity will arise. This still leaves us wondering why it is that these groups make such a limited comparison, and some sociologists have even suggested that they couldn't face the true realization of their situation. When Marx suggested that religion was the opiate of the people he was suggesting that it dulled the senses so that they were unable to see their real situation. He was, in fact, suggesting another argument as to why the deprived are not more radical. The values and expectations created by religion prepare, it is argued, the main body of society for the very values and social expectations requisite for an industrial economic system. This particular argument is discussed at greater length in the chapter on Beliefs Values and Norms.

EDUCATION AND CLASS   Working-class children are generally educationally under-privileged as a direct result of the economic under-privilege of their parents. They are under-privileged in the schools that they attend, many of which are victorian in construction and without adequate facilities such as toilets. Teachers, being merely human, have less desire to work in these areas (unless very dedicated) than in the more splendid surroundings of the suburban school. Urban schools in the inner areas, especially of large cities, were recently designated as Educational Priority Areas, and given extra finance for staff and facilities. In relative terms, however, this was very inadequate and of very little use unless the living standards from which the children came was also changed. In Britain children are not given the same educational treatment, for some are assessed and selected for special *kinds* of education in specialized schools, and the school system is itself stratified into different types of schools with different ability classes. Many of the middle classes opt out of the state education system (just as they opt out of the NHS) and send their children to private and public schools. Because schools are staffed mainly by middle-class teachers (if they were not middle class to start with, they are by virtue of their education and occupation) they often impute *meanings* to the children they teach. One study showed that head and class teachers of secondary modern schools saw their C stream pupils as dirty, smelling and stupid, aggressive and lacking in ambition; in other words they might have interpreted the pupils' behaviour differently, or given a different meaning to it, had it been exhibited by middle-class children.

CORRELATES OF STRATIFICATION

Many of those who occupy high social-class positions in society feel that they deserve much of what they receive as extra recompense because of the responsibility that they have to bear. But the disparities in social class are reflected in the income they receive and also in patterns of health. For one thing, certain occupations carry with them a high risk of mortality and also a high risk of crippling diseases. Infant mortality rates are higher the lower the social class involved. Mental or psychiatric disorders show a social-class distribution.

The pattern of sexual intercourse varies not only from culture to culture but from social class to social class within any given culture. For example, the working class are more likely to experiment less in sexual positions, have sexual intercourse with the lights out, and with some of their clothes still on. Michael Schofield found that the lower classes learned the facts of life later than the middle classes (respectively 12·7 for boys and 12·5 for girls as compared with 12·3 and 11·9 for girls). One reason suggested for class differences is implied by the fact that middle-class girls reach puberty earlier which, coupled with the extended way of talking mentioned by Bernstein, may mean that the facts of life were explained to them earlier. Probably middle-class parents are more aware of the need for sex

TABLE 5.5
Babies, mothers and social class

	Professional managerial (I–II)	White collar (III)	Skilled manual (III Man)	Semi-skilled (IV)	Unskilled (V)
Mother's age	%	%	%	%	%
21 or less at first birth	24	25	40	46	53
Breast feeding: at 1 month	60	50	50	51	34
at 3 months	39	34	24	22	12
at 6 months	20	12	11	11	7
No bottle after 6 months	10	9	4	1	1
12 months	50	47	29	21	15
Dummy: at some time	39	53	71	75	74
still at 12 months	26	38	55	57	46
Bottle or dummy to go to sleep	23	36	47	52	51
if wakes	24	36	40	47	42
Bedtime: 6.30 p.m. minus	47	31	29	24	31
8.0 p.m. plus	7	12	20	23	26
Sleeps in room alone	54	42	20	18	3
Diet inadequate	5	10	13	13	32
Potty training not started					
(12 months)	12	16	17	13	32
of those started, never					
successful	36	38	46	42	79
Genital play checked	25	50	57	69	93
No smacking	56	38	32	42	35
General smacking	39	53	60	54	58
Frequent tantrums	9	8	14	15	23
Father's participation:					
high	57	61	51	55	36
little or none	19	6	16	18	36
Baby-sitting once or less p.a.	25	36	42	42	59

Source: John and Elizabeth Newsom, *Patterns of Infant Care in an Urban Community.* London, Penguin, 1965, p. 229.

education. Similar patterns can be seen with delinquency and crime, which we examine in more detail elsewhere. Several studies have been done on the way in which social class affects child rearing. Some of the ways in which it does can be seen by examining Table 5.5.

SOCIAL MOBILITY

The degree to which a society exhibits movement between social classes or strata is termed *social mobility*. Two types are generally noted. When movement is up or down from one stratum to another this is termed *vertical mobility*, and when it is from one social position to another without in fact changing the social stratum it is known as *horizontal mobility*.

THE CAUSES OF MOBILITY   There is a high social mobility when certain conditions prevail in a society, for example in periods of rapid social change such as we have during revolutions or war or conquest of some kind. Large immigrations can change the pattern of social mobility, as for example with the influx of European peasantry into America or the Asians into Africa. A political revolution can change the mobility pattern in quite a drastic manner, as occurred in the revolution in Russia in 1917. Sociologists tend to classify the factors as follows:

1. Opportunity structure—in relatively open societies there is opportunity to move which is lacking in closed societies such as the caste system. Very advanced societies have educational, business and entertainment mobility.

2. Demographic factors—new immigrants, coloured or white, generally tend to push the older inhabitants automatically up the social ladder. Similarly, internal migration from the countryside to the towns or from one part of a country to another is often done for the purpose of improving one's position.

3. Automation—tends to displace blue-collar workers and attract white-collar opportunities.

4. Levels of aspiration—Achievement varies from one stratum to another, and although it might well be present in all social classes it tends to be higher in the middle classes.

THE ACHIEVEMENT OF SOCIAL MOBILITY   Vertical or horizontal mobility can be achieved in a number of ways. For example a person can gain much from attendance at a school with a good reputation, from staying on at school beyond the statutory period, by going on to higher education, and so on. Degree of mobility is directly related to education, which in turn is closely tied to occupation. One of the ways in which one can achieve a higher social status is by being recruited to a higher-status occupation. Yet another way is by economic success, which can open many avenues to social mobility if not in itself (at least in Britain) a very important factor.

To control power, for example political power, can also bring social mobility, but power in a general sense is usually tied to the above avenues of social mobility such as education, economic success and education. Finally, new ways have appeared through show business and pop music, and through athletic and sporting prowess.

Social-mobility studies tend to be concerned with differences in social mobility between different countries, increase or decrease in social mobility, and the theory known as *embourgoisement* (the convergence of the working class towards the middle class), and finally the suggestion that there are a number of 'top people' who are firmly entrenched as the ruling elite in both the political religious, social, military and economic spheres. ARE WE ALL MIDDLE CLASS NOW? As societies become more industrial there is a tendency towards equilibration, in which the members of one stratum become more like others in some respects. This is usually taken to mean that the working class is crossing the threshold of the middle class either by acquiring material possessions, acquiring new norms, values and standards of the middle class, and that the members of the working class are being accepted as social equals. Much of the research brought to bear on this argument is far from satisfactory. It is further complicated by the fact that many who are working class tend to consciously identify themselves with the middle classes by their voting behaviour. The answer seems to lie along the lines that while there has been a general trend in both America and Britain towards a general equalizing of wages, there is no evidence that middle-class life styles have been aspired to in any significant form, for example in entertaining, visiting, social participation and so on. Evidence from work dissatisfaction, work conditions, and other areas suggest that a gulf still exists. The child-rearing philosophies, from work both in England and Detroit, suggests further large gulfs between the social classes. In some ways—for example, by ownership of a television set—the working class are catching up with the middle classes. But this is not to take into account the actual viewing habits. Other indices such as the ownership of a car, telephone, and so on are also seen by some as indicative of a narrowing of the gulf. But it appears that as the gulf starts to close the middle classes jump one step ahead (for example by having two cars, two telephones, a colour television, holidays at home in England and not in Spain where the working class go to in increasing numbers). Further division is maintained by the middle classes being able to purchase social advantage in the form of private education and private medical treatment.

OCCUPATIONAL RANKING STUDIES Cross-cultural studies tend to display a certain similarity of ranking between different occupations. However, there may be many reasons why we should cast some doubt on any claim for such studies *really* proving anything because often the occupational titles vary and interviewing procedures may be incomplete or dubious. Certainly it appears that professions come at the top with semi-skilled and unskilled occupations ranking low.

TABLE 5.6

Occupational ranking in 4 countries

Indonesia	Rank	USA	Rank	Great Britain	Rank	USSR	Rank
Physician	1	Physician	1	Medical officer	1	Doctor	1
Univ. professor	2	College professor	2				
Engineer (chemical civil, architect)	3	Chemist/architect/civil engineer	3			Engineer	2
Lawyer	4	Lawyer	4	Country solicitor	3		
Member: People's Representative Council	5	United States Congressman	5				
Head of government department	6	Head of department in government	6	Civil servant	4		
Military officer	7	Army Captain	7			Officer, armed forces	4
Director of private corporation	8	Director of large corporation	8	Company director	2	Factory manager	3
Airline pilot	9	Airline pilot	9				
High school teacher	10	Instructor in public school	10	Elementary-school teacher	6	Teacher	5
Newspaper reporter	11	Reporter, daily paper	11	News reporter	7		
Artist, pianist, author	12	Artist	12				
Farm owner operator	13	Farm owner operator	13	Farmer	5	Chairman of collective farm	6
Small businessman	14	Small store manager	14				
Non-commissioned officer	15	Corporal in army	15				
Electrician, machinist	16	Electrician, machinist	16	Fitter (electrical)	10		
Owner-operator of lunch stand	17	Owner-operator of lunch stand	17	Newsagent tobacconist	8		
Policeman	18	Policeman	18	Policeman	9		
Truck, bus driver	19	Taxi driver	19	Carter	11		
Labourer (servant, messenger, janitor)	20	Dock worker/janitor	20	Road sweeper	12		

Source: R. Murray Thomas, 'Reinspecting a Structural Position on Occupational Prestige', *American Journal of Sociology*, March 1962, **67**, p. 564.

STATUS

We tend to get our initial status from our family of origin. This ascribed status can, in time, become achieved status as we leave the family of origin and carve our own way through the world. A nurse from working-class parents, for example, may well mix in very different circles from her own colleagues whose parents are middle class. In other words, the social status of an occupation may be different from the person who occupies it. Some occupational groups rise suddenly in the status hierarchy, for example technologists. The behaviour of individuals often reflects their status. Thorstein Veblen coined the term *conspicuous consumption* to describe the competitive way in which wealth was used to portray one's social status. In advanced societies such as America and Britain, economically unproductive occupations or behaviour, such as fox-hunting, often carry with them high social prestige, while the opposite is the case for economically productive work. It seemed to Veblen, writing at the very end of the last century, that the very highest prestige was given to those who did not need to work in order to live. Very 'flashy' diamonds and cigars are examples of conspicuous consumption or pecuniary emulation. It seemed to him, moreover, that women were attributed high social status if they possessed a useless beauty, and dogs gained a high value if bred into an ugliness out of all proportion to their actual utility. In many ways society, with its insistence on accrediting high status to often utterly useless people and objects, was in effect emulating or resembling some tribal societies, notably the Kwakiutl tribe's custom of *potlatch* (involving either the destruction or giving away of such items as blankets, which brought with it an enormous status) and the Melanesian yam display and *kula*. In these complicated processes status was maintained by ostentatious displays of wealth. Similarly, the colonial British felt obliged to give cocktail parties which were successively better and more elaborate than the previous one. Not to do so was to lose face. Again, to fail to return in like kind a birthday or Christmas gift is regarded as a loss of honour and a slight in western countries.

In England the kind of vocabulary used (as well as the accent, of course) is regarded as an indicator of whether a person is middle or lower class. Some examples are given in Table 5.7.

TABLE 5.7

U	Non-U
pudding	sweet
sick	ill
wireless	radio
master	teacher
luncheon	dinner

CONCLUSIONS Every person employed as a nurse or doctor both comes from a family occupying a position in the social strata and is also in an occupation which is itself socially ranked. Furthermore, the patients who come into contact with medical and para-medical staff come from a wide variety of social background. In many cases, the NHS services get a gross distortion because the 'elite' have tended to purchase their treatment elsewhere. Many of the patients may appear coarse and vulgar to a nurse or doctor from the middle classes, and often some difficulty may be experienced in even understanding the speech of some patients. Very often, too, communication relating to illness may be severely hampered due to lack of understanding and the attributing of different meanings by the participants involved. Some of the implications of social differences are encountered here.

SUGGESTIONS FOR FURTHER READING

BERTRAND, A. L. (1967). *Basic Sociology*, Appleton Century Crofts, New York.
BOTTOMORE, T. B. (1965). *Classes in Modern Society*, George Allen and Unwin, London.
RUNCIMAN, W. G. (1966). *Relative Deprivation and Social Justice*, Routledge and Kegan Paul, London.
WORSLEY, P. (ed.) (1970). *Modern Sociology: Introductory Readings*. Penguin Books Harmondsworth.
WORSLEY, P. (ed.) (1970). *Introducing Sociology*, Penguin Books, Harmondsworth.

6

SOCIAL DEVIATION

In every society there are some individuals and groups whose behaviour is regarded by others in that society as deviant or odd or peculiar or in some way a problem. Such behaviour can vary to the extent that in one society it may be regarded as odd but in another as perfectly normal. The kind of behaviour regarded as odd can also vary both within and between societies. Furthermore, one kind of behaviour may be unacceptable to one group in society and yet fully welcomed by another group and even encouraged. A psychological viewpoint usually regards such abnormal behaviour as being the result of some impairment of what is termed *personality* or *temperament*. Freud, for example, saw disorders of the personality resulting in abnormal behaviour as being due to innate biological impulses. Inside every individual there was a constant battle in progress between such things as needs and drives.

Whatever the limitations of such a view such theories nevertheless tend to indicate that the period of early socialization is important for later behaviour, and that when something 'goes wrong' in early childhood this has often a considerable effect on later behaviour resulting in an abnormal or deviant pattern. But although what happens in the biography of each individual is obviously important, such accounts and descriptions would not take enough notice of the variation in the kinds of deviance in society nor its distribution among the different social classes and groups in society. In addition, there are different frequencies of deviance in society. For example, crime and suicide rates can vary from one period of the year to the next and from one year to another. What some medical students do on Rag Day may well be regarded as 'pranks', but the same actions carried out by working-class youths may be seen as delinquent. Thus such concepts as *meaning* and *interpretation* enter into the sorts of actions which we may or may not regard as abnormal. Certain types of abnormal behaviour are largely confined to one stratum of the population: for example, robbery with violence which is mostly working class, or embezzlement which is more often a middle- and upper-middle-class phenomenon. Problems such as the variation, distribution and frequency of abnormal or deviant behaviour are capable of being dealt with by sociological or socio-psychological approaches which take into account the concepts which we have so far discussed such as role, social organization, socialization.

THE ANALYSIS OF DEVIANT BEHAVIOUR

Deviant behaviour is any behaviour that fails to meet some specified standard which is socially or culturally expected by a society, social group or system. Obviously in day-to-day behaviour we witness a large number of deviancies, for example when people are too early or too late in turning up for an appointment. In one sense the idea of deviance is a departure from some ideal statistical norm or standard and as such is atypical. But a purely statistical approach to the problem does not help us very much. Another approach to a definition is to refer to deviant behaviour as the kind of behaviour which violates institutionalized expectations (expectations shared and recognized as legitimate within a social system, a departure from culturally expected rules of conduct).

We tend to assess nonconformity by the degree of the deviation from some specified standard, and its direction, for example people who are two minutes late for an appointment are regarded differently than those who are one hour late, and those who arrive early are regarded somewhat differently than those arriving late. The standards from which behaviour deviates allows only a certain amount of such deviation and to become too deviant can involve the introduction of sanctions by the group or society. The situation in which an action occurs plays a part in determining whether it is called deviant. For example, people can become drunk at parties and on New Year's Eve but not at other times, people can kill others in wartime but not in peacetime, and so on. The limits which are tolerated by groups and societies are constantly changing and behaviour regarded as deviant a generation ago may not be so regarded today.

Some deviations are *approved* by society and some *disapproved*. We therefore tend to look at society as shown in Table 6.1.

TABLE 6.1

	Disapproved deviations	Approved deviations
	the poor	the wealthy
	the sick	the healthy
	the intellectually stupid	the intellectually able
	the ugly	the beautiful
	the aggressive	the meek

One of the problems in analysing deviance is how to define the specified or accepted standards from which people deviate. In the case of criminality which involves the infringement of a law, the problem is still with us, but to a lesser extent. In the case of crime we have a legislative set of laws and an intricate machinery for dealing with any infringement. When certain deviations are also at the same time illegal, as suicide and homosexuality were some time ago, the problem is less acute (although there are still problems). In terms of 'ordinary' deviation, however, because the norms or rules are not codified or written down, it becomes more difficult to discover just what the 'standards' are which are held by any group. One suggestion that some sociologists make is that we should first try to look at the social deviations themselves and then try to deduce what the commonly accepted standards of society are, and Emile Durkheim suggested that the deviant was a 'moral frontiersman' who acted as the agent through whom society was reinstated on the right 'track'.

LEARNING TO BE DEVIANT

The problem of how we come to learn deviant actions and beliefs involves a number of approaches, some of which see deviance as 'achieved' by the individual and others as 'ascribed', that is becoming deviant as contrasted with being made deviant.

CONDITIONING A child can be punished for doing something wrong by being smacked or by the withdrawal of affection or approval, and because children (and all humans) are constantly seeking to achieve pleasure (*hedonism*) and reduce pain most children learn by this method of conditioning *not* to do the wrong thing. This kind of theory is popular with behavioural experimental psychologists such as G. Trasler and H. J. Eysenck.

IMITATION Individuals simply copy the behaviour of approved models and reproduce such behaviour in similar situations. Such a theory involves not simply a straight copying but a consideration of the decisions involved in whether they should or should not copy.

THE DEFINITION OF THE SITUATION The learner, according to this theory, is encouraged to make sense of the situation with which he is confronted. He interprets previous rewards in order to apply such conditions to a present or future situation.

DIFFERENTIAL ASSOCIATION Sutherland tried to discover the epidemiological characteristics of deviance by relating behaviour to the degree of disorganization or organization in the environment. He summed up his theory in the phrase 'crime causes crime' by which he meant that individuals reared in a criminal environment were more likely to become deviant than those who were not. He did not suggest a simply mechanistic situation, because individuals both *define a situation* and place a *meaning* on events which surround them.

THE LEARNER'S CONTRIBUTION Individuals do not simply absorb the external world without discrimination. They possess their own beliefs and values, meanings and interpretations, and the result is a 'continuous interchange between reality and subjective experience'. This has two consequences. Firstly, an individual does not become deviant overnight but undergoes a series of assimilations and accommodations, with the result that two individuals subjected to the same reality may react differently.

83

Secondly, although a pattern or norm of behaviour exists 'out there', individuals receive it differently.

THE FIVE PERSPECTIVES ON DEVIANCE

These attempts at establishing a theory of how individuals learn to become deviant can be incorporated into the five ways or perspectives with which sociologists have traditionally viewed the process.

SOCIAL PATHOLOGY

Society, according to this view, is analogous to an organism. Moreover, it is an organism in a healthy state. Deviant situations or individuals are seen as the 'ills' or 'sickness' of society and a danger (usually moral) to its well-being.

The key to this perspective of society lies in the process of socialization through which the moral norms are transmitted to entrants. In the early years of the theory deviants were regarded as deliberately rejecting the teachings of society, but subsequently they came to be regarded as having learned the wrong values.

Early theorists saw deviance as inherited by in-breeding and confined to certain lower strata in the population, but later this view was modified to mean that social pathology was rarely to be found without a bad environment.

SOCIAL DISORGANIZATION

This view regards society as a system consisting of an ordered relationship of parts. From time to time this ordered system fails, generally in three main ways: (a) *normlessness*—a lack of specific rules on which action can be based; (b) *culture conflict*—at least two opposing sets of rules on how to act; (c) *breakdown*—rules exist but conformity to them does not produce the expected rewards. The basis of social disorganization is *social change*, which results in some parts of the ordered system becoming out of joint with other parts. Such social change may be caused by technological or cultural changes which produce a change in the relationships between individuals.

If a society is socially disorganized, this produces stress, with the result that persons in the society experience personal disorganization and adopt behaviour patterns such as alcoholism or mental illness.

Robert Merton constructed a typology which was concerned with *culture goals* and *institutionalized means*. An individual or group can reject either one of these resulting in a fourfold classification (Table 6.2). This

TABLE 6.2

Goals		Means
Innovators	+	—
Ritualists	—	+
Retreatists	—	—
Rebels	— (+)	— (+)

means that an innovatist rejects current means and introduces new ones to achieve the societal goals that he accepts; the ritualist abandons the goals and yet adheres to the means (the petty official or bureaucrat); the retreatist abandons both means and goals (the addict or dropout); and the rebel abandons both goals and means and erects new ones (members of religious sects or political fringe movements). Although this type of approach is relied upon quite heavily it is not always easy to distinguish between means and goals nor is it obvious that such means and goals are held in common by any group or society.

VALUE CONFLICT

In this perspective social problems are seen as social conditions which do not 'mesh' with group values or values held by society because these values *conflict*. Such conflict can be seen between social classes such as the rich and the poor, or between races such as white and black, and results from the competition and frequency of contact between such groups.

DEVIANT BEHAVIOUR

This view has much in common with social disorganization. Indeed, Merton's approach is an example of one which would fall into either class. This perspective views social problems as arising from violations of normative expectations, and behaviour that departs from these norms is deviant. The causes of such departures lies in the learning of deviant ways either due to a lack of socialization in 'proper ways' or over-contact with 'improper' patterns of behaviour. One of the classic studies representing this perspective which we shall elaborate on below is expressed by Albert K. Cohen's study of working-class delinquent gangs in America. The concept of *anomie* as a state of relative normlessness in society is central to this perspective.

LABELLING

Labelling or *typing* can be summed up by the saying 'Give a dog a bad name ...' As Rubington and Weinberg remark, 'central to the labelling perspective is the notion that what is socially problematic exists in the eyes of the beholder'. According to this view social problems and deviants are defined by society's reaction to what it presumes to be a violation of expectations. By labelling someone as a homosexual, a pervert, or an alcoholic we go a long way, so this theory would argue, towards making a deviant out of them. The process is clearly displayed, although on a slightly less deviant level, in the educational system. Both the teacher and the pupil's behaviour will be adversely affected if the notion that the child is stupid is revealed to either or both. Such a view implies that we can socially construct deviants.

Rubington and Weinberg see the perspectives as follows: the social pathology perspective stresses *persons*; the value conflict perspective stresses *values*; the social disorganization perspective stresses *rules*; the deviant behaviour perspective stresses *roles*; and the labelling perspective stresses *social reactions*. Actually, of course, all five perspectives interrelate and contribute to an understanding of social problems. There may be faults and criticisms to be levelled against all of them to some degree, but on the other hand they each contain several aspects of some significance. Rules, roles and social reactions are at the present time the most commonly used perspectives out of the total of five.

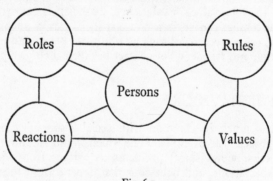

Fig. 6.1

DEVIANCE IN THE MEDICAL SETTING

We shall be dealing at greater length with two types of behaviour that some sociologists would designate as deviant, namely illness and death, but there still remain a number of other categories of deviant behaviour which are of concern, namely role and status conflict in old age, alcoholism, drug addiction, delinquency and crime, mental disorder, suicide and sexual deviance. There may well be other types of deviance arising out of extreme prejudice, marital and family conflict and so on. Those engaged in medical and para-medical occupations are inevitably thrown into contact with deviation in one form or another. Illness is itself, as we shall see, an extremely good example of a type of deviance and the medical categorization of a 'sick' person fulfils in an admirable fashion the classic sociological exploration of deviant behaviour. Other forms of deviation are distributed throughout the population, not necessarily randomly but certainly to the extent that such deviationist behaviour contains other elements of physical impairment that require medical treatment and diagnosis. For example, alcoholism eventually produces a variety of diseases including cirrhosis of the liver and peripheral neuritis, and an addict may appear several times in the same casualty department feigning symptoms which he knows will result in his obtaining the drug he requires. (Indeed, if he is not known by the casualty staff he may get as far as being admitted with the same symptoms to the hospital ward.)

Contacts such as the ones we have mentioned require a knowledge of both the deviation concerned and also some knowledge of how to deal with the deviants themselves, who in most instances are not strange 'monsters' but unfortunate individuals who have 'come to the surface' from a pool of latent deviants in the general population. Often those engaged in the treatment and care of such individuals can exhibit quite damaging prejudice which interferes with the quality of the relationship required. By recognizing the subtleties of the process by which a person becomes a deviant, much can be done to benefit staff and patient.

SEXUAL BEHAVIOUR

The sociological study of sexual behaviour differs from both the biological and psychological approach in the way that certain assumptions are made as to its origin and also to the unit of analysis used for study. For example, biology might be tempted to think of origins or aetiology in terms of organic and genetic, while sociology concentrates more on behavioural and developmental aspects, stressing such themes as socialization, together with an interpersonal aspect with its stress on the situational. In cases of deviance, biology would use as the unit of analysis (and medicine is heavily dependent on biology) the diseased organ or sick person, while sociology would use as the units of analysis requiring attention the act, behaviour, deviant person, categories of deviance, and so on.

The sociological study of deviant behaviour has tended to fall into three categories. It has first of all looked at the ecology and styles of sex as a physical act. Secondly, it has examined the normative implications of the physical act. Thirdly, it has looked at the societal implications of the physical act, together with how these implications relate to the individual.

It is now well documented that frequencies and techniques of sexual behaviour vary widely among individuals according to the variables of social class, ethnic group, level of education, age and sex categories. A survey of over two hundred societies on a cross-cultural basis showed that heterosexual behaviour is almost universally favoured but that as many societies condemned homosexual behaviour as condoned it. Among the Siwans of Africa a male who indulges exclusively in heterosexual behaviour is singled out as peculiar. During male puberty rites among the Aranda of Australia and Keraki of New Guinea homosexuality plays an important part. Nearly every male in Afghanistan is homosexual until he marries. In contrast to this, and for no immediately apparent reason, nearly all societies strongly disapprove of masturbation. Bestiality is acceptable among the Eskimos, joked about among the Tswana of Africa, and strongly disapproved of by the Hottentot of South Africa. The forms of family structure vary, as we discuss in Chapter 3, but all societies have some sort of stable relationship, although they differ in the degree to which they entertain degrees of extramarital relationships. In most societies women initiate sexual advances as much as men.

A. C. Kinsey's research on sexual behaviour in the human male and female was based on 12 000 American males and 8000 females. Although his sample has been criticized for including an over-representative number of Jews and college-educated people, nevertheless some indication can be seen of the extent of sexual behaviour. (1) *Masturbatory behaviour* was practised by 93% of males and 62% of females, and is more common among better educated urban dwellers and less common among devoutly religious believers. Males worry and experience guilt feelings while females do not appear to do so. (2) *Extramarital sexual relationships* were allegedly experienced by 50% of males and 26% of females by the age of 40. Males felt more strongly about such relationships if experienced by their wives, and 51% thought such behaviour grounds for divorce as compared with only 27% of females. Such behaviour did not appear to vary much with social-class differences, although devout females appeared more inhibited than those who were not devout. (3) *Homosexual behaviour* to varying degrees was experienced by 50% of males and 28% of females by the time they reached 45, and was found to increase with the level of education for both sexes, and especially among single females. (4) *Sexual contact with animals* was experienced by 8% of males and 3·6% of females by the time they reached 21, primarily those living in rural areas. Although after 21 this decreased almost to zero in the males it did so by only 50% in the females (mostly unmarried).

THE SOCIOLOGICAL PERSPECTIVE

Sociologists regard sexual behaviour as a part of social action, because it not only influences, and in turn is influenced by, other factors but it also supplies a motive for action. Often it interferes with other social behaviour, and in the case of deviants can be interpreted as often *disruptive* to normal societal processes. The early theorists such as Freud thought of *all* behaviour (not just overt sexual behaviour) as modifications of the 'sex instinct'. Researchers such as Kinsey and Masters and Johnson are working mainly in the physicalist tradition and place a heavy emphasis on styles of sexual behaviour and the ecology of the sex act. Sociologists differ from this view because they tend to concentrate on institutionalized forms of sexual behaviour. For example, the importance of procreative behaviour lies in its demographic consequences and the institutional arrangements a society establishes for the birth and rearing of children.

Some sociologists have talked of the *eroticized role*, by which they mean that we possess social roles such as lover, wife, prostitute and so on, which have a heavily sexual element embedded in them together with economic or affective exchange. Sexual behaviour, because it is under the control of the cortex is regarded as implying degrees of normative and decisional control. Urination and defecation are associated during the process of socialization with the sexual motivation of infants. The work of Kinsey and others have provided strong evidence that although sexual behaviour may be biogenic in origin the particular aspects adopted by persons in order to achieve sexual gratification is *socially learned*. Because social disapproval induces anxiety most of us refrain from deviant behaviour. Because of the eroticized role we interpret sexual behaviour as being meaningful to the actor and capable of being understood by the observer by placing it in the context of other aspects of the personality of the individual.

Individuals are recruited to the eroticized role (i.e. they become wives, husbands, lovers, and so on) on the basis of social norms, personality, and societal mechanisms of control. Variances, disturbances of the personality and various breakdowns in the mechanisms of the process of socialization and societal response result in a breakdown of sexual relationships—or at least a malfunctioning.

NORMS OF RECRUITMENT

Social types are constrained in who they can recruit because of the prescription and proscription of social norms. For example, white does not marry black, royalty does not marry commoner, Catholic does not marry Protestant. Special rules may be in force prohibiting some of these marital ties, such as in South Africa. Individuals may, as is almost universally the case, be excluded from incestuous relationships, or form exogamous or endogamous ties. Numbers of any individuals in any society are excluded from recruitment to the eroticized heterosexual role, for example, the inmates of prisons or asylums, or those in certain religious orders. Certain occupational conditions may also make it difficult to become recruited into the eroticized role.

Another important aspect of recruitment is the means of sexual communication used, for example language, dress, ritual courtship, and make-up. Deviant sub-groups, for example homosexuals, develop private signalling systems to cue a potential partner.

Society controls the types of sexual behaviour as well as the recruitment by such mechanisms as attitudes which reflect disapproval, gossip and scandal. Social control may also be institutionally arranged, as for example in the Nazi youth camps in Germany, various community prohibitions among religious orders, and chaperonage. Sometimes there is control over the form of the sexual act, such as the prohibition against oral-genital contact in some American states. Some elements of the population such as dwarfs, the crippled, the blind and deviants present a special problem because their identity is spoiled but their sexuality unimpaired. Erving Goffman's *Stigma* gives a good account of how such problems are managed by cripples, prostitutes, homosexuals, ex-mental patients, alcoholics, unmarried mothers, and so on. We shall return to the problem of stigma below.

DEVIANT OCCUPATIONS

Some sexual deviations tend to be linked in the mind of the general public with certain kinds of occupations. Actors, for example, are thought of as being proportionately over-representative among homosexuals than perhaps boxers or bank managers. One study of homosexuality suggested that it was linked to the stratification system in a society. Because of the seasonal variation of the entertainment industry such work offers a low level of average earnings, insecurity, and low male economic status. Unless actors are very successful they are generally accorded a low level of prestige by the general public. Societal norms regard many of the theatrical accoutrements as more 'normal' for women (e.g. make-up), and although the same economic conditions apply, such recruitment characteristics as 'good breasts', 'beauty', and so on are carried over into the non-theatrical world and ensure female entertainers greater access to the higher levels of the stratification system. Consequently, the male entertainer is a less desirable marriage choice and furthermore has to compete with males of a higher socio-economic status. This considerably inhibits the male entertainer's access to the females with whom he works. Obviously some males are attracted to the entertainment world *because* it offers opportunity in a homosexual career.

An American study of striptease artistes showed, as one might expect, that their physiques were larger than average women, they were Caucasian and generally urban, and almost all were first-born children. They also had a high rate of homosexual behaviour compared with the general population because their occupational choice made it difficult to formulate 'normal' relationships with the male sex. A further study of burlesque comedians gives additional substantiation to this approach.

STATISTICS OF SEXUAL OFFENCES

It is important to realize that recorded criminality is only a sample of the total criminality. But although it is impossible to arrive at an *exact* statistical picture due to the nature of the subject, nevertheless the figures which are recorded do give us a broad indication of trends in sexual behaviour. There is certainly no clearly uniform picture. One-third of heterosexual offenders appear to be under 21, although only one-tenth of homosexuals. 7% of those convicted of heterosexual offences were over 60. Quite a number of homosexual *and* heterosexual offenders are married with three or more children (17·7 and 34·2% respectively). Most cases of indecent exposure occur among males with one child or during the wife's first pregnancy (nearly 45%). One in five of homosexual offenders were engaged in some form of personal service, domestic work or entertainment (16% were domestic workers, hairdressers, cooks, waiters and barmen, and 5% were actors, musicians and artists).

Since 1947 there has been a total increase in the heterosexual class of offenders of 49% and for the homosexual class 128%. Many of the indictable sexual offences occur in areas where the offender *and* the victim live. In the Metropolitan Police District only 1·5% of the indictable crimes were classified as sexual. In the country areas the proportion was 4·9%; in the larger towns it was 3%. In 1954 sexual crimes per 100 000 of the population according to police areas were as shown in Table 6.3.

TABLE 6.3

Police district	Number per 100 000
London	16·8
Five cities (over ½ million)	39·2
Eleven cities (up to ½ million)	35·6
Smaller urban areas	37·5
County areas	41·8

For the five large cities the figures were as follows: Liverpool 44·1, Birmingham 43·9, Manchester 34·6, Sheffield 34·6 and Leeds 33·3. The incidence of sexual crime per 100 000 was very much lower in the London and South Eastern Region and highest in Wales. Part of the reasons for the variation is the different emphasis given by different police areas as to what constitutes a crime. For example, many police in Metropolitan London may turn a 'blind' eye to an incident which a policeman in rural Wales may not. Other differences may be accounted for by the willingness displayed by victims or relatives in approaching the police. It has been suggested that only 5% of sexual misconduct is reported to the police.

Seasonal variation in sexual offences is generally as shown in Table 6.4.

TABLE 6.4

Spring (March to May)	24·5
Summer (June to August)	35·1
Autumn (September to November)	23·1
Winter (December to February)	17·3
	100·0%

The incidence of offences against victims under 16 was highest in the summer and lowest in winter, while for those over 16 the highest incidence was in winter.

What has been said so far, then, suggests that the concept of deviancy is implicitly tied to that of a norm. Such norms, however, are variable from age to age, society to society, and social class to social class. The ancient Greeks' acceptance of homosexuality and the Egyptian Pharaohs' encouragement of incest are examples of how these norms can vary.

Most sexually deviant offences are more of a nuisance than a menace, and many of them arouse pathos in the majority of 'normal' people. Neither is it correct to think that a minor sexual offence will lead to progression to a major sexual offence, exhibitionism to rape. In fact, eight out of ten offenders are first offenders, and persistent sexual offenders form only 3% of those convicted of sexual offences. One examination of 2000 victims of sexual offences showed only 9% suffered any physical consequences. Similarly, child victims also appear to show little effect from their experience, the damage often being done by their subsequent questioning and 'spotlighting' by the police courts and police personnel. In Israel there exist specially trained personnel who interview child victims.

HOMOSEXUALITY

Homosexual behaviour is the establishment of sexual relationships with one's own sex. As Kinsey suggested, a significant number of both males and females have some experience of reaching orgasm with a member of the same sex at some stage in their lives. However, it is useful to distinguish adolescent experimentation from the act of socially identifying with homosexuals, for it is only a small proportion of the former who become homosexuals. Deviation of this type is classified by some as *primary* (sporadic, situational and unorganized) and *secondary* (deviant behaviour organized as part of a deviant identity). Primary homosexual behaviour can develop into secondary behaviour according to a variety of contingencies such as frequency (how often), visibility (is it 'spotted' and what is the reaction), tolerance, exclusion from normal channels and so on. Lemert sees primary deviance as having only marginal implications for the psychic structure of the individual, whereas secondary deviation is deviant behaviour.

The homosexual, once labelled, tends increasingly to have all his actions interpreted through his homosexual 'framework'. The obsession with the search for the aetiology of homosexuality has led to various interpretations not far removed from the earlier Freudian ones. Such an explanation suggests the importance in the child of a model; lacking such a model, or with a poor model to emulate, the child grows up 'deficient'. The growing girl projects upon other women an image which actually springs from within herself, with the consequence that she no longer adores femininity in other women because she herself possesses it. Some women do not develop this far and end up by regarding themselves as deficient females. This results in the girl turning away from heterosexual contacts (because she considers herself undesirable) and at the same time retaining an adolescent interest in her own sex. Such explanations assume a necessary relationship between the development of masculinity and femininity and heterosexuality and homosexuality, with the consequences that it is believed that the homosexual models himself upon heterosexual roles. Homosexuals vary enormously in the extent to which their sexuality becomes the organizing feature of their lives and yet we tend to view the *total* of their lives through the homosexual label. Surveys tend to show, however, that homosexuals, despite the stigma attached to them, manage their lives fairly well.

Because of the stigma, and until recently the fear of prosecution, attached to being a homosexual, it was little wonder that such individuals tended to frequent disreputable places such as public lavatories and found what little comfort they could in transitory and promiscuous relationships.

The 'coming out' period of a homosexual, the self recognition of a homosexual identity, is generally a period of excess coitus. It is at this time that many appear to go through a crisis of femininity ('going in drag'). The period of ageing is another crisis in the life cycle of homosexuals because they then find themselves unattractive to younger homosexuals.

The genetic basis for homosexuality is uncertain, although many regard it as an inherited constitutional abnormality. There is certainly no reason to suppose it is determined by a specific gene. Male homosexuals tend to be born of elderly mothers, and to arrive later in their families than their brothers or sisters. This might suggest a chromosomal abnormality, but late comers to families are very often much slower to develop. There is, however, much to suggest that homosexuals are made and not born, and that homosexuality is learned and not inherited. The proportion of brothers to sisters of a large population, according to one piece of research, usually works out at 105 or 106 to 100. In major research studies of homosexuals the brother–sister ratio was higher than expected— 119 to 100—and higher still among older homosexual males. Female homosexuals are found to have an excess of sisters compared to the general population. Another unusual feature, as we have mentioned, is the age of the mother, who tended to be older than the normal control group. Lang put forward the idea that human homosexuals were intergrades which appeared to be males but had a female chromosomal pattern—which would account for the excess of brothers and elderly mothers. Pritchard, after examining the Y chromosomes of a number of male homosexuals, found no evidence or any abnormality, male homosexuals having a male chromosomal pattern and female homosexuals a female pattern. One of a pair of uniovular twins who is a homosexual often has a brother or sister who is also, but this is to a far lesser extent the case with binovular twins. Whatever the aetiological answer there is a good deal of evidence to suggest that such theories as labelling and societal reaction play an important part in becoming homosexual.

Three types of treatment are common. Large doses of drugs help the more bizarre aspects of homosexual behaviour; psychotherapy has also helped those wanting to become heterosexual; behaviour or aversion therapy may also be used.

TRANSVESTISM

Some men experience an exhibitionist and sexual pleasure in dressing as women (and vice versa). This is not to be identified with homosexuality, which is a separate phenomenon. Often such individuals perform their deviation in secret in front of mirrors, achieving orgasm by seeing themselves in women's apparel. Sometimes the constriction of women's clothes occasions intense excitement. Female impersonators and transvestite entertainers tend to recruit these.

PAEDOPHILIA

Both in and out of prison child molestors are regarded with intense loathing. Their behaviour usually takes the form of genital display or fondling of the child, and is common to both homosexuals and heterosexuals. One example of 126 homosexuals showed only three as being interested in boys under 16 but 84% of another survey had been indicted for sexual offences against this age of boy. The suggestion here is that most homosexuals who come to the notice of the courts are specialized homosexuals or paederasts, said by many psychiatrists to exhibit compulsive behaviour. As we said earlier, the actual physical damage done to the child is usually non-existent. The damage is emotional, being done by the legal mechanisms, physical examination by doctors, anxiety of the parents, and the gossip of the neighbours and friends.

STIGMA

By *stigmas* Goffman does not mean simply a physical blemish such as scars, deformities and so on. Prostitutes, homosexuals and dustmen have stigmas to a larger or lesser degree. But a person can have a scar, for example, which can be interpreted as something positive (he gained it in the war). Generally, 'by definition, of course, we believe the person with a stigma is not quite human. On this assumption we exercise varieties of discrimination, through which we effectively, if often unthinkingly, reduce his life chances'. He goes on to suggest that on the basis of the original imperfection we impute a wide range of further imperfections.

Such stigmas are gross physical defects, defects in character, and stigmas associated with membership of some particular group which is looked down upon by society. These stigmas are ascribed at birth or acquired in the course of a life, and although people receive their stigmas at different periods they nevertheless share basic common problems and adopt common strategies which help them to manage their spoiled identity. Having a stigma such as colostomy does not necessarily in itself produce a peculiar way of life, but this may result from the way the person is viewed by others.

People with a stigma such as prostitution may (1) refrain from mixing with 'normals', (2) refrain from telling 'normals' the true facts, (3) meet the situation directly. In other words, a prostitute can mix with others of the same occupation or with sympathetic 'normals', an illiterate can pretend to be actually literate, a limbless man can ostentatiously light a cigarette with his artificial hands which is 'sufficient to warn the audience that there is no need to go beyond the normal set of social understandings'. In a similar vein, which we shall discuss in more detail later, the sick person is often stigmatized, especially in the hospital setting, and 'talked down' to by the staff.

COURTESY STIGMA   Some people, simply because they share a web of affiliation with a stigmatized person, are themselves spoiled in their identity. They are 'normal' and yet very 'different' in many ways. Often such individuals manifest their differences by conversation, slips of the tongue, and so on. In any society there are people who are friends or relatives of stigmatized individuals and groups such as homosexuals, criminals, and deformed children. Different types of adaptation are possible for those with courtesy stigmas. They can affiliate wholeheartedly with the stigmatized; they can eventually cease to be regarded as 'normal' by society; they can try to convey that they are unsoiled or unconnected. One study of the mothers of mentally retarded children showed how their adaptations were in fact examined through their relationships with family, friends and other parents of retardates. These mothers helped to maintain membership of the 'normal' community by altering the meanings of these relationships and limiting participation in the organized world of mental retardation. Further, by recognizing the priorities of conventional family life they helped to provide additional ways of conveying an image of normality.

ALCOHOLISM

To a large extent alcoholism is a cultural product being very much the most suitable means that individuals have to help them overcome various social or psychological difficulties. Tension is found to some degree in all societies, although distributed among individuals in unequal degrees, and because alcohol is a means of relieving tension then theoretically the probability of becoming alcoholic is distributed according to the degree of tension. One suggestion is that some individuals find in alcohol a means of relieving various anxieties and conflicts that are generated by the demands of society and to which they cannot accommodate.

In extremely simple societies alcoholism simply consolidates group cohesiveness. It also aids certain forms of religious actions and rituals. When drunkenness does occur it usually takes the form of a shared revelry, which is not surprising, for in such societies most experiences are shared. Horton studied 118 primitive cultures in Africa, Asia and North and South America and related the frequency of drunkenness to two indices of social anxiety: insecurity about food supplies and stresses from acculturation by contact with Western civilization (which weakened social patterns and kinship ties). The more these factors operated the more Horton discovered there was a high rate of drunkenness. Hallowell shows from the literature of the seventeenth and eighteenth centuries that the Northwestern Woodland Indians of North America were suffused with anxiety because the witchcraft of sorcery systems which they had were, in fact, a highly institutionalized means of aggression. When alcohol was introduced by the white men this simply made the situation much worse. Another study by Ruth Bazel examined the role of alcohol in two Central American communities. She examined the patterns of drinking in relation to the distinctiveness of the character structure of the Chichicastenango in Guatemala and Chamula in Mexico, as seen in relation to the full context of their economic, social and religious institutions.

Group differences in the rates of various pathological phenomena have been observed since Emile Durkheim first discussed them in his classic study *Suicide*. In Scandinavian countries there are 12 male alcoholics to every female alcoholic. In America the ratio is 5 or 6 males to every female, and in London it is $1\frac{1}{2}$ males to every female. In America there are differences in different ethnic groups, the Irish and Scandinavians being high and the Jews and Southern Italians being low. All this suggests a sociological dimension in addition to any psychological or physiological one. R. F. Bales outlined three major sets of variables in the aetiology of alcoholism: (1) dynamic factors—the incidence of level of acute psychic tensions in the group; (2) normative factors or orientations—drinking is embedded in the cultural tradition of the group; (3) alternative factors—culturally patterned behaviour, normal or psychological, which may serve as functional equivalents or alternatives to drinking as modes of adjustment to acute psychic stress.

In France, more than three million of the electorate are dependent on the production and sale of alcoholic drinks, and in Italy more than two million earn their livelihood in this way. Yet in France alcoholism is a national problem, whereas in Italy it is not. In Anglo-Saxon countries patterns are different, and drinking occurs mainly at night, leading to a sharp increase over a short space of time in the level of alcohol. The nature of any public house in Britain is largely determined by the locality in which it is to be found. In Britain it is estimated that over the age of 16 32% are regular beer drinkers, 10% regular spirit drinkers and 5% regular wine drinkers, with roughly half a million being employed in the drink trade.

Further sociological factors include the rate of alcoholism to be found in various societies and groups. We have already mentioned that alcoholism appears to affect men much more often than women. There is also a pronounced peak between 40 and 50 years of age, the average ages being 44 in men and 47 for women. Individuals have twice as much chance of becoming alcoholic if they live in urban areas (although no correlation has been found by size of city) than if they live in a rural area. Alcoholics have more broken marriages than the average population (33% are divorced or separated) and a significant number of the males are widowers. In terms of social class more Class I occupational groups die from cirrhosis of the liver but Class III frequent Alcoholics Anonymous groups and Alcoholism Information Centres. As R. F. Bales pointed out, the Irish Americans present an interesting sociological phenomenon when compared with the Italian Americans, for the former have from two to three times the rate of alcoholism than any other group. A possible explanation is the Irishman's close dependence on his mother, the father's position in the family being insignificant and weak. Irishmen also marry later than other nationalities.

DEFINITION OF TERMS A few people are teetotallers. Some are social drinkers. Some are excessive or heavy drinkers. A number are alcoholics suffering from the *disease* of alcoholism. The World Health Organization defines alcoholics as:

> ... those excessive drinkers whose dependence on alcohol has attained such a degree that they show a noticeable disturbance or an interference with their mental and bodily health, their interpersonal relations and their smooth social and economic functioning; or who show the prodromal signs of such developments.

There are between 300 000 and 412 000 alcoholics in Britain, with some

70 000 chronic sufferers. In other words 6·2 per thousand of adult males and 1·4 per thousand of adult females have been estimated as suffering from some degree of alcoholism in this country. Part of the problem in trying to estimate the extent of alcoholism is in arriving at a workable definition of what constitutes the disease, together with the fact that many alcoholics are extremely clever at concealing their illness. One in four males admitted to mental hospital in Scotland in 1962 was alcoholic.

In terms of cost to the nation economists have estimated that the 70 000 to 100 000 chronic sufferers in this country cost the nation £6 million a year by being unable to work, with absenteeism and poor productivity of the remaining 300 000 costing an estimated additional £40 million. Alcohol probably causes 1200 deaths and 50 000 injuries on the roads per year and it is the fourth major cause of premature death. In England and Wales in 1959, 26 men and 6 women per million were admitted to hospital for the first time with a diagnosis of alcoholism. The corresponding rates for Scotland were seven times as high for men and five for women. Some occupations are classified as 'high risk' because they exhibit high rates of alcoholism and a high mortality rate from illnesses associated with alcoholism. Publicans, for example, have nine times the rate expected of all men of comparable age and barmen have five times the rate. Seamen and commercial travellers have a high rate.

DETRIMENTAL EFFECTS OF ALCOHOL ON THE BODY Somatically malnutrition is the most serious consequence. Loss of appetite (anorexia) is often accompanied by morning nausea, and this results in an inflamed stomach (gastritis) or a diseased liver (cirrhosis).

CAUSES Some theories claim that alcoholics show an immature personality stemming from an unduly close relationship with their mothers. Others tend to be self-indulgent. Some have sexual problems, either having little sexual drive, impotence or shyness with the opposite sex, or sexual deviance of some sort. Some have a self-punitive personality. Yet others under stress or in conflict drink (a) to lessen the frustration with an increase in gratification, (b) for temporary attainment of a surer social footing, (c) for release from social inhibition. These sorts of theories are broadly psychological.

There appears to be no differences in anatomy, physiology or pathology, nor any abnormalities of metabolism or of tissue chemistry. There is no evidence of an allergic factor in alcoholics. Similarly there is no evidence to support endocrine factors. There is slight evidence for loss of brain substance, and nutritional factors (N_1 factors) have been evidenced, as also has metabolic disturbance. The reason why the children of alcoholics are more prone (one survey estimated 11%) is not biological or genetic but due to example.

There remain social and cultural theories of causation. These fall into three categories: incitement, opportunity and example. Opportunity consists in increased leisure and money, and in the way a particular society is structured and organized. Included in this section are the occupational opportunities and the distribution of pubs (1 for every 80 men in Scotland). The most effective cause appears to be the power of example. *Alcohol Abuse* sums it up as follows: 'The common characteristics of high rates of alcoholism include social pressure to drink, inconsistent nonexistent social sanctions against excessive drinking, utilitarian or convivial goals, drinking outside a family or religious setting and ambivalence towards moderate drinking.' The answer seems to lie in regarding alcoholism as a disease which is multi-causal.

VARIETIES OF DRINKING EXPERIENCE AND STAGES IN BEING ALCOHOLIC It is now recognized that there are several different types of alcoholic. We have, for example, the unsuspecting alcoholic, the regular and sustained alcoholic, the neurotic alcoholic, symptomatic alcoholics (indicative of depression, schizophrenia, and so on), and bout drinkers. These are responses to varieties of drinking experience.

Individuals do not suddenly become alcoholics but progress through a series of stages in drinking behaviour. It is only in the later stages that physical and mental symptoms dominate and we witness the onset of serious physical diseases.

THE ALCOHOLIC'S FAMILY Do alcoholics select certain types of wives and are those women particularly attracted to alcoholics? The wife of an alcoholic is much more frequently than chance the daughter of an alcoholic. Alcoholics frequently marry women older than themselves, and it is much less common for a wife to leave an alcoholic husband than vice versa. Women alcoholics, like female delinquents, have a more disturbed personality than their male counterparts. The children of alcoholics are generally well cared for, and in later life tend either to drink excessively themselves or to be strongly opposed to the habit.

TREATMENT Among treatment agents are the GP, the hospital doctor, the psychiatrist, antabuse, psychotherapy, aversion treatment, and so on. Antabuse (disulfiram) is used fairly widely in this country, and emetine or apomorphine are used in aversion therapy.

Alcoholics Anonymous or AA has a world total membership of more than 350 000, with 250 groups in Britain with 2500 members. The programme is based on a form of group self-confession. Al-Anon and Al-Ateen groups have recently been formed for the wives and the children of alcoholics. Two other bodies are the National Council for Alcoholism and the Medical Council on Alcoholism founded in 1963 and 1968 respectively. Both these bodies exist to help the alcoholic in some way, the former by educational and referral means and the latter by sponsoring research.

Success is correlated positively with male sex, youth, social stability, employment, marriage, balanced personality, motivation to treatment, and negatively with female sex, old age, social instability, unemployment, single or divorced state, psychopathic personality disorder and poor motivation for treatment.

DRUG ADDICTION

There appears to have been a successive tradition of drug use throughout history. The Sumerians, the Chinese and the Incas all used drugs extensively. Cannabis is used in many religious rites, as is also peyote. The Peyote Religion is found in over 50 North American Indian tribes.

TERMINOLOGY The word *drug* denotes a chemical substance used medicinally. A secondary meaning associates it with addiction. In 1950 the World Health Organization described *addiction* as a state of periodic or chronic intoxication which was detrimental to the individual and subsequently to society, and which was produced by the repeated consumption of a drug which was either natural or synthetic. *Habituation* differs from addiction because it creates a desire (but not a compulsion) to continue taking the drug for the sense of improved well-being. In 1964 the World Health Organization recommended that *drug dependence* be substituted for these two terms.

Drugs themselves fall into two categories: *hard* or dangerous restricted drugs such as heroin and cocaine and *soft* drugs such as barbiturates (phenobarbitone), amphetamines (pep-pills, benzedrine), cannabis, and LSD 25 (d-lysergic acid diethylamide).

The growth in the rate of addiction is one of the significant factors in addiction with the average age of new addicts becoming less. There are more male addicts than female addicts, and there is some indication that new addicts in Britain are male rather than female. In America addiction is mainly a problem associated with minority groups, whereas in Great Britain this is not the case.

Narcotic addiction is more of a problem in some countries than others. In Hong Kong the rate is 120 times the rate in Great Britain, and in Iran it is 264 times the rate. In America the problem is 12 times that in Britain. It has been estimated that the number of new addicts doubles every one and a half years, in which case by 1984 the number of new addicts in that year alone would be roughly one million. Naturally the increase of this nature is purely statistical and the process of levelling out inhibits any such phenomenal growth. Addiction growth seems to have been stimulated among 'non-therapeutic' addicts (obtaining the drug from another addict) as compared with 'therapeutic' addicts (who obtain their drugs from medical treatment), the latter being a comparatively static group. The former seem to have begun as a small group in the late 1940s or early 1950s who were aided by Canadian and American addicts, and the over prescribing of some GPs in this country.

THE SOCIOLOGY OF THE ADDICT It seems that one has to work hard to become an addict. Not all who come into contact with addicts become so themselves. Some are not really affected in any significant way, others simply do not attempt it even though given ample opportunity, and so on. An experiment in which two successive doses of morphine were given to

150 healthy young men resulted in only 3 being willing for the injection to be repeated. One researcher has stated that the danger of addiction 'resides in the person and not the drug'. Even addicts realize that the positive aspects of heroin last only for some 18 months, after which time the doses are to prevent withdrawal symptoms.

Different societies at any one time entertain a variety of beliefs and attitudes towards certain drugs. Certain individuals whose use of drugs differs to some extent from the norm are labelled by others as deviant. This encourages such individuals to identify with others like them in order to form a drug sub-culture. Such sub-cultures tend to fall into two distinct kinds comprising those from the educationally and culturally under-privileged and those from the educated middle-class 'rebels'.

Drug addicts are generally young people who live in large urban areas and who occupy a minority status in society. The high rates in America are generally to be found among ghetto negroes and Puerto Ricans, but the addicts themselves do not differ in education and intelligence from others who share their position but are non-addicts. Because of the economic demands of being an addict, most of them tend to be unemployed and living on the fringe of society.

Generally, addicts seem to come from homes where the mother is dominant and the father weak and ineffectual. Addicts also appear to entertain more than their fair share of negative attitudes, of 'opting out' of the male ideal, to experience difficulty in establishing social relationships, being easily depressed and frustrated and so on. Three factors seem important in any individual becoming an addict; (1) a psychological, predisposing inadequate personality, (2) a crisis such as a death or other traumatic event, (3) the timely offer of drugs.

MENTAL ILLNESS

There is evidence that mental illness as such occurs in all cultures. We must be careful to distinguish *social concepts* relating to mental illness, such as madness, lunacy, from *medical classifications* such as psychoses and schizophrenia. The three main causal classifications are as follows: (1) mental disorders resulting from organic lesions (for example syphilis of the central nervous system, (2) mental disorders resulting from psychological experiences, (3) mental disorders resulting from social experiences. The main areas of traditional demarcation are: (1) *psychoses* entailing a gross derangement of mental processes and inability to evaluate external reality correctly; (2) *neuroses* entailing some impairment of functioning, often of a segmentary nature but involving no distinct break with reality; (3) the *psychosomatic* disorders entailing organic malfunctioning. Examples of psychoses include schizophrenia, of neuroses various anxiety reactions, and of psychosomoses asthma, rashes and hypertension.

AETIOLOGY The old explanation in terms of mental illness arising from the strain of modern living is no longer tenable. Research of incidence over a century found no evidence of a rise in rates over this period below the age of 50. The hypothesis that people living in a *gemeinschaftlichten* community are less prone is not tenable either. Eaton and Weil's study of the Hutterite settlements in Montana and the Dakotas showed the same rate of mental disorders as for New York State. Mental illness seems to be societally distributed, and the mental disorders known to western psychiatry occur just as much among primitive peoples throughout the world. Wherever schizophrenia, for example, has been reported, the society in question has been in the process of *acculturation*, a sociological concept involving further concepts of culture conflict, marginality and shock.

The following social characteristics have been found in a number of studies to be associated consistently with a relatively high incidence of diagnosed schizophrenia: aged between 20 and 35; low socio-economic status; living in anomic urban area; being a migrant; unmarried; being introverted. There is inconclusive evidence of the relation of mobility to functional psychoses. The aetiology of schizophrenia is now regarded as arising from various combinations of hereditary vulnerability and stress from the environment, the former arising from a combination of genes rather than from a single one. Other theoretical formulations include the *double-bind* theory, in which the individual is regarded as being involved in an intense emotional relationship and involves two orders or messages, sent by the mother to the child, one contradicting the other. This seems to have support in a situation in which a mother cannot tolerate an affectionate relationship with her child but cannot accept the feelings that she has. Absence of a strong father figure who might help the child discriminate messages is also conducive to this. Wynne developed a similar theory. He observed the extent to which the families of schizophrenics attempt to maintain an illusion of complementarity that does not in fact, exist, denying differences and directing joint efforts towards achieving what Wynne calls *pseudo-mutuality*.

SOCIAL CLASS, OCCUPATION AND EDUCATION Social class is an important indicator of the kind of experiences to which an individual has been subjected during his life and his expected reactions to these experiences. One theory, concerned with schizophrenic patients, suggests that their generally low socio-economic status can be accounted for by their drift down to that level. Another theory suggests that low status of many schizophrenics is the result of their being born into a socially disadvantaged situation. One survey found that in the USA 91% of schizophrenics were in the same social class as their family of origin compared with 36% of the general population; which suggests a remarkable absence of general mobility. Morrison found that the occupations of schizophrenics were distributed normally as one might expect for the general population. It is more than likely that the origins of the patient determine the care he receives from his relatives. The fewer the letters and visits a patient gets the more likely he is to stay in hospital. The patient's treatment has been shown to be related to his social class. In America, at least, the middle and upper classes are more likely to get psychoanalytic treatment and the poor physical treatment. A patient's socio-economic status may influence the physician in his diagnosis either by the *parataxis* of the socially disadvantaged (inability of expression) or reluctance on the part of the physician to diagnose schizophrenia in those who approximate closest to his own socio-economic status.

FAMILY ENVIRONMENT AND MENTAL ILLNESS In cases where the nuclear family is not properly formed, as we indicated in our discussion of the work of Bowlby and the Harlows, there is a slightly higher tendency to produce schizophrenics. Various adverse features occur in schizophrenic-producing families, basically what Lidz and others have called schism and skew. Usually the mother forms a close though anxiety-ridden relationship with the child while the father is excluded; the reverse occurs occasionally when the patient is a daughter. Disturbances in family life in early years can and do produce varying degrees of disability and often characteristics of a psychotic type.

Mental retardation, long thought to be organic in origin, is in some cases brought about by faulty family mechanisms. The feeble-minded, the educationally sub-normal and the defective can come from high intelligence, high socio-economic homes but also, of course, from low intelligence, low socio-economic status homes. At one time these facts were explained by reference to the theory of multifactorial inheritance, i.e. that the child inherits gene combinations which are unfavourable. Another explanation will refer to environment. Relatively severe mental defects can be caused by what Bourne has called 'grossly perverted rearing'. The mother may be of low intelligence (and therefore incapacitated) but it is difficult to pin down the causal or associative factors involved. Children from poor homes also suffer more in childhood from bronchitis, pneumonia, infective diarrhoea, and vomiting. They also have more home accidents than children from good homes. The mothers of defectives from good homes tend to have experienced disturbances in their relationships with their own parents during adolescence and to have entered into marriage and motherhood with generally unfavourable attitudes. A great deal of research indicates that the essence of mental illness might lie in the area of disturbance in interpersonal relationships.

SOCIAL BEHAVIOUR OF MENTAL PATIENTS The behaviour of mentally disturbed individuals is a result of their illness and also a means of recognizing and diagnosing their particular disturbance. *Schizophrenics* stand at odd distances from others when engaged in interaction; their posture and gesture are utilized to express the bizarre; they lack gaze contact; their speech fails to synchronize and there are long pauses; they are introverted in a very special way and do not engage in social behaviour; they give no reward in interaction and resent criticism; they lack social skills. *Depressives* are miserable, sombrely dressed but neat and clean; their posture is drooping with lowered head; they speak little and their voice is low and slow; they can engage in a social behaviour; they show little interest in opposite sex; they are socially unrewarding and lack confidence; 10–15% try to kill themselves. *Manics* are cheerful and wear loud clothes; they have a dramatic gaze; they speak a lot; they are dominant, extroverted, and possess poor skills; they misperceive situations and cannot see anyone else's view; they can be rewarding or non-rewarding. *Paranoics* are introverted; they dress to suit the mood they are in; they don't trust or reveal anything; they are socially unrewarding, and are arrogant and touchy; they have poor skills and misperceive situations. *Anxiety neurotics* have a tense and awkward posture; their movements are jerky; they indulge in face-touching, speak fast with breathy voices; their faces are tense; they show lack of poise and don't enjoy social occasions; they worry what other people think; their social skills are strange and destructive; their perception is over-sensitive and they are afraid of rejection. *Hysterics* take great care of their clothes and general appearance; they emphasize bodily complaints; they blink excessively; they are extrovert but socially unrewarding; they are flirtatious.

THERAPY Some studies have suggested that individuals recover under psychotherapy and also when under no treatment. 70% of neurotics are self-cured after two years and 90% after four years. Reasons for this vary from the suggestion that they adopt a new style of life, or have amateur help from friends. Sometimes there is improvement for no apparent reason, for example when a great number of mentally ill people recovered at the death of George V. Three methods of treatment are generally used: (1) *psychoanalysis*, which involves interpretation; (2) *non-directive therapy*, in which no direct help is given; (3) *existential therapy*, in which the patient is directed to his own goals.

In the 1950s there seemed to be no faster rate of recovery for those treated compared with those on the waiting list, but since 1960 those treated have a greater rate of recovery than those not treated. One suggestion is that psychiatrists and psychoanalysts have improved, and that recovery does depend on the manner of psychoanalysis rather than any particular school. Young and intelligent psychoanalysts produce a greater degree of confidence and a higher rate of recovery. *Behaviour therapy* has had some success (88%) with enuresis by the use of avoidance therapy. *Aversion therapy*, mainly with drugs, has had some success with bizarre forms of sexual deviation. *Desensitization* has been very successful (some 81%) and uses a light hypnotic state to discover what factors are found upsetting (for example, a fear of death) and gradually subjecting the patient to increased 'doses' of the fear stimulus (starting with photographs of cemeteries and finally ending with the glimpse of dead bodies). *Assertion therapy* is the acting out of dominant situations. *Social skills therapy* consists of neurotics being put in a situation where they are required to talk, and involves the use of role-playing, feedback, social-skills training which are utilized to deal with different age and personality categories. Individuals are taught to emit appropriate signals and simple social situations are explained to them.

MENTAL ILLNESS AS A SOCIAL ROLE   Lemert's conception of primary and secondary deviance is important because it may determine whether mental illness is a transitory phenomenon or whether it becomes part of the identity of the individual concerned. In other words, subsequent social experience may in fact *worsen* one individual whose handicap is identical with that of another. One example is when some children with polio are more socially disabled than another group even though their actual physical handicap is less.

Thomas Scheff has argued that mental disorders are residual deviant behaviour and emerge from very different sources. He also argued that the amount of illness recognized and treated is a tip of a much larger iceberg the existence of which is denied, not recognized, or is so transitory as to change quite rapidly with the change of circumstances. The behaviour which comes to notice, however, is the result of particular social forces which induce the individual to grasp on to the notion of playing the role of the mentally ill, often because such individuals have retained a stereotyped image of the behaviour associated with such illness. Various rewards may accrue to individuals who adopt such roles which, once undertaken, may in the long run prevent a return to the 'normal' role. It is very often the case that when a mental patient denies that he is sick, this is taken as a further indication of the illness he is thought to be suffering from. To try to revert to the original and normal role is difficult because of the stigma and suspicion attached to the role of the mentally ill. Finally, Scheff thinks that the transition from the primary to the secondary type of deviation can occur during crisis, when the individual is most open to suggestion.

Thomas Szasz believes that the term 'mentally ill' is used in modern society to designate areas that have no foundation in biological malfunction, and that such designation is based upon ethical or psychosocial criteria. Despite Szasz's criticisms the disease concept of mental illness may still be useful.

Erving Goffman described the mental hospital as a *total institution* comparable with a prison. The criteria which qualify for admission vary enormously and include the seeing of visions and the hearing of voices. However, there are still important contingencies which determine admittance within certain limits, such as the socio-economic class of the patient and the extent to which his offence is 'seen' by others. But Goffman sees the whole situation as a dramatic occurrence in which the patient is gradually relieved of his freedom, and the 'self is systematically, if often unintentionally, mortified'.

ASSOCIATIONS FOR THE EX-MENTALLY ILL   Just as ex-addicts are sometimes able to join an organization such as Daytop or Synanon in America which exist to help them, mostly by group psychotherapy and community living, so the ex-mental patient can affiliate to such movements as Recovery, Inc. in America and Neurotics Nomine in England. Some of these groups are lay-run while others are under the general supervision of professional medical personnel.

SUICIDE

Psychiatrists are more likely to commit suicide than most of their patients. They have an annual suicide rate of 70 in 100 000 compared with 11 in 100 000 in the general public. Other surveys have shown that doctors in other fields are also likely to kill themselves more frequently than other professional men. Up to the age of 39 one in four deaths among doctors was suicide compared with one in ten in the under 30s for the general public. 1 in every 50 doctors takes his own life. In England and Wales 5000 people kill themselves each year and 40 000 attempt to do so. Suicide rates vary between nations, with West Berlin one of the highest and Italy and Southern Ireland among the lowest (although in Catholic countries authorities may be loath to return a suicide verdict because of the stigma involved). Suicide also varies according to the time of the year, the social class of the individual concerned, and in the methods used. All this suggests what has long been recognized, that is a social tendency to suicide.

Stengal found suicide to be positively correlated with the following factors: male sex; increasing age; widowhood; single and divorced state; childlessness; high density of population; residence in big towns; a high standard of living; economic crisis; alcohol consumption; history of a broken home in childhood; mental disorder; physical illness. Among factors inversely correlated to suicide rates are female sex; youth; low density of population (but not too low); rural occupation; religious devoutness; the married state; a large number of children; membership of the lower-socio-economic classes; war. The most common factor appeared to be social isolation.

The incidence of suicide showed distinct seasonal variations. Contrary to what might be expected the peak seasons for suicide are not autumn and winter but the spring and early summer. One suggestion for this has been that it may be the time when a rhythmical biological change is manifested, but a sounder suggestion is that it is also the most 'popular' time for depressive illness, which would partly account for the seasonal increase in the incidence of suicide. It may also be because it would be a time of the most marked contrast between the internal state of an individual who was feeling depressed and the external state of nature at its sunniest and best.

Freud postulated a 'death instinct' which existed alongside the sexual drive and which manifested itself as a tendency to disintegration and destruction. Another factor which has been suggested is that of imitation, which might be true in suicide epidemics and suicides that run in families but not applicable to the majority of suicides.

PSYCHOLOGICAL SIGNS

Some, although by no means all, would say that a person must be mentally ill in order to undertake suicide. If we consider the four broad categories of mental impairment—the neuroses, psychoses, mental retardation and the abnormal personality—some substantiation might be made for associating suicide with mental illness, as one-third of people who kill themselves are estimated to be suffering from a neuroses, psychoses or disorder. Suicide is rare among those suffering from *organic dementia* and mental defectives. Psychologists and psychiatrists would generally look for the following criteria indicating suicide, according to Stengel: (1) depression with guilt feelings, self-deprecation and self-accusations associated with tension and agitation; (2) severe hypochondriases, i.e. tendency to continuous complaining, usually about physical symptoms; (3) sleeplessness, with great concern about it; (4) previous suicidal attempt; (5) fear of losing control; (6) suicidal preoccupation and talk; (7) suicides in the family; (8) life in social isolation; (9) serious physical illness; (10) alcohol or drug addiction (there is a high incidence of drug taking among doctors, which might partly account for their high suicide rate); (11) the end of a depressive illness; (12) dreams of catastrophes; (13) unemployment and financial difficulties.

SUICIDE NOTES AND CORONERS' REACTIONS TO SUICIDE

A number of studies of the notes left behind by suicides reveals them to be far less dramatic, and much more matter of fact, than simulated notes. Such notes are among the criteria used to arrive at the real suicide rate in society which lies beneath the official statistics. However, recently serious doubt has been thrown on this real suicide rate as it has become apparent that different societies and different groups in society view the behaviour designated 'suicide' differently. It is really a blanket term used to cover different kinds of behaviour which has different meanings attributed to it. A further suggestion is that coroners act as 'front-line' individuals who help to establish a shared definition of suicidal situations by interpreting the meaning of the evidence. A similar role is served by the mass media who popularize or focus attention on a particular kind of suicide (for example, among students) which then becomes firmly established in the mind of the general public.

DURKHEIM'S CONTRIBUTION One of the earliest sociologists to point out the social tendency of suicide was Emile Durkheim. He postulated three main types of act. (1) *Egoistic* suicide, arising from the individual's lack of integration with his group. He had in mind here the lack of social controls as illustrated by the single being more prone than marrieds, Protestants (with the stress on individualism) being more prone to suicide than Catholics, and so on. (2) *Anomic* suicide represents the failure of the individual to adjust to social change and the weakening of social constraints. The limits society imposes on the individual's desire make them more reasonable and realizable. High employment in wartime is an insufficient cause of the drop in the suicide rate, and rather (a) there is more opportunity for disguised suicide, (b) there is an increase in 'causes' and 'partisanship'. (3) *Altruistic* suicide is when the group's authority over the individual may be so compelling that he loses consciousness of his own personality and its claim upon life. Examples are the aged Eskimo going into the snow to die, the captain going down with his ship, and the Indian widow's suttee—all exemplifying a suicide which is socially and culturally imposed.

OTHER CONTRIBUTIONS Cavan formulated a combination of factors that caused suicide: (1) a personal crisis that either disturbs the individual's customary ways of realizing his needs or introduces a conflict between them, for example when one's spouse dies or there are rows; (2) a personality factor when a rigidity in some people makes for difficulty in adjustment; (3) the factors arising from social disorganization.

PSYCHOANALYTIC EXPLANATIONS Four determinants of personality may be distinguished: (1) *constitutional*—the inherited and biological aspects of personality; (2) *situational*—chance and accidental events and experience such as being an orphan or only child; (3) *role*—the cultural determinants of how statuses are to be put into action or performed on the basis of age, social class, occupation, and so on; (4) *group membership*—of school, class, nation and so on. The psychoanalytic approach talks in terms of a wish to kill some unidentifiable characteristics within the self or a wish to be killed or atone. Sometimes this is expressed as a wish to die and seek reunion with a loved one or God. There is some evidence that some suicides wish to identify with a parent or parent surrogate who died at a crucial time in the child's development.

ECOLOGICAL STUDIES Sainsbury's study of suicide in London boroughs found the following factors associated with the act: *social status*—poverty, unemployment, overcrowding, and middle-classness were none of them important by themselves but there was a tendency for the poor to commit suicide less frequently than the middle class; *social isolation*—people living alone, living in boarding houses, and lodging-house keepers were found to be of significant numbers; *social mobility*—people entering and leaving, those of foreign birth, that is, all transients, were significant; *social disorganization*—divorce, illegitimacy and delinquency were factors, and there was a correlation of suicide with the rate of admission to mental hospitals, increasing age and rapid changes in an individual's economic position.

CRIME AND DELINQUENCY

A. K. Cohen's theory of delinquent behaviour sees it occurring as a result of thwarted status problems faced by working-class youths. Children learn to become delinquent by becoming members of groups in which delinquent conduct is already well established. Within each age group cultures exist which are shared by only a few, and these are termed *sub-cultures*. There are sub-cultures within these again, belonging to neighbourhood cliques and so on. What Cohen is saying is that in many ways becoming a delinquent is like becoming a Boy Scout. The characteristics of delinquent sub-cultures lie in its non-utilitarianism, maliciousness and negativism. Taking its norms from the larger culture it actually turns these upside-down, and the conduct of a member becomes right precisely because it is wrong in the eyes of the larger culture. Such a sub-culture is also versatile in the sense that stealing often goes hand in hand with vandalism, trespass and truancy. It is also a form of short-run hedonism, in which pleasure is immediate and transient. It exhibits group autonomy because social pressures comes from within the group.

The middle-class values which are presented by society to working-class youths are for the most part unobtainable. There is no thought in the working-class culture of postponing gratification for future rewards, nor are they encouraged to be rational, responsible, ambitious or have a respect for private property. Denied status in the world outside, such youths create their own status systems in which values are prized which are not accommodated in the larger culture.

Cloward and Ohlin distinguish three types of delinquent gang: (1) *criminal* gangs are chiefly engaged in theft and money-making activities; (2) *conflict* gangs look upon violence as a major source of status; (3) *retreatist* gangs stress drugs as a means of escaping from the immediate. Basically the origin of these three types stems from the gulf which exists between goals and opportunities.

FACTORS IN DELINQUENCY Barbara Wootton selected twenty-one major investigations and found twelve different factors connected with delinquency: (1) the size of delinquent's family; (2) the presence of other criminals in the family; (3) club-membership; (4) church attendance; (5) employment record; (6) social status; (7) poverty; (8) the mother's employment outside the home; (9) school truancy; (10) a broken home; (11) health; (12) educational attainment. None of these, says Wootton, are *causes* in the accepted sense, but there is a correlation in the sense that some of these factors accompany the fact of being a delinquent.

Some have argued for the existence of *formal* and *subterranean* values in society. The former are deferred gratification, planning, routine, predictability, non-aggression, for example, and the latter are short-run hedonism, spontaneity, new experience, excitement, aggressive masculine role, peer-centredness and so on. Although we all hold subterranean values to some extent and usually express them in our leisure pursuits, certain groups such as working-class youths tend to accentuate these values at the expense of the formal ones.

David Matza and Gresham Sykes have tried to account for a theory of delinquency by suggesting that working-class youths do not set out to violate the formal values of society but try to be accepted by the system by adopting a set of strategies or justifications which he thinks will be accepted by the wider society. These *techniques of neutralization* are five in number: (1) responsibility is denied, for example, 'I'm sick'; (2) denial of victim, 'we weren't hurting anybody'; (3) denial of injury, 'people like that can afford it'; (4) condemnation of the condemners, for example, 'everybody does it'; (5) appeal to higher loyalties, 'I didn't do that because of myself.'

Individuals become delinquent (or deviant) as a result of exercising certain choices in the context of *affiliation* (contagion or conversion) and *signification* (being signified or identified as a thief as opposed to becoming one). Matza goes on to give a picture of the delinquent as not essentially very different from normal youths in society. 'The delinquent is casually, intermittently, and transiently immersed in a pattern of illegal action.'

Wardrop suggested five categories of delinquency as follows. (1) *Organic*—largely the result of brain damage due to an early history of birth trauma, early injury, illness involving encephalitis. There is a persistent tendency to hyperkinetic behaviour with poor muscular co-ordination. In adolescence the behaviour form is outbursts of temper, overtly delinquent behaviour which is often motiveless, together with a lack of ability to form stable relationships. Subjects also possess a poor *self-image* due to poor abstract reasoning ability. (2) *Grossly deprived delinquent*—illegitimacy and rejection produces an affectionless character and hostility resulting in poor impulse control. Such children, with a history of statutory child care and fostering, have a low tolerance of frustration and require immediate impulse gratification. (3) *Emotionally disturbed delinquent*—this group is sick, as opposed to the first two, which are disturbed: (a) neurotic reaction— a history of rejection and a delay in psychosocial development which takes the form of stealing in boys and promiscuity in girls (both are attempts to identify with a sex role); (b) psychotic reaction—taking the form of 'odd' behaviour or persecution. (4) *Family problem delinquents*—delinquency in this case is reactive to interpersonal tension in family relationships. (5) *Situational delinquency*—typical problem delinquents produced by culturally and economically deprived backgrounds without any psychiatric or emotional problems.

THE GENETICAL BASIS OF CRIME AND DELINQUENCY Following on Lombroso's work on the 'atavistic' criminal in terms of skull shape and size were the attempts of Kretschmer and later Sheldon to distinguish body types, namely *ectomorph*, *mesomorph* and *endomorph* to which a particular kind of temperament was attached. The endomorph preferred comfort, the mesomorph was aggressive and active, and the ectomorph introverted. Subsequent research found that there were twice as many mesomorphs among delinquents than could occur by chance. One answer is that delinquent gangs and behaviour is more suitable to those with a mesomorphic physique and such children are more likely to be admitted to gangs than more 'weedy' children.

A recent suggestion that genetics may be a clue to violence is the result of research showing a link with genetic abnormalities in the sex chromosomes. Patients in a special security hospital in Scotland included a group sharing a genetical abnormality—their bodies contain two Y male sex chromosomes instead of one. They also shared gross personality disturbance and had a history of early conflict with the law. Although physically healthy (but unusually tall) the majority were mentally subnormal, from normal home backgrounds, but given to violent temper and unresponsive to treatment. A study of Rampton prisoners revealed an extra X chromosome (female) resulting in eunuchoid proportions, a tendency to breast development and infertility. In the general population XXY is 1 in 1000 or 1 in 1500 but at Rampton it was 1 in 200 and in some places 1 in 100. Klinefelter's syndrome, XXY, is found 1·3 times in every 1000 male babies. Although such theories as these may explain a small proportion of pathological offenders they still leave much unexplained. XYY males, because of their height and build, may be singled out in societal processes and be victims, partly at least, of societal reaction, labelling or typing processes.

CONCLUSIONS

It has been stated that criminology is the study not of problem-solving but of problem-raising. Certainly many of the areas we have discussed highlight grave faults in our society rather than solve anything of any importance. The contribution of sociology is not only to understand societal processes but to glimpse some of the motivations and meanings that individual actors impute in their interactions.

Some forms of deviance are undoubtedly in need of medical treatment, especially the grosser forms. Medical personnel, however, may come across such deviance masquerading under other forms, for example injuries on a small child, cirrhosis of the liver, and so on, which are not immediately apparent as symptoms of larger aberrations of behaviour. It is useful to know also that an attempted suicide is not just a suicide that failed but a cry from the heart of one isolated individual for some form of help.

SUGGESTIONS FOR FURTHER READING

COHEN, S. (ed.) (1971). *Images of Deviance*, Penguin, Harmondsworth.
LEFTON, M., SKIPPER, J. K., and McCAGHY, C. H. (eds.) (1968). *Approaches to Deviance*, Appleton Century Crofts, New York.
RUBINGTON, E. and WEINBERG, M. S. (1968). *Deviance: the Interactionist Perspective*, Macmillan, New York.
RUBINGTON, E. and WEINBERG, M. S. (1971). *The Study of Social Problems: Five Perspectives*, Oxford University Press, New York.
TAYLOR, I., WALTON, P. and YOUNG, J. (1973). *The New Criminology*, Routledge and Kegan Paul, London.
TAYLOR, L. (1973). *Deviance and Society*, Nelson, London. (First published by Michael Joseph, London, 1971.)

SEXUAL DEVIANCE

STORR, A. (1964). *Sexual Deviation*, Penguin, Harmondsworth.
GAGNON, J. H. and SIMON, W. (eds.) (1967). *Sexual Deviance*, Harper and Row, New York.

ALCOHOLISM

KESSEL, N. and WALTON, H. (1967). *Alcoholism*, Penguin, Harmondsworth.
OFFICE OF HEALTH ECONOMICS (1970). *Alcohol Abuse*, No. 34, April.
PITTMAN, D. (ed.) (1967). *Alcoholism*. Harper and Row, New York.

SUICIDE

SAINSBURY, P. (1955). *Suicide in London*, Maudsley Monographs, Institute of Psychiatry, London.
STENGEL, E. (1964). *Suicide and Attempted Suicide*, Penguin, Harmondsworth.

DRUG ADDICTION

OFFICE OF HEALTH ECONOMICS, (1967). *Drug Addiction*, No. 25, October.
LAURIE, P. (1967). *Drugs: Medical, Psychological and Social Facts*, Penguin, Harmondsworth.

CRIME AND DELINQUENCY

VAZ, E. (ed.) (1967). *Middle-Class Juvenile Delinquency*, Harper and Row, New York.
HUGHES, H. M. (ed.) (1970). *Delinquents and Criminals: their Social World*, Allyn and Bacon, Boston.

MENTAL ILLNESS

SPITZER, S. P., and DENZIN, N. K. (eds.) (1968). *The Mental Patient*, McGraw-Hill, New York.
SCHEFF, T. J. (1967). *Mental Illness and Social Processes*, Harper and Row, New York.

7

ILLNESS AND DEATH

The German poet Rainer Maria Rilke wrote that 'In hospitals, where people die so agreeably and with so much gratitude towards doctors and nurses, one dies a death prepared by the institution: they like it that way. If, however, one dies at home, one chooses as a matter of course that polite death of the better circles with which, so to say, the funeral first class and the whole sequel of its touching customs begin.' It has been estimated that between 53 and 88% of all deaths occur in hospital settings, this figure rising to 95% in the under-45s but decreasing by slightly over 10% for the 65s and over. Many more women than men die in hospitals, and a large number of both sexes die on the first day of admission. Many of those admitted to hospitals take a considerable time to die. Again, many people, admitted to hospitals, to the care of health professionals, are a long way from death. They are simply ill.

HOW HEALTH PROFESSIONALS VIEW ILLNESS AND THE PATIENT

Many theories used in contemporary medical settings are based on the biological models of disease. There are other, and sometimes similar, models used by such practitioners as faith healers and herbalists. Undoubtedly, the scientific nature of the models and the framework used by doctors, nurses and so on owes much of its success to being closely linked with the scientific areas of biology and chemistry. The use of scientific diagnosis provides a prediction of how the patient will fare from having a particular kind of illness, an aetiology of the illness in question, and lastly may suggest a course of treatment for the illness. David Mechanic states, 'correct and reliable diagnosis is the basis of the sound practice of scientific medicine'. Sometimes a diagnosis can be made and a course of treatment effectively carried out, such as in the case of pernicious anaemia. At other times, however, even though a diagnosis is made, no substantial prediction can be made of the disease's course, the aetiology is doubtful and the treatment ineffective. Mechanic cites Boeck's sarcoidosis as an example, and adds, 'although it is helpful to make the diagnosis, it does not lead to a clear course of action'. Similar problems are presented by the diagnosis of raised arterial blood pressure. In itself a correlation between hypertension and mortality is statistical rather than individual, and high blood pressure is not itself a cause of death or of a person being admitted to hospital. The first stage of hypertension shows no organic change in the cardio-vascular system and generally no treatment is prescribed. Indeed, because 10% of the population display raised blood pressure at this stage such treatment would be very expensive. The second and third stages reveal left ventricular hypertrophy and ischaemic heart disease, but those making the diagnosis are usually aware of such traps as the false positives of the electrocardiogram and some of the negative side effects of treatment with hypertensive drugs. In addition, there are difficulties involved in the measurement of hypertension by the two most commonly used methods, the intra-arterial method and the cuff and sphygmomanometer. The individual's own blood pressure may vary according to such factors as his emotional state, room temperature, previous physical activity and so on. Several factors emerge in this area which have a bearing on the biological model such as the difficulty of diagnosis (after about fifty years of age, for example, it is 'normal' to have 'abnormal' blood pressure), the quantitative relation between raised arterial pressure and mortality, doubts about effective treatment at stage one, and so on.

The diagnosis made by the physician is based on his previous medical knowledge, both clinical and arrived at by scientific research, but also his observation of the patient and the latter's account of his symptoms. Therefore, interpretation and selection enters into the area of diagnosis and disease. Individuals differ enormously according to age, socio-economic class, climate, culture and so on, which in turn affect the patient's and the health professional's interpretation and selection of the criteria.

MENTAL ILLNESS   We have mentioned Thomas Szasz elsewhere. Basically he has put forward the theory that what we term mental illness is observed and diagnosed from patterns of behaviour and thinking which deviate from the 'normal' rather than by a systematic study of organic brain lesions. 'Mental illness' is a term usually used to classify problems associated with problems of living rather than problems related to a biological breakdown of some sort. Often diagnosis which masquerades as medical or psychiatric diagnosis is actually social diagnosis.

THE RELIABILITY OF DIAGNOSIS   Apart from problems associated with raised arterial blood pressure there are many other instances of difficulty associated with diagnosing illness. Many psychiatrists, for example, differ as to what constitutes 'sickness'. R. D. Laing is one psychiatrist whose views often run counter to orthodox psychiatry. The interview and the consultation are situations very open to errors of interpretation. Some surveys have suggested that agreement between psychiatrists on the diagnosis can be as high as 55% and as low as 28%. Other surveys have suggested that agreement between psychiatrists can sometimes be as varied as 0·05 per hundred to 51 per hundred, as, for example in the case of military psychiatry. The diagnosis of different mental conditions varies very much.

Schizophrenia, psychosis and mental deficiency have a high agreement, but paranoid psychosis and cerebrovascular psychosis have a low agreement level.

Medical diagnosis is, as we might expect, higher among specialists than in general practice in the degree of accuracy. Mechanic cites the example of between 20 to 25% error in even a well-trained person's reading of X-rays. Many other areas of research have shown varying differences in both the kind and the accuracy of medical diagnosis.

ILLNESS AS SOCIAL DEVIANCE Illness is viewed by many sociologists as social deviance because it is not only deviant statistically but also from some standard or norm. Although it is true that disease can be 'there', what really matters is how we think or conceive it. Freidson puts it this way: 'Diagnosis and treatment are not biological acts common to mice, monkeys, and men, but social acts peculiar to men. Illness as such may be biological disease, but the idea of illness is not, and neither is the way human beings respond to it. Thus, biological deviance or disease is defined socially and is surrounded by social acts that condition it.' Illness as deviance contains both a biological and a social aspect. The sociologist's task is not to accept illness as something which indisputably exists but to try to explain the social processes whereby certain symptoms and signs arise in the first place, how we call such signs and symptoms 'sickness', and how the person designated as 'ill' adopts the role of the sick person, cripple, dying, incurable and so on. The situational theory of deviance, which we discuss in the chapter on deviance, throws light on the concept of illness as social deviance by regarding deviance as imputed (rather than 'out there'), not necessarily motivated by the individual, and responses to it are organized or managed socially. Like beauty, deviance to a considerable extent is in the eyes of the definer.

SOCIOLOGICAL FORMS OF ILLNESS Parson's classic representation of the sick role sees it as containing the following norms: (1) Exemption from normal social-role responsibilities which, of course, is relative to the nature and severity of the illness. (2) The institutionalized expectation that the sick person cannot be expected by 'pulling himself together' to get well by an act or decision or will, he is in a condition that must be 'taken care of'. (3) The definition of the state of being ill as itself undesirable with its obligation to want to 'get well'. (4) The obligation—in proportion to the severity of the condition, of course—to seek technically competent help, and to cooperate with (the physician) in the process of trying to get well.

Thus, to claim the sick role gives us an excuse not to perform certain responsibilities, puts upon others the obligation to look after us, makes us reluctant to be ill and anxious to get well, and makes us seek the help of a doctor or some other qualified person. Sick-role variations are bound to occur in instances where individuals are not given or expected to have exemption from normal roles, the degree to which they are expected to 'get well', and to the extent to which they cooperate with the treatment agent, and finally the extent of their being held responsible for their condition. Freidson argues that Parsons' conceptualization of the sick role is heavily tailored to modern Western industrial society, and that the extent of the exemption is a *consequence* of the seriousness imputed to the condition. In a trial classification of deviance, Table 7.1 might emerge (adapted from Freidson, p. 231).

TABLE 7.1

Imputation of seriousness	Imputation of responsibility	
	Individual held responsible	Not held responsible
Minor deviation	Parking offence	A cold
Serious deviation	Murder	Heart attack

The degree of seriousness of the deviation reflects middle-class views. However, he makes the point that often the medical profession holds individuals responsible for medically labelled illness as in the case of venereal disease, abortion and attempted suicide. Furthermore, the above classification merely distinguishes between 'crime' and 'illness'. A more sophisticated table (Table 7.2) is consequently presented by Freidson (adapted from p. 239). The Parsonian definition of the sick role occurs in cell 5, Goffman's stigmatized roles are in cell 4, and chronic sick or dying roles are found to cell 6.

TABLE 7.2

Imputed seriousness	Illegitimate (stigmatized)	Conditionally legitimate	Unconditionally legitimate
Minor deviation	Cell 1 'Stammer' Partial suspension of some ordinary obligations; few or no new privileges; adoption of a few new obligations.	Cell 2 'A cold' Temporary suspension of few ordinary obligations; temporary enhancement of ordinary privileges. Obligation to get well.	Cell 3 'Pockmarks' No special change in obligations or privileges.
Serious deviation	Cell 4 'Epilepsy' Suspension of some ordinary obligations; adoption of new ones; few or no new privileges.	Cell 5 'Pneumonia' Temporary release from ordinary obligations; addition to ordinary privileges. Obligation to cooperate and seek help in treatment.	Cell 6 'Cancer' Permanent suspension of many ordinary obligations; marked addition to privileges.

THE LAY CONCEPTION OF ILLNESS AND DISEASE

To a very large extent it is true to say that illness behaviour is a culturally and socially learned response. Thus middle-class people are quicker and more eager to seek medical advice than working-class people, and in certain cultures the witch or folk-doctor is relied upon in preference to the medical practitioner. Illness differs in response and recognition according to ethnic differences, and response to pain also varies according to ethnic culture. The higher the socio-economic class the greater the possibility of reporting illness behaviour. Such classes, Mechanic reports, 'were more likely to buy health insurance, to get a periodic medical check-up, to receive polio immunisation, to eat a balanced diet, and they more frequently had eye examinations and dental care'.

Not only are the signals of distress (what we will call pain) felt or interpreted differently by different cultural and ethnic and social groups but they are also interpreted differently. Other symptoms, such as tiredness or irritability, are also interpreted differently and have different *meanings* attributed to them. Some cultures regard certain symptoms as of little consequence and do not follow these up by reporting them to the medical authorities. In a sub-culture of violence any individual act of violence is unlikely to be regarded as symptomatic of mental disturbance.

The lower the social class of the group concerned the more likely they are to be ignorant of the functioning of the human body. 'They are prone to think of and describe their experience with illness in the now-antiquated notions still exploited by patent-medicine advertisements—notions of qualities of the blood, of the necessity to "purge the system", of the importance of the state of the liver and kidneys to health, and the like.' Freidson suggests that such a person is more likely to seek the help of folk or patent remedies. This is born out by research carried out by the office of Health Economics in their publication *Without Prescription*. The group to which one belongs determines to a large degree the extent to which any one lay-person refers to (a) his fellows, (b) a medical practitioner.

Mechanic has found it useful to distinguish between *self-defined* and *other-defined* illness, the major distinction being that in the latter case 'the person tends to resist the definition that others are attempting to impose upon him'. He uses this distinction in listing ten factors affecting the response to illness, as follows:

(1) visibility, recognizability, or perceptual salience of symptoms;
(2) the perceived seriousness of symptoms;
(3) the extent to which symptoms disrupt family, work, and other social activities;
(4) the frequency of the appearance of symptoms, their persistence, or frequency of recurrence;
(5) the tolerance threshold of those who are exposed to and evaluate the deviant signs and symptoms;

(6) available information, knowledge, and cultural assumptions and understandings of the evaluator;

(7) perceptual needs which lead to autistic psychological processes;

(8) needs competing with illness response;

(9) competing possible interpretations that can be assigned to the symptoms once they are recognized;

(10) availability of treatment resources, physical proximity, and psychological and monetary costs of taking action.

Mechanic cites the example of a man who has occasionally become inebriated. This may become more frequent and persistent, and his behaviour or situation will probably become more evident to his family and colleagues. His behaviour will become more disruptive and people will become less tolerant. Information will be sought, and the perceived seriousness will, most probably, overcome the perceived stigma. The final exemption from obligations is death. It is also when illness, seen as an active struggle by individuals to control their life situations and environments, ceases.

DYING AND DEATH IN THE MEDICAL SETTING

Julius Roth's study, *Timetables*, is concerned with the way in which the inmates of a tuberculosis hospital structured the passage of time. When individuals are uncertain about what might lie ahead of them they tend to draw upon the experiences of others who have either been through the same experiences or are at that time experiencing the same. The formation of group norms focused upon reference points becomes an essential part of the *career* of the inmate. Roth means by the *career* of the institutionalized TB patient, 'a series of related stages or phrases of a given sphere of activity that a group of people goes through in a progressive fashion (that is, one step follows another) in a given direction or on the way to a more or less definite and recognisable end-point or goal'. The group norms that are formed serve to measure the progress of the individual and are, in fact, *benchmarks* or events of significance that occur in the average career. In a hospital setting two groups of people, those in authority and the patients, each construct *career timetables*. By this Roth means that 'when many people go through the same series of events, we speak of this as a career and of the sequence and timing of events as their career timetable'. The authority group and the patients both establish a timetable for the same series of events, but because they 'see' the same events differently (professional versus lay, hospital versus patient) and differ in their goals the timetable norms developed differ from each other to some extent. Hence there arises, according to Roth, a constant bargaining relationship between 'the expert, the professional, the authority, the controller on the one hand, and the client, the subordinate, the controllee on the other hand'.

Roth's study can be usefully applied to a number of medical settings other than a tuberculosis hospital. Elizabeth Gustafson applies the concept of career to a study of the dying nursing-home patient. In such an institution the majority of patients are terminal cases who although perhaps not willing to admit the fact at least know that they are in that setting until they die. 'For the aged patient, the passage of days itself brings him noticeably closer to the end of the road. Admission to the nursing home immediately launches him into a new, regressive career ending in death.' Timetable scales in a nursing home career are illustrated by Gustafson as in Table 7.3.

TABLE 7.3

Physical deterioration scales			Mental deterioration scales
Social activity	Mobility	Functional control	Mental control
1. Passes to 'outside'	1. Walks	1. Continent	1. Occasional forgetfulness
2. Responsibility for own affairs; social contacts			
3. Hobby or job	3. Hobbies		
4. Physical recreation			4. Occasional incoherence
5. Spectator recreation	5. Wheelchair	5. Incontinent	5. Considerable disorientation
6. Minimal activity	6. Bed		
7. Lassitude	7. Extreme weakness		7. Total *non compos mentis*
8. Coma	8. Transfer to general hospital		

Source: Adapted from Gustafson, p. 229.

Bargaining as a process of interaction with authority is not so firmly articulated as described by Roth because, as in terminal wards, many may have become too ill to maintain a bargaining position. Anyway, the nursing staff have little control over the terminal outcome. The process involves in many cases bargaining for more time 'directly with his disease, or death, or God'. Despite the forced cheerfulness of the medical staff the patient 'finding the staff unresponsive to the real meaning of his bargaining, becomes frantic and eventually lapses into despair . . .' The distinction between a *social phase* of death and a *terminal phase*, preceding the final termination occasioned by psychological or biological death, enhances the value of the social phase during which the patient is reacting against the desire of relatives, staff, visitors and peers to force him into a premature social death. 'This kind of bargaining will and should continue in the best of institutions. But it will become effective and wholesome when the staff members and visitors respond by doing all they can to facilitate the preservation of the patient's maximum status according to the timetable scales. The staff member with this positive goal will find it easier to acknowledge (sometimes directly to the patient) that death is the inevitable end of the career. The patient who feels he has been valued and respected during this phase will find it easier to approach the end of his life willingly.' When the terminal phase is reached medical staff can help the patient move into a positive position *beyond* the process of bargaining in a full acceptance of death. 'It should become the common goal of staff and patients that each dying career should end in this positive way.'

A different setting for dying is offered by Glaser and Strauss' (1965) study of a terminal cancer ward. In such a setting the articulated bargaining process suggested by Roth may not apply. In contrast there may arise a certain amount of *confusion* about the form that staff–patient interaction should take. For example, the patient may feel that he will survive but the nurse knows that he will die. A form of mutual pretence exists when both know that the outcome will be terminal but both act as though it will not be so.

A TIME TO DIE

David Sudnow's study examines the way in which dying is socially organized in the hospital setting. From the observation of 250 deaths he concluded not only 'The categories of hospital life, e.g. "life", "illness", "patient", "dying", "death", or whatever, are to be seen as *constituted by the practices of hospital personnel* as they engage in their daily routinised interactions within an organisational milieu", but we also see that the very way of handling the dying patient may itself be a reflection of the needs of the staff to attempt to cope with their routine work. Occasionally this may result in the committing of improprieties such as the closing of a terminal patient's eyelids before death (it is more difficult after), and leaving a patient near to death in a room not adapted to terminal cases such as a laboratory or supply room. Sometimes, on a busy ward, 'portions of the wrapping are done before death, leaving only a few moments of final touch-up work with the dead body ... they will occasionally go into the room of such a patient (one they believe will die shortly), change the bed-sheets, insert dentures, and, in several cases I know of, diaper a patient who is still 'alive'. Such predeath treatment is likely to occur only during the night shift, when aids are assured that relatives will not visit and discover their work'.

Glaser and Strauss' later study, *Time for Dying*, written in 1968, is concerned with dying as a temporal process which takes place 'over time'. A secondary consideration of the study is that the process of dying in hospitals is influenced by the training and codes of the medical staff. Lastly, an individual's death is a *social* event to the extent that it influences others and is noticed and recorded.

DYING TRAJECTORIES   Glaser and Strauss talk of the course of dying as a *trajectory* (the path made by a body moving under a given force—a term used in physics) which has duration (it takes place over time) and shape (it can be plotted or graphed). The hospital, doctors and nurses must deal with a series of critical phases during the process of dying: '(1) The patient is defined as dying. (2) Staff and family then make preparations for his death, as he may do himself if he knows he is dying. (3) At some point, there seems to be "nothing more to do" to prevent death. (4) The final descent may take weeks, or days, or merely hours, ending in (5) the "last hours", (6) the death watch, and (7) the death itself. After death, death itself must be legally pronounced and then publicly announced.' Often the relationships between doctors and nurses is such that the latter are not taken into full medical confidence and have to pick up 'cues' about the patient's condition. Such cues are gleaned from the physical state of the patient himself and from temporal references made by nurses or doctors.

The dying trajectory is a status passage. Originally the term was used by Van Gennep to describe the passing of a person from youth to adulthood, or from spinsterhood to marriage, and so, which is characterized by clear and precise rules. Such passages from one status to another are scheduled, regulated and prescribed, although some are not. Furthermore, to move from one status position to another may or may not be desirable, inevitable, reversible, repeatable, individual, shared, clear, voluntary, controlled or legitimate. Dying as a trajectory 'is almost always *unscheduled*; second, the sequence of steps is *not institutionally prescribed*; and third, the actions of the various participants are only *partly regulated*'. Generally, we regard death as undesirable.

IMPROVING THE CARE OF THE DYING More people than ever before are dying in institutionalized settings such as hospitals or nursing homes. Often the care given to terminal cases is described in the popular press as 'inhuman', 'insensitive' and so on. Nevertheless, the care and devotion lavished by nurses and doctors on terminal cases is of a high order. The Glaser and Strauss works are part of a six-year study specifically concerned with the dying patient. The second contribution in the series is by Jeanne Quint, *The Nurse and the Dying Patient*. Certain general recommendations arise from the research.

1. 'Training for giving terminal care should be greatly amplified and deepened in schools of medicine and nursing.' Sociological and psychological approaches to death and dying with regard to the dying patient and his family should be introduced with particular reference to the 'web of social relationships that grows up around a patient who lingers while dying'.

2. 'Explicit planning and review should be given to the psychological, social and organizational aspects of terminal care.' Particular patterns of dying as demonstrated by the different types of trajectories require varying organizational efforts.

3. 'There should be explicit planning for phases of the dying trajectory that occur before and after residence at the hospital.' Often the patient is dying and yet well enough to be only an out-patient visitor to the hospital. Similarly, post-mortem grief is no longer supposed to be the concern of

the hospital. New mechanisms offering some form of trained therapeutic service could be introduced to care for the relatives of the dead, and perhaps even for those who die at home.

4. 'Finally, medical and nursing personnel should encourage public discussion of issues that transcend professional responsibilities for terminal care.' Such issues as the withholding of addictive drugs until near the death and the apparent senseless prolonging of life are, according to the researchers, public issues which are neither the province nor within the capabilities of the medical and nursing professionals.

CONCLUSIONS

Diagnosis of illness is based firmly on the biological model. The process of bargaining can enter into diagnosis just as much as into the setting described by Roth. For example, Balint's study shows how the diagnosis made by a general practitioner results from a kind of negotiation made between the patient and the doctor which entails the patient making 'offers' of various symptoms and illnesses which the doctor can reject, accept or modify until there is a kind of common agreement satisfactory to both. Part of the process involves some sort of reconciliation between the lay and professional perspectives of illness, but the interpretation and selection of data are also important. The acceptance of a diagnosis of illness excuses us the performance of certain roles. Generally speaking, individuals are not normally held responsible for illnesses and are exempted from obligations.

The concept of career timetables as developed by Roth, although applied initially to a TB unit, was extended by Gustafson to death and dying. The varying trajectories of dying as studied by Glaser and Strauss resulted in some concrete recommendations for improving the care of the dying.

SUGGESTIONS FOR FURTHER READING

BALINT, M. (1957). *The Doctor, his Patient, and the Illness*, Pitman Medical Publishing Co., London.
FREIDSON, E. (1970). *Profession of Medicine*, Dodd, Mead and Co., New York.
GLASER, B. G. and STRAUSS, A. L. (1965). *Awareness of Dying*, Aldine Publishing Co, Chicago.
GLASER, B. G. and STRAUSS, A. L. (1968). *Time for Dying*, Aldine Publishing Co, Chicago.
GUSTAFSON, E. (1972). 'Dying: The Career of the Nursing Home Patient', *Journal of Health and Social Behaviour* 13 (3), 226–235.
LAING, R. D., ESTERSON, A. (1964). *Sanity, Madness and the Family*, Tavistock, London.
MECHANIC, D. (1968). *Medical Sociology*, The Free Press, New York.
PARSONS, T. (1951). *The Social System*, Free Press, Glencoe.

QUINT, J. (1967). *The Nurse and the Dying Patient*, Macmillan, New York.
ROTH, J. (1963). *Timetables*, Bobbs-Merrill, Indianapolis.
SUDNOW, D. (1967). *Passing On: the Social Organisation of Dying*, Prentice-Hall, Englewood Cliffs, New Jersey.
SZASZ, T. (1964). *The Myth of Mental Illness*, Harper and Row, New York.

8

HUMAN ECOLOGY AND DEMOGRAPHY

The world population is currently around three and a half billion, but in 30 years the figure will be nearer six billion if the current growth rate continues along the same course. Such an area of study is known as *demography*, which deals with the distribution of population, its composition (usually sex, age and marital status) and its change. *Ecology* refers to the study of relations between human groups and their environments. Such studies have a direct practical application to long-term planning of schools, hospitals, new towns and so on, and originated in very early times (for example the census at the time of Jesus' birth or during the reign of David) when they were regarded as important sources of information useful for the organization of armies and economic resources in the ruling of a conquered people. In recent times such a study has been shared not only by sociologists but also by social geographers and historical demographers, and knowledge has been pooled in order to arrive at a general picture of the kind of planning that might be required for transport, the building of new communities, facilities for the young and old, and the distribution of industry.

DEMOGRAPHY

MEASURING CHANGES IN THE POPULATION   A crude way in which we could begin to measure changes in population is simply to count the number of children born in any particular country. The demographer, however, in order to arrive at a more accurate picture, uses rates and ratios. To arrive at a rate he divides the total of the population into the number of births in a given year, which gives him the *crude birth rate*. To arrive at what he calls the *refined birth rate* he divides the number of children born during a given year by the number of females of childbearing age (15 to 44):

$$\text{crude birth rate} = \frac{\text{number of births per year}}{\text{total population}} \times 1000$$

It is useful to introduce another term here known as the *population at risk*, because simply to take any thousand would be a very crude way of arriving at a true picture. Thus, in order to arrive at a birth rate we would use the 'risk' population as women of childbearing age and not just any thousand in the population:

$$\text{refined birth rate} = \frac{\text{number of births per year}}{\text{females of childbearing age}} \times 1000$$

It is also useful to give quite different figures for each sex because of different life expectancies and also because to take a thousand from either sex (rather than females) would not be of much use. Similarly, different age groups are given different figures because each age group contains different numbers of the population and has different mortality rates.

Similar methods are used to analyse the death rate. The rate of natural increase is measured as follows:

$$\frac{\text{births per year} - \text{deaths per year}}{\text{total population}} \times 1000$$

The population change in any given society can be reduced to four variables. These are fertility (births), mortality (deaths), emigration (movement from an area) and immigration (movement to an area). Any other event which occurs to affect the size of population does so by influencing one of these *basic demographic variables*.

In the nineteenth century, Great Britain experienced the introduction of relatively sophisticated medical services, a number of scientific improvements, improved sanitary provisions, and legislation affecting general public health. The sociological changes from a nation of high fertility and mortality to one of low fertility and low mortality began in the middle of the nineteenth century. Families began to get smaller and people began to live longer; this trend began with the upper and middle classes, with their family planning and improved hygiene and dietary standards, and eventually spread to the working classes. Fears that such trends might result in a population *decline* led to the establishment of a Royal Commission on Population in 1944. The trend varied considerably from an ultimate family size of over six for the marriage cohorts of the 1860s, over five in the 1880s, over four in the 1890s, and over two in the 1920s. From 1956, however, the rate has begun to increase rapidly again due to a number of interesting factors. (1) There are increasingly *less* spinsters in the female population (of women between 20 and 39 in 1911, 552 per thousand were married compared with 808 per thousand in 1961); (2) more males are marrying; (3) people are marrying earlier; (4) there is a rise in the number of illegitimate births; (5) immigration.

Up to the turn of the century infant mortality rates remained fairly constant, and certainly the rate in the nineteenth century did not give a true reflection of the rapid improvement in medical and sanitary practice. R. K. Kelsall and others have suggested that 'It seems that it was not until the midwifery service was statutorily recognized and progressively extended in the early part of the twentieth century, and until standards of hygiene were improved, that any improvement in the infant mortality rate could be achieved.' The discovery and application of penicillin and vaccines has resulted in a reduction of 90% in post-neonatal deaths (from five weeks to the first birthday) and 60% in neonatal deaths (first four weeks after birth) compared with the early part of this century.

Life-expectation tables are used by insurance companies to give a theoretical picture of the duration of the life of persons born at the same time. They are calculated by taking *age-specific rates* (number of deaths per thousand of certain ages) of a population and predicting a person's expected longevity. Because such tables assume the mortality rate (the current one) to remain constant they actually underestimate the longevity of any age category. *Life span* refers to the age limit of man and *life expectancy* to the average length of life reached at the time of death by individuals born during a certain time.

There are considerable sex differences in mortality rates. The ratio of male to female infants is 106 to 100. The general picture, however, reveals that many of these male children die off so that there tend to be about 95 men to every 100 women in the general population. There are several reasons for this including the higher rate among males of death from accidents, heart disease, tuberculosis and cancer, the fact that males tend to consult their doctor less frequently than females, and the generally acknowledged stresses and strains which men are subjected to in their occupations. In the age groups of 75 and over women outnumber men almost twice as much, no doubt partly due to the large mortailty rate in the Great War, but also to the general mortality rate of males from a number of specific diseases.

Immigration and emigration are additional demographic variables which influence the population trends. From the beginning of the nineteenth century until the outbreak of the Second World War an estimated twenty million emigrated from Britain. In the ten years after 1946 an estimated 50 millions left their homes and migrated, mainly to the USA, Great Britain and France. Commonwealth immigration into this country has generally meant a settlement in one of the six large conurbations. An estimated 350 000 have settled in Greater London; 70 000 in Birmingham; 12 000 in Nottingham and Bradford; 10 000 in Liverpool and Manchester. These migrations have considerable importance in terms of such factors as housing densities, health, education and general services.

One of the interesting features of migration appears to be that many highly qualified individuals move from their country of origin. Many of the recent Asian immigrants to Great Britain were highly trained professional people. Such a feature has been referred to as the *brain drain*. In the 1960s many well-qualified scientists, technologists and university lecturers left Britain for the USA and Canada and Australia, where they regarded prospects as better than in this country. One category of emigrants were medical doctors who were leaving at the rate of some 400 a year. Although not in itself alarming, this figure appeared quite significant when compared with the output of a medical school or with the increase in population in this country, for it really meant that we were in fact losing more than the figure actually represented in relation to the general trends in the population. Of course, Great Britain also benefits from the large number of Asian medical and paramedical personnel who come to work in this country.

Another factor of migration is its occurrence *within* or *internally* to a country. Generally the trend is from the poor areas to the more prosperous regions and from the rural areas to the urban conurbations. In this country this trend was already firmly established and illustrated in the novels of the nineteenth century. The trend has also meant that large urban areas have also gained at the expense of the smaller ones. One third of the population of Britain live in seven conurbations: Clydeside; Greater London; South-East Lancashire; West Midlands; West Yorkshire; Merseyside and Tyneside. Advanced industrial nations have a constantly shifting distribution of population, more than often tied to specific occupations which have to move to where the employment is to be found, but increasingly shared by other occupations. In one year in the USA 38 million people changed their place of residence, giving a rate of one in every five. The reasons why there is internal migration are as follows: economic consideration; retirement; change in marital status; and miscellaneous reasons such as a search for adventure.

POPULATION SIZE AND LIVING STANDARDS Thomas Malthus, writing about 1800, was concerned with the consequences of an unchecked population which might grow at the rate of geometrical progression (2, 4, 8, 16, . . .) more rapidly than the supply of food. Two courses of action would reduce this rate. Firstly, war, famine and pestilence. Secondly, celibacy and moral restraint. The pessimism of Malthus overlooked the efficiency of modern birth-control methods and the technological achievements in food production.

The question of *optimum population* has an upper limit set by the supply of food and resources available. Similarly, if the population were not to be replaced by new members it would very soon decline. The optimum size of a population, however, will be set by the scale of cultural values held in a given society at any time one: (1) technology; (2) values relating to levels and standards of living; (3) valuation placed upon children; (4) social regulation of sex; (5) post-conception regulation of child survival (e.g. abortion); (6) attitudes and practices regarding health and mortality. These mean that a highly technological country can keep a large population in food and operate a surplus, will operate constraints to keep its population within certain living standards and will generally place the same value on either sex of its children. In countries with a strong emphasis on the male child there is usually a high fertility rate. In some societies extra-marital and other sexual relationships are strictly regulated. A high value may be placed upon the males to die in battle or to enter a religious order, thereby regulating the population. Lastly, certain foods may be culturally prohibited although nutritious.

SOCIAL CLASS VARIATIONS IN MORTALITY AND FERTILITY The higher infant mortality at the lower end of the social scale was found, by J. W. B. Douglas, to be due to the higher incidence of premature births, itself associated with such factors as early childbearing, poor antenatal care, working too much or too hard, births close together, and a greater post-neonatal mortality due to a greater risk of infection from pneumonia, bronchitis and gastro-enteritis. Even with a general increase in the standard and level of living it is likely that the same differentiation would betray itself and that differing rates would show themselves in different social classes. Social class variations also occur, as we discuss elsewhere, in mortality rates other than those of infants. The social class gradient in fertility rates tends to adopt a U curve, so that upper and working class rates are higher than middle-class rates.

OTHER IMPLICATIONS OF DEMOGRAPHIC DATA Women today are finished with childbearing and rearing at a comparatively early age, leaving them free to enter into other areas of activity. They also tend to live longer than they did a half century ago. This has considerable implications in terms of career structure and training and for the economy in general. If we couple with this the fact that spinsters are disappearing at an alarming rate then such occupations as nursing and teaching will, in the words of R. K. Kelsall, have either to rely on a male recruitment or adapt themselves to married women. This, again, will have implications in terms of training and educational provision, and it may well be that a form of lifelong education, or recurrent education will have to be introduced on a large scale in the Western world in order to cope with these trends.

The consequence of an ageing population is that many resources from the economically viable will have to be increasingly diverted to a large section of non-producers. In 1966 22·9% of the population were under 15, 64·8% between 15 and 65, and 12·3% over 65. This pattern throws extra burdens on the health and welfare services and the national economy. Over a million of these over 65 are women and living alone (forming one-person households).

WORKING MOTHERS Hannah Gavron, in *The Captive Wife*, demonstrated that 90% of middle-class mothers had some clear occupational patterns before entering marriage, and of these 77% wanted to return to their work when the job of raising the children was over. The significance of this was that these wives no longer saw their lives as a process of long-term subservience to the role of mother and wife. With the middle-class wives, 37% continued to work when they had young children, compared with 29% of the working class. As we might expect, the latter found it more difficult to combine home and work roles. Studies reveal no damage to children whose mothers work, and in fact there is a slight suggestion that these children do better in educational attainment.

HUMAN ECOLOGY

The study of *human ecology* deals with the manner in which community organization distributes people, services and facilities in time and space. A *community* is a population consisting of human beings who live within a specified and limited geographical area and who live in a style of life involving interdependence on one another. Such a community is to be distinguished from a family or a neighbourhood and provides systematic linkages for social and structural relationships to be erected. The emphasis is upon the relationships of the community rather than the individuals who comprise it, for communities survive both individual births and deaths and people entering and leaving.

COMMUNITY AND NEIGHBOURHOOD. A *neighbourhood* is a structural entity where everyone knows everyone else. This is not expected in a community. Neither is the neighbourhood a self-sufficient entity providing for the whole range of basic needs for its inhabitants. Neighbourhood interaction patterns include knowing people by face if not by name, having a nodding acquaintance, a speaking relationship, visiting each other's houses and so on.

TYPES OF COMMUNITY Although there is no common agreement as to what constitutes a community it is generally held that it has a specific territorial focus. Some writers emphasize subjective criteria such as identification, whereby individuals identify with a given community. By mapping the zone to which individuals claim to belong, some sort of picture or delineation can be established. Others use the *neighbourhood-cluster* method which is an objective means by which we identify the location of each neighbourhood and the trade centres used by the people in it.

Rural communities include settlements which are small in size and stress a *gemeinschaft* set of relationships. Primitive food-gathering communities are examples of this type. A later development is the village community. This can exist as a *nucleated* village where the inhabitants cluster together. Another form is the *line* village where development is along a main track or road. The *plantation* community is one in which the workers' settlements are in relation to the employer's house. *Frontier settlements*, as found predominantly in Canada and the USA, are another form of rural community.

Urban communities are dominated not by agriculture, in the way that rural communities are, but by commerce, industry and service occupations. In urban communities there is a complex division of labour and social relationships, a high density of population, and social control is exercised by means other than kinship, such as a complex police force. The features of urban communities include a growth in impersonality, with the result that the majority of one's social contacts are superficial, transitory and segmental, and a growth in the division of labour to meet market expansion. Urban communities can be classified into manufacturing communities, retail and wholesale communities, mining communities and holiday and retired people's communities and so on.

Urban communities offer a varied pattern of social interaction that is very complex. For example *natural areas* develop by being distinguished according to some identifiable characteristics such as dockland, doctors' and hospital areas, Skid Row, China Town and so on. E. W. Burgess suggested the *concentric-zone* theory, which viewed urban communities as having five zones: zone I is the central business area; zone II is the area with older houses converted into small hotels and boarding establishments and housing some of the poorer inhabitants; zone III includes better working-class homes; zone IV is the middle-class area; zone V is the area of fashionable suburbia. The drawback with the concentric-zone theory is that urban development is not uniform. H. Hoyt argued for studying the urban community by the use of *radial sectors* stemming from the centre of cities and following major transportation routes. The *nuclei* analysis sees the city as exhibiting clusters of activities and population which appear in various parts of a city.

THE REGION Somewhat larger but still a homogeneous social structure, the *region* is characterized by homogeneity related to social life, a conscious uniqueness and identification by the inhabitants, and the absence of distinct boundaries. An area becomes a region because of geographic and physiographic forces such as soil, climate and topography which often produce distinctive dialects and dress. In addition, certain historical developments can mould or contain people within a region such as the Scottish Highlands. Finally, cultural experiences can distinguish an area and identify the inhabitants by music or culinary specialities.

COSMOPOLITANS AND LOCALS Two types of orientation have been usefully distinguished in the life-style of individuals, which also dominate their personality. These are known as the cosmopolitan, who identifies with a way of life outside local boundaries and interests and is not constrained by neighbourhood ties, and the local, who is constrained by the *gemeinschaftlichten* of the local community with its interests. Inhabitants of the inner city areas generally fall into five classes: (1) the cosmopolites; (2) the unmarried or childless; (3) the 'ethnic villagers'; (4) the deprived; and (5) the trapped and those who are downwardly mobile. The first two categories are generally known as cosmopolitans and centralists who are distinguished by a basic orientation to a large city. Locals are to be contrasted because their orientation is basically parochial and they express no interest in 'the Great Society'. This kind of orientation also imposes patterns of friendship on the respective 'orienters', so that locals cultivate a large number of friends, in whom they take a pride, while cosmopolitans are not so interested in meeting as *many* people as possible.

Groups within cities vary, also, and it has been found useful to distinguish between 'exclusive membership' groups and 'inclusive spatial' groups. The former type tends to select from a total population in an area on the basis of some criterion, such as prowess or interest in sewing, and cuts across neighbourhood lines. The latter includes all those active in a defined area.

INNER CITY AREAS AND SUBURBS Because of the spatial restriction of inner city areas people crowding into them become homogeneously segregated into distinct localities. However, because of the lack of distance between these localities there was frequent interaction which led, at least in America, to the 'melting-pot' effect. A phenomenon known as the *ethnic villager* emerged in the inner city areas of large cities everywhere, but particularly in the great urban areas of the USA. These 'urban villagers', as they are sometimes called, still lived much in the way that they did in their Puerto Rican or European peasant communities, exhibiting little contact with the facilities offered by inner city areas other than their place of employment. Although living in the inner city they still possess the characteristics of *gemeinschaftlichten*, that is, close kinship, lack of anonymity, weakness of secondary-group contacts and of formal organizations, and are very suspicious of anything outside their immediate neighbourhood.

The suburbs of cities are more than likely to be dormitory areas. They are farther away from the work and play facilities offered by cities and are more modern because they developed later. They rely quite heavily on the car as a means of transport. The density of housing is less than in the inner city, and houses are single family dwellings rather than multi-family. The population is more homogeneous and includes few immigrants who tend to be concentrated in the inner areas. The inhabitants of suburbs are younger, have white-collar occupations, higher incomes, and include a greater proportion of married people than the occupants of inner areas.

THE CULTURE OF POVERTY AND THE INNER CITY SLUMS   The last two of the five categories mentioned above—the 'deprived' and the 'trapped'—have no other choice than to live in the city (unlike the first two types). The 'deprived' population are the very poor and those mentally or emotionally disturbed who live in the fringe or grey areas. The 'trapped' are those caught in a neighbourhood invaded by immigrants or industrial and commercial development, who are unable to move out. It is to this sort of area that the downwardly mobile (coming down the socio-economic hierarchy) gravitate. An area such as this might include the widowed and widowers of retirement age.

The distinctive kinds of behaviour exhibited by these categories differs from that of the suburban dweller to quite an extent. Such a way of life as the former may well include racketeering and gang activities which, although beyond the law, is nevertheless a part of accepted behaviour in the areas. A study of such an area in Liverpool showed that petty pilfering was an accepted way of life. The vicious circle of poverty, unemployment, low attainment and disease and ignorance makes such areas as this blighted.

Such areas as these are structured in a kind of inevitability by the economic system. Because wages are low and unemployment is high such an area stands in marked contrast to the upwardly mobile and prosperous middle-class areas. The desirable, being unobtainable, forces such individuals into what Oscar Lewis has described as the culture of poverty. This is an attempt to adapt, adjust and cope with the dominant values of

Western society, and is thus a *sub-culture*. 'It is both an adaptation and a reaction of the poor to their marginal position in a class-stratified, highly individuated, capitalist society.' The culture of poverty is absorbed by slum children by the age of six or seven, and little else will ever have any real impact on them. The distinguishing characteristics of the sub-culture are as follows: (1) disengagement from the major or dominant institutions of society; (2) chronic lack of money and employment; (3) matrilocal (woman dominant) structure; (4) hostility to control agencies such as the police and 'welfare'; (5) a sense of community; (6) emphasis on character traits such as masculinity and localism.

ECOLOGICAL AND DEMOGRAPHIC CONTRIBUTIONS TO MEDICINE

We shall later be discussing some of the ecological studies in greater detail. Essentially such studies are carried out on groups rather than individuals and involve the comparison of one set of characteristics of a population with another set of characteristics in an attempt to account for variations among the *populations* (an aggregate of objects about which certain information is desired). Such correlations are known as *ecological correlations* and are generally popular in the statistical data produced by public health departments and medical officers of health. The census returns provide sufficient evidence on such areas as density, for example, which can be related to infant mortality, cancer, and so on. However, although ecological studies can say things about populations, e.g. that a population characterized by low income and status also has high mortality, this does not in any way guarantee that persons with low income and status will have a short life. To impute that individuals or persons have the characteristics revealed by groups or populations is to be guilty of the *ecological fallacy*. In other words, such a fallacy imputes individual correlation on the basis of a group correlation. It is a common error in the sociology of education where group or population characteristics are attributed to individual children. It is also common in the lay mind which draws individual inferences about cancer, rabies, home accidents, hypothermia and so on from ecological studies graphically described in the *Sunday Times* and *Observer*.

By far the best application of ecological and demographical data, although they do have their uses in indicating areas of research on the individual, is in the area of the planning of medical resources and personnel.

THE PLANNING OF AN URBAN HEALTH SYSTEM   The problem is not only to find the best location of doctors and hospitals and health centres but also to satisfy the basic health requirements of the patient population. The patient, in seeking health care, will be affected by such factors as the following: (a) his relative need for care; (b) the distance-cost of the travel required; (c) whether he is a NHS patient or a private one; (d) the social attributes of the doctors, clinics or hospitals; (e) the present environment in which he lives.

An important approach in such a study utilizes the concept of *life space* in which the individual lives and of which he is aware. Although much life space is economically determined, there also exist areas which are socially defined and referred to as *social space* or *social field*. These are heavily reliant upon the notion of status and role. Thus a trip to a hospital or a doctor may be viewed in two ways. Firstly, taking the life-space view of the trip, it is merely a line of interaction but secondly, taking the social-space view, it involves such questions as whether the patient is uncomfortable in a doctor's room or hospital because he is concerned about his status or his 'social appearance'. Such a concept as social space may restrict an individual to situations and encounters in which his status is high, such a feeling whether real or imagined being determined to some extent on his socio-economic situation and origin. The *action space* of an individual consists of his day-to-day moves, excluding trips to the seaside and to hospitals, which are not run of the mill. The action space of individuals is determined by such factors as age and socio-economic standing. Uncongenial spaces such as hospitals and surgeries may tend to have a limited and undesired use by individuals because of a number of factors such as poverty (social spaces are constricted and social distance increased), religion (Jewish areas may feed Jewish hospitals and doctors and Roman Catholics may prefer their own schools, hospitals and ethnic physicians), race (a negro may travel a greater distance to encounter a negro physician, especially in the USA), ethnicity (Poles and Asians may have their own medical preferences), and age (the surgery in the young, middle-class suburban area which contains many children may be more popular for someone setting up practice than an area that contains mainly retired people).

'Becoming ill', which is dealt with in detail elsewhere, has a variable threshold. Earickson, in his study of hospital patients' spatial behaviour in Chicago, found that 'becoming ill' was influenced by many different factors such as fear, concern about cost (peculiarly American, but in Britain there may be worry about *earnings* rather than the cost of medical treatment), and the relative perception of the need for treatment. It may well be that those of low educational attainment and low income may be *more* ill, and certainly they tend both in the USA and Britain to be found in high-density areas which are also high in noise and pollution. Such individuals, when they finally realize that their symptoms may be serious and quack remedies not sufficient, may find it difficult, especially in America, to obtain proper medical care. 'As most physicians' intellectual values find their closest counterpart in middle and upper-class patients, they are far less willing to locate their offices where they will have many poor patients.'

In America the siting of hospitals, viewed as business concerns, can be modelled on a commercial pattern provided that the above variables such as age, ethnic preference and socio-economic factors are taken into account. In Britain hospitals are sited usually in inner urban areas, near universities or in the suburbs, and the establishment of new hospitals is not subject to the same constraints as in America. Nevertheless, ecological and demographic features are essential in future long-term planning of geriatric and maternity units, and also for family-planning services. If the rate of such diseases as coronary thrombosis and cancer continues to increase at the present high level, then further provisions will have to be made both for the training of personnel and the erection of specialized units.

SUGGESTIONS FOR FURTHER READING

EARICKSON, R. (1970). *The Spatial Behaviour of Hospital Patients*, Department of Geography, University of Chicago.
KELSALL, R. K. (1967). *Population*, Longmans, London.
OPEN UNIVERSITY (1973). *The City as a Social System*, Open University Press (Urban Development Course), Bletchley.

9

THE BEHAVIOUR OF INDIVIDUALS
IN SMALL GROUPS

Social interaction in small groups is found in a number of different species such as monkeys, apes and humans. Much of the behaviour of humans is, in fact, learned in such groups, and as individuals grow older such behaviour as they have learned in childhood groups is constrained, modified and stimulated by further contact with groups of a secondary nature.

WHY STUDY SMALL GROUPS? The phenomena of human interaction in societies can be viewed from a number of different perspectives. One perspective may be called 'social history' or 'social geography' and another 'sociology' or 'social psychology'. These are not necessarily conflicting perspectives but very often complement each other in 'rounding off' what after all is a very important study. Sometimes such perspectives break down even further into sub-categories. The study of small groups as such is commonly regarded as the special province of social psychology, and is one which overlaps with both psychology and sociology. In one sense it is useful to make such a distinction, but at a higher level such essentially artificial boundaries break down. *Social interaction* and *socialization* are areas both central to sociology and social psychology.

Sociology has traditionally been concerned with macro-scale interpretations and generalizations about large organizations of people such as societies, civilizations or nations. It has also been concerned with the movements of collectivities of people through the social structures and systems of these large organizations. However, it has been pointed out that the only historical continuity of men in society is in the small groups. Other categories such as guilds and trades have been disrupted and broken up, but small groups have survived, suggesting the latter as the basic social unit.

There has been much disagreement over what is meant by 'small group' but generally it can be taken to mean a number of persons engaged in meaningful interaction with one another in which there is some recognition of mutual expectancy.

Small groups such as the family, adolescent groups, work groups, T-groups, therapy groups, and committees are the kind studied by researchers interested in this area. Several reasons have been suggested for studying small groups. Firstly, such groups as the family provide us with our primary and basic experience in the socialization process. Secondly, some have hoped for a new sociological synthesis arising out of such study which would furnish a series of 'laws' which could eventually be applied to all human behaviour. Thirdly, small-group research is regarded by a few as perhaps providing an empirical testing-ground for sociological theory. Fourthly, a number of areas appear to converge on small groups such as counselling, clinical psychology, problem-centred groups, and so on. Fifthly, it is safe to say that many large-scale models which sociologists work with, such as the *conflict model*, can be examined in miniature. Sixthly, many pragmatic processes such as therapeutic mechanisms, so useful with groups such as Recovery, Inc. for ex-mental patients and Alcholics Anonymous for excessive drinkers, can be scrutinized at this level. Seventh, and lastly, small-group production rates affecting output can be examined in this small and relatively concise area.

A CRITICISM OF SMALL-GROUP RESEARCH Before we begin to discuss the positive contributions of small-group research it might be useful to suggest some of the main weaknesses in such an approach, which often is open to attack from both sociology and psychology. Small-group research is often guilty of using obtuse and difficult language which critics regard as an attempt to cover up a weak methodology. Many small-group research situations are very artificial ones taken from the world of American boys' summer camps, girls' dormitories, bomber crews, laboratory groups and so on.

The theory of small-group research is concerned with discovering the social counterpart of the discovery of the atom in physics. Thus the small group is held by many social scientists to be the simplest unit of human phenomena—the social counterpart of the atom in physics and of the cell in biology. However, neither the cell nor the atom is the simplest unit but is in fact a generic element of the biological or physical structures.

J. L. Moreno pioneered a method of measuring the internal structure of small groups. This method, *sociometry*, is concerned with the likings, dislikings, repulsions and attractions between members of these groups. It usually involves each member of a group specifying, usually in private, a number of other persons in the group with whom he would like to do something (such as sit next to) and those with whom he would *not* like to participate in any activity. The limitations in the use of such methods include: (a) it is only *one* way of viewing interpersonal relations; (b) sociometry doesn't bring out the differences in 'choice'; (c) there is an inadequate quantitative treatment of data.

Another criticism levelled against small-group research is that the term 'small group' is itself an arbitrary classification. This is not to say that small groups cannot be studied as a religious sect, the family, and so on, but that it cannot be studied as a typical example of all the heterogeneous groups of small size. Further, a small group is not necessarily simple because of its size. On the contrary the social organization of the General

Nursing Council is infinitely less complex than a hospital ward, and *gemeinschaft* communities are not necessarily more complex than Ford Motors.

THE FORMATION OF SOCIAL GROUPS It is useful to designate different kinds of groups on the basis of why they come together in the first place. For example, we talk of a leisure or interest group, a work group or a religious group and so on. B. W. Tuckman suggested that there are four major phases in the formation of groups and that group structure and the activities of groups develop in similar ways. He designated these as *forming, storming, norming*, and *performing*. In other words, the group locates itself around a leader, there is conflict between various sub-groups, a development of group cohesion, and finally a resolvement of interpersonal problems. Groups vary in the time they take to pass through one of these four phases and other factors such as the introduction of new members often interferes with the smooth flow. Group cohesiveness is very important in group formation because it indicates the level of attraction to a group (sometimes designated as the 'we' feeling). Individuals may be attracted to a group because of its prestige, because of other members, or because of the task that the group is performing. A group with relatively high cohesiveness displays a large amount of interpersonal interaction between members and a common agreement on the goals or task in hand.

INTERACTION PROCESSES IN SMALL GROUPS Potential members of groups often share something in common, such as an alcoholic addiction problem, but having joined a particular group they also begin to develop shared ways of looking at problems, of interacting, and so on. Social groups can therefore be said to form social norms through (a) having a common (or near common) goal at which to aim; (b) the development of a specialist language to facilitate communication and goal attainment, and the establishment of quite clearly defined rules; (c) the establishment of a set of beliefs and attitudes which are held in common; and (d) the formation of a set of norms about physical appearance, clothes, etc. Thus Alcoholics Anonymous recruits share a desire to attain sobriety and develop a special language and ritual in their groups to facilitate the achievement of this goal. They also develop the same attitudes towards their problems. The recruit to such groups must comply with such norms and later, after membership is established, the norms which initially have to be learned become familiar or internalized. Sometimes individuals in small groups do not conform to the norms. When this occurs they are either made to conform by the other members, are excluded from the group, form alternative groups of their own, or become innovators in the existing group. The reasons why an individual may not conform include a number of factors such as a strong personality, a wish to challenge the leader, or the influence of another group which he regards as important. If recruits place a great deal of importance on joining a group they are more likely to conform to its norms. Also, certain personalities are more likely to conform. Argyle reports that several studies have shown that conformers are likely to be female, unintelligent, lacking in self-confidence, and authoritarian. There is some suggestion that different nationalities conform more than others and that different sub-sections vary in the degree of conformity.

ROLE DIFFERENTIATION AND THE STRUCTURE OF THE SMALL-GROUP HIERARCHY Although small groups have a normative pattern, individuals in such groups often behave differently from one another because they have different tasks to perform and because their personalities differ. Very often a large group requires a firm leader, whereas a small group operates on the principle of a democratic consensus. Some groups have a system of offices, privileges and so on built in to their structure. These formal groups are distinguished from informal groups, which have an absence of such offices and titles.

There are a number of processes by which a leader emerges from a small-group situation. Leadership was initially studied in terms of the leader's attributes, but more recently it is regarded as emerging from effects induced by the demands of the situation. It is increasingly being seen as a process of interaction involving a person who influences and those who are influenced. Usually those who attempt leadership are those who successfully attempted earlier leads and who have ability to cope with the group's problems. Such individuals also display a higher self-esteem and self-accorded status. Whether or not leadership succeeds depends on the perception by other members of the similarity of this situation to ones in which the would-be leader was successful earlier. Sometimes the emerging leader is in a position to coerce other members due to his power to reward or punish them. Persuasion by a would-be leader that he can successfully lead is another factor.

The trait approach to leadership sought to identify unique characteristics in the leaders, and people were regarded as 'born' leaders. The situational approach views leadership in the life context in which it occurs. While certain minimum abilities are required of all leaders, such abilities are also distributed among non-leaders as well. Furthermore, the traits of the leader which are effective and necessary in one group or situation may be quite different from those in a different setting. Leaders tend to display a better verbal effectiveness and social perceptiveness than non-leaders. A further distinction made is between the social specialist leader whose activities are mainly constructive in contributing to group organization, maintenance and internal harmony among members, and the task specialist leader whose main concern is with the group's successful attainment of its collective aims and goals.

The two main styles of leadership normally distinguished are those of autocratic versus democratic leadership. Power and influence may be exerted in an essentially autocratic style through direct coercion and authoritative manipulation, or in a more democratic style through indirect cajoling, seduction and persuasion. Very limited and culture-bound research has tended to suggest that democratic styles of leadership are not only preferred by most people but also they that tend to facilitate the effective performance of the group.

Several factors may influence the style of leadership adopted by an individual in a group. His own personality and needs may dispose him to adopt a particular style. Characteristics of the group itself and even the pattern of communication among members may also affect the style. A person cannot display leadership functions unless others display the reciprocal role of follower. Social power is not an attribute of an individual but a relationship between an individual and others. Limited evidence suggests that good leaders are people who are (a) sensitive to specific needs and demands of their group and each of its members, (b) able and flexible enough to adapt their behaviour to suit their needs, and (c) responsible enough to initiate new actions when needed.

Status is an important concept in the study of small groups for a number of reasons. Status is a position occupied by a person in the social system. This position can also be occupied by a family or a kinship group. Any position is relative to others within the social system, and determines a whole range of relationships with persons of differing status. Socio-logists generally regard status as the static aspect of role and role as the dynamic aspect of status. Status entails a series of prescribed rights and duties. As we have already suggested, the bases of status differential and allocation varies considerably from society to society and from one historical period to another within the same society. Status may rest, for example, on personal achievement or on some group-recognized status-giving factor. Status may be based upon differences of birth, wealth, occupation, political power, race, IQ, and so on.

That differences exist within the system does not in itself account for status discrimination. It is the process of symbolic interpretation which gives significance. Apart from the distinction between ascribed and achieved status some have gone on to identify six main criteria: (1) birth; (2) possessions; (3) personal qualities; (4) personal achievement; (5) authority; (6) power. When there is a good 'fit' between a person's position in each of these six major rankings this indicates a high degree of *status consistency*. *Status inconsistency* is where there is a bad 'fit', for example a teacher has education but low income.

We generally talk of status as accruing to a position which any person occupying acquires or is ascribed. However, even within a given position an individual's achieved status may vary upward or downward from this base depending upon features of his performance in that position. That is, a person's role enactments or performances tend to validate his status and so may modify it. Consequently, ineptness in role enactment lead to a loss of status. An inept ward sister loses status in the eyes of the rest of the ward staff. Strictly speaking status is attributed to positions and not people. Since each person occupies multiple positions within the social system, each of which accords him a status, we can think of persons as being characterized by status.

The concept of status which we have briefly reiterated here can be related to small-group study. Every position that is recognized and continues to be recognized by the members of a group contributes in some way to the purposes of the group. Social position determines role behaviour. A position has been described by one social psychologist as a locus of influences. Not only this. Relationships between different persons' position influence their role relationships. In other words, positions are related along a dimension which are regarded as 'higher' or 'lower' or 'superior to' others. These are commonly referred to as status differentiations. These differentiations occur in some form in all group situations and a few of these can be classified as follows; *professional prestige* occurs between members of a group and is characterized by deference on the part of low-status members towards those of high status, and expected deference from the former on the part of the high-status members; *popularity status* occurs because people tend to associate with those who are equivalent to them in popularity status; *power and authority status* is distributed in families, organizations and so on which entail a host of concomitant behaviour patterns; *knowledge status* occurs because certain groups and individuals within groups are delegated deference on the grounds of special skill or knowledge.

The basis of power in small groups is the relationship between a person and an agent (which can be another person, a role, a norm, a group or a part of a group). There are five bases of power which are important: (1) *reward power*, which is defined as power whose basis is the ability to reward; (2) *coercive power*, which is based on the individual's perception that the agent has the ability to mediate punishments for him; (3) *legitimate power* involves the individual's acceptance of a code or standard by virtue of which the agent can exert power; (4) *referent power* is based on the individual recognizing the agent as a reference group; (5) *expert power* is based on the perception that the agent has some special knowledge or expertise. Some have distinguished between power of two kinds—*behaviour control* and *fate control*. In the former, by varying his behaviour *A* can make it desirable for *B* to vary his behaviour too; in the latter, *A* can affect *B*'s behaviour regardless of what *B* does. Thus power can be looked at in terms of the degree to which the less powerful person can affect certain outcomes on his own behalf.

A highly cohesive group possesses all or some of the following characteristics: (a) a high level of mutual attraction among its members; (b) shared attitudes and rules; (c) well-developed structural integration. Each of these properties confers power on the group over its members.

Communication in small groups is largely the same as that in bigger social organizations. *Horizontal communication* characterizes the majority of interaction in such groups. If we take the example of a hospital and a ward within a hospital most communication is between individuals occupying the same status positions. For example, student nurses tend to communicate more with each other than with a staff nurse or a ward sister. Interaction takes place between student nurses on a ward in terms of cooperation and help over certain tasks. Sometimes student nurses communicate with others from other wards, and certainly individuals occupying the same status positions communicate much more with each other than with either superior or inferiors. Communication also tends to centre around friendship and social support either in the residential quarters or coffee breaks or during leisure. *Communication downwards* in a hospital setting takes the form of information, orders or instructions. It also takes the form of communication by experts. In a bureaucratic organization such as a hospital such communication is usually filtered down through the hierarchical channels. *Upward communication* takes the form of seeking help, of reporting on progress, and sometimes of making suggestions.

FIVE DIFFERENT KINDS OF SMALL GROUP The *family*, which we treat separately elsewhere, is found in some form in all species of mammals. it is in the family that the important process of socialization occurs, where positions are allocated and interaction patterns established. *Adolescent* groups are generally the first secondary associations that individuals join as completely separate entities from the family. It is in such adolescent groups that the majority of crimes, rebellion and non-conformity (to adult values, that is) occur. Some sociologists have suggested that adolescence is a creation of industrial societies and that primitive societies have no such indeterminate span between childhood and adulthood. Certain adolescents are more popular than others. For example, an American study suggests that beautiful girls and athletic boys are more popular than intelligent ones of either sex. Although generally adolescent groups have no special task they tend to be over-concerned with sex and with the establishment of an ego-identity which characterizes itself with a fastidiousness over clothes, haircuts and so on. Relationships in adolescent groups tend to be more intense than at other periods of the life-cycle.

Work-groups are essentially concerned with the performance of a task. *Problem-solving* groups usually succeed at their task better than individuals. Finally, *T-groups* and therapy groups are the setting for behaviour which, although some would regard it as atypical or abnormal, may nevertheless be a magnified example of a less obvious form of similar behaviour occurring elsewhere.

TWO CASE STUDIES OF SMALL-GROUP INTERACTION From 1927 until 1932 the Western Electric Company carried out a series of studies under the direction of Elton Mayo into monotony, morale and fatigue. Once famous as the 'classic' investigation these studies are now one of the supreme examples of really bad research. The company, based at Hawthorne, Illinois, and now called the Hawthorne Experiments, were directed at the problem raised by unexpected results of the effect of lighting conditions on output. The experimenters were expecting an increase in production to coincide with an increase in illumination and vice versa. Contrary to expectations production increased not only with the improvement of lighting but also when such lighting deteriorated. To test what the 'human factors' were that apparently intruded on their experiment those involved set up another test known as the Relay Assembly Test Room. The six girls involved in this experiment, despite whatever alteration in their conditions of work, continued to improve their production. What emerged finally was that it was not a physiological relationship between the girls and their work which was important but various psychological factors such as the attitudes of the girls and how they regarded their work.

The Bank Wiring Room experiment was supervised by an anthropologist, Lloyd Warner, and was a study of a section of a normal workshop. Fourteen workers were studied including nine 'wiremen', three 'soldermen' and two 'inspectors'. Several findings emerged from the long and detailed observation which followed. Firstly, the men shared a set of norms which were not officially defined in any way and to some degree militated against the management. Having set their own standards of what constituted a day's work the men were very much against anyone breaking their set rate. Such norms as these were enforced by such means as group criticism and symbolic reminders that any one individual was breaking the group's norms. Secondly, the workers in the group came to regard the inspectors as superior to some extent and the soldermen as inferior. In other words, a set of social relationships and interaction was established by the group.

The impact of such a study is that it characterizes the way in which a whole series of informal relationships can develop even within a tightly regulated system. A more popular example is afforded by the BBC series *Colditz*, which demonstrates how officers held in captivity and regulated by a very strict regime can still manage to form a whole pattern of unofficial and informal activities. Another factor which emerged from the study was that the work performance to an extent depended on their social relationships. Such studies as these were the beginning of the *human relations* approach, which has tended to dominate managerial and bureaucratic studies.

The Western Electric Company study has produced the term 'the Hawthorne effect' which describes how the observer influences his object of study by merely being there. One of the reasons why the girls in the Relay Assembly Test Room showed such large increases in output was simply that they liked being observed. To put it another way they worked better when watched. A more serious criticism is summed up by Argyle: 'the results of that experiment could however be accounted for entirely in terms of uncontrolled factors, such as changed incentive arrangements, the replacement of the two slowest girls by two faster ones, and the reduced variety of work done'.

A study of the Norton Street gang by William F. Whyte examined a group of Italian slum neighbourhood dwellers in Boston. The study was produced in 1943 after a number or years spent living with the group in the area. The group consisted of a number of young men (13) between 20 and 30, who were unmarried. The study showed quite graphically a small group sharing common norms and interacting together in a structural manner. There was a certain hostility to outsiders and these were safe-guarded by a shared set of attitudes. The most prestigious sexual targets were Anglo-Saxon Protestant women, but women inside the neighbour-hood were taboo. The group was structured into a formal hierarchy as follows:

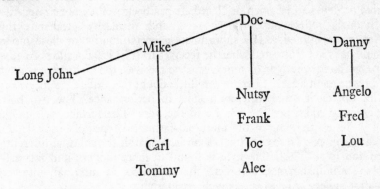

Evolving during the Depression, the gang was an avenue of mobility and a means of achieving social status and recognition. The group had its own corner (Norton Street) and a regular evening meeting place at a cafeteria where table positions were fixed by custom. Athletic skill and toughness were highly prized characteristics. Doc was the person of the highest status, the leader, together with his two lieutenants, Mike and Danny. These three were less restricted to gang activities than the other members. Doc was expected to lend money to others but not to borrow himself. He was expected to be fair in his dealings with others. Basically, group members derived their satisfaction from their shared activities and relationships. The study is important because it shows how a leader can effectively structure a group, and also because it highlights well-organized groups and activities even in an area which might be described as anomic or disorganized. In other words, a slum ghetto possesses a number of primary groups which offer an intimate atmosphere.

THE SUPERVISOR IN THE SMALL-GROUP SITUATION Leadership involves some degree of supervision. It is generally felt that leaders/supervisors should be high in dominance (effectively doing the job), rewarding, skilful (in leading and supervising), and able to take the role of the other (why *did* someone act as he did). Other related characteristics that a supervisor should show are the ability to initiate structure and to show consideration for others.

Supervision in a small-group situation can take many forms, as follows:

(a) S   (b) S   Sd   (c) S   S   S   (d)   S

   Sd   Sd   Sd   Sd   Sd Sd Sd

(S is supervisor and Sd is supervised) but the most common form is still (d). The supervisor receives little or no training in human skills or problem solving, nor in communication.

The manner or style by which a person is supervised elicits a different response in that person depending on whether the supervision is authoritarian or democratic, open or closed. It has been well demonstrated that individuals reflect supervisory styles and themselves transmit this reflection or influence. If a subordinate expects punitive or close supervision, he is not frustrated when he receives it. If he has not the normative expectation for the type of supervision he receives, then a form of conflict and resentment arises. There is very little doubt that different supervisory styles can elicit quite different results in performance. The two basic supervisory styles are the *closed* and the *open*. The former style might still be found in some of the more old-fashioned types of hospitals and medical schools. Here the supervision is formal, hierarchically differentiated and total. The latter style is found in more modern and forward-looking establishments, and here the supervisor is informal, interacts with the supervised and is relatively egalitarian.

Such work as that on supervision is directly applicable to medical settings where much of the work involves the supervision of subordinates by doctors, tutors, ward sisters and so on. Furthermore, hospitals are full of small work groups. Even hospital wards are examples of small groups where relationships and patterns of interaction can be observed and acted upon by staff. In the course of their working lives many medical staff come into contact with small groups, both therapeutic and otherwise. Despite the criticisms of small-group research mentioned above, the way in which such groups are formed and persist over time can be of immense interest to social scientists and of value to those interested in medical care.

SUGGESTIONS FOR FURTHER READING

ARGYLE, M. (1969). *Social Interaction*, Methuen, London.
CHINOY, E. (1967). *Society* (2nd ed.), Random House, New York.
KELVIN, P. (1970). *The Basis of Social Behaviour*, Holt, Rinehart and Winston, London.
KLEIN, J. (1967). *The Study of Groups*, Routledge and Kegan Paul, London.
McDAVID, J. W. and HARARI, H. (1968). *Social Psychology*, Harper and Row, New York.

10

THE PROFESSIONS AND NURSING

The work a person does tells us a great deal about other aspects of that person's life. It helps us to place him or her quite firmly in a whole pattern which we have learned to associate with that work, including the *stereotypes* that we have. Equally importantly, the kind of work that a person does to a large extent determines activities in the non-work sphere. For example, we would be very surprised if a barrister lived in a council house or frequented dog races.

We spend most of our lives working. Sometimes we find it intensely satisfying but most people, unless they fall into this lucky category, 'each day sell little pieces of themselves in order to try to buy them back each night and weekend with the coin of fun'. C. Wright Mills was referring to the monotony of work that so many in the population face as a daily occurrence. We have moved away from the *gemeinschaft* economic existence of pre-industrial times to the large impersonal technical work situations of the twentieth century. The whole pattern of work has changed. Now people no longer work in isolated folk communities but congregate in large masses in factories and offices.

Because it is difficult to arrive at a definition of *work* as a term, partly because some people are lucky enough to enjoy what they are doing but also because a large number of people such as housewives work without being paid, then sociologists prefer to use the term *occupation*. This latter term refers to that which a man does to determine his *market situation*, i.e. which enables him to receive services and goods for money or some other form of exchange. Some work, of course, falls outside the market situation. By this we mean the kind of work that people might perform in their leisure time, such as decorating their house. Another way of classifying work is to designate it as either *expressive* (enjoyable or intrinsically satisfying) or *instrumental* (merely a means to an end).

The social system has the task of filling the multiplicity of job-roles available in a given society. Depending on the society in which we live, this can be achieved either through coercion or socialization. In a slave society or a totalitarian society, or even in South Africa or the southern states of America, there are few options available to large sections of the population, because individuals are coerced, either by force or by a severe limitation placed on the options to enter certain occupational categories. In a more open society, however, individuals are brought up in particular socio-economic strata of the population, which nevertheless theoretically offers them an unlimited choice of occupations. In a society such as this other factors enter into the freedom of choice, such as education. In other words, children of working-class parents usually choose the occupations of their parents, their friends or relatives, and very rarely either wish to break away from this or indeed have the necessary qualifications to do so.

REALISM OF ASPIRATIONS Sociologists of occupations have argued that working-class children, whether consciously or unconsciously, limit themselves to their class horizons, regarding it as natural that they move into the same occupational level as their parents. They do not choose from the whole range of occupations because their *milieu* has dictated to a considerable extent the possible occupations in terms of which they think. Other research has shown that children from non-selective schools rank very low in the scale of ambitiousness, and working-class children set the horizon of their expectations at the level of their classmates, neighbours and friends. The working population tends to fall into three categories. Firstly, those with high aspirations who obtain the jobs of their choice. Secondly, those who have no great expectations of work. Thirdly, those who use work as a means of achieving status and remuneration.

OCCUPATIONS AND THE ECONOMY Occupation, because it has implications for the non-work sphere, is the most important indicator of the position an individual occupies in a market situation. It also gives a strong indication of a person's status and also his income. In modern industrial society some sociologists such as Marx have argued that highly impersonal modes of production have led to man being alienated. Even non-Marxist sociologists of work have argued that men employed in industrial occupations are alienated, that is, alienation is used as a shorthand description of the impact of modern industrial life on the manual worker. Generally speaking, the word alienation can be broken down into the following categories: (1) in a factory technology the workers are dominated and their alienation expressed in their relative *powerlessness* before the machine system; (2) robbed of a sense of purpose due to the fragmentation of the work task, the worker develops *meaninglessness*; (3) having no claim to the property institutions of capitalism there arises the employee's sense of *isolation* from the system of organized production and its goals; (4) modern technology and capitalist economic institutions have negated the human perspective in the work situation, resulting in *self-estrangement*. However, most social scientists today would argue that alienation is not a consequence of capitalism *per se* but of employment in the large-scale organizations and impersonal bureaucracies that pervade all industrial societies.

Within modern industry a vast process of structural differentiation has taken place, resulting in variations in the form and intensity of alienation. The best example of alienation is probably among car assembly workers, as many as 61% in some surveys claiming that their work is monotonous all or most of the time. Alienation refers particularly to the quality of personal experience which results from ways in which the social world is organized, and in particular the socio-technical settings of employment. When men feel that they are manipulated as objects, are without either control or power, and are without the *gemeinschaft* type of community that could compensate in some way for this feeling, they develop symptoms of fragmentation which we call alienation.

Some sociologists have pointed out that alienation follows a U-curve. During the old cottage and craft industries, when the *gemeinschaft* community was at its greatest, alienation was at its lowest. The industrial revolution, with the mass exodus from the agrarian division of labour to the cities, saw the end of the cottage industries and an increase in alienation. In the twentieth century with a large section of the labour force in assembly-line industries the feeling of alienation is at its highest, but already, in fully automated industries such as chemicals, there is evidence of a counter trend as the labour force is thrown back upon its own resources. The work of Goldthorpe on Vauxhall car workers bore out much of the research on alienation, but the particular factory studied had a long record of good relationships at the time of the study, and possibly the sample used (229 affluent workers) was too small to draw any valid conclusions. In the words of the French writer Albert Camus, 'Without work all life goes rotten. But when work is soulless life stifles and dies.'

WORK SATISFACTION Work satisfaction varies greatly by occupation, and as one might expect, the greatest satisfaction is displayed by professional and business occupations. The same pattern is displayed for those asked whether they would enter the same occupation again (mathematicians 91% to unskilled car-workers 16%) and those asked whether they would continue working after the age of 65 (professionals 68% to unskilled 16%). Although similar results are born out by a number of studies the samples in most of them tend to be quite small.

There are many factors which account for occupational differences in satisfaction. Firstly, occupational prestige which is invariably carried over into the non-work area. Secondly, control over time, physical movement and place of work, or control over the technical and social environment (coalminers and steel workers appear to derive some satisfaction from this), or control as the freedom from direct supervision (which appears to give satisfaction to miners, lorry drivers and railwaymen). Thirdly, integrated work groups where the evidence suggests that the greater the extent to which workers are members of integrated work groups on the job, the higher the level of job satisfaction and the less the degree of work alienation. Fourthly, occupational communities such as those described in *Coal is Our Life* and *The Fishermen* have a high level of off-work association which is rarely found among urban factory workers, and in which the occupation itself is used as a reference group utilizing its standards of behaviour, its system of status and rank, as a guide to conduct carried over into the non-work area. This stands in marked contrast to the alienated assembly worker, who is characterized by a separation of his work-sphere from his non-work-sphere.

OCCUPATIONAL VALUES   Different occupations carry with them differences in the prestige allocated to them in society, so that we normally rank unskilled and manual work as prestigiously low and non-manual work as high. There is considerable agreement from the surveys completed in this area that members of the general population tend to rate occupations roughly on the same point of a prestige scale so that professionals are ranked higher than middle-management who in turn come higher than skilled manual workers. Income by itself is not a sufficient criterion upon which to base a judgement. A poorly paid nonconformist minister of religion will be credited with more prestige than a second-hand car dealer, for example. Such notions as 'service' and 'usefulness' to society are also important in evaluating occupational rankings.

OCCUPATIONAL STUDIES   Dennis, Henriques and Slaughter's study of a coalmining town, *Coal is Our Life*, showed that 69% of the male population were employed in mining and the town had a high dependability on the industry. Teamwork was important, for many of the miners worked in groups. The important findings of the study show that many of the experiences and social relationships in the work area were carried over into the non-work area.

Other research on the Hull fishing industry showed that those employed live within a mile of the docks. In 1960 only 3% of the population of Hull were engaged directly in the fishing industry, though many others were engaged in closely connected trades. The work is dangerous and involves periods away from home. There is an insecurity of long employment and income with uncertainty about old age. The fishermen live in an area where houses have a low purchase price and low rental value and where there is a strong community pull.

BUREAUCRATIC ORGANIZATIONS   Many people spend a large part of their working life in what are termed bureaucratic organizations in both the public and the private sector. Bureaucracy emerged in China, but it now characterizes much of present-day western industrial society. Because such organizations vary, sociologists find it useful to employ an ideal type of bureaucratic system based on the work of the German sociologist Max Weber, and which includes (a) carefully defined *offices* or positions, (b) a *hierarchical* order with clearly distinguished lines of responsibility and opportunity, (c) selection of personnel by methods based on *technical* or *professional* qualifications, (d) *rules* and *regulations* for social action, (e) security of *tenure* and the possibility of *career* and (f) a minimum of emotional involvement. All procedures are carried out by a *rational* procedure. Obviously an ideal type does not really exist and instances only approximate to it. We can all think of instances in which the system breaks down, when for example a firm sends out several reminders which cost more than the small amount owing. We can also envisage employees without technical competence, confusion and conflict among roles, and arbitrary and ridiculous rules.

Generally, bureaucratic systems are criticized for dampening personal growth, developing conformity and the 'organization man', and because they are hierarchical. There are dysfunctional and unintended consequences of bureaucracies, which are often inefficient and fail to achieve their intended goals.

INFORMAL WORK STRATEGIES Individuals in employment frequently develop strategies for coping with stress and the feeling of powerlessness which they experience in their work. Some workers strike or stay away from work. like the dock workers, or break up the working day with cups of tea or frivolities. The collective action of unions is a major way of establishing independence. Many occupations which are striving for status increase, for example clerical workers, have no desire to use the same sorts of strategies as manual workers. Professional associations have different strategies of negotiation from trade unions.

PROFESSIONS

Professions stand out from occupations and the surveys of occupations carried out on them as distinctly different. A profession is a very different type of occupation from all others, particularly in the distinction that a professional has the right to control his own work, that is he possesses a deliberate autonomy to such right and is granted such rights as to be able to deliberately ignore outside intervention. There remains a distinction between 'scholarly' professions and 'practising' professions and between professions and paraprofessions, which it is hoped will become apparent.

Some professions, for example dentistry and pharmacy, are autonomous in their own right, without being as prestigious as medicine. Others are very much dependent on the paradigm profession of medicine and are called *paramedical*. Nursing is a good example of a paramedical profession because although it becomes legitimate for nurses to receive orders and be evaluated by members of the medical profession the opposite is not the case. Nursing therefore becomes classified as a paramedical profession because, in the words of Freidson, they specifically and generically occupy positions round a profession. The search for full professionalism by paraprofessionalists is usually instituted by the latter setting up roughly the same standards as the profession that they are trying to emulate, principally training and licensing.

CHARACTERISTICS OF A PROFESSION A profession is usually characterized as possessing the following characteristics, derived from William J. Goode: (1) the profession determines its own training and educational standards; (2) the practice of the profession is generally recognized by some form of licensing; (3) the boards which grant the licence are manned by members of the profession; (4) legislation is decreed by the profession; (5) standards and their control are laid down by the profession. Training in particular is prolonged, specialist and relatively abstract. The nursing profession on these criteria fails to possess the autonomy and control over training, and neither is it felt to create the knowledge, despite claims to the contrary. Even the possession of a criterion of 'service organization' is not felt sufficient to warrant the label of profession, because it is basically an institutional attribute rather than an individual one. It is only when society acquiesces in granting an autonomy from supervision by lay personnel that the category of profession can be awarded.

THE DIVISIONS OF MEDICAL LABOUR

Medicine historically sought the exclusive right to practise its arts. Many other kinds of healing art became dissociated with such a claim and with the state monopoly which accompanied it. It has now become established that it is illegal for anyone to practise medicine who is not qualified to do so.

Many tasks of medical healing, which were once thought the sole prerogative of physicians, are now practised by non-medical personnel, but it is the *control* of the situation and of the division of labour which is distinctive. One of the categories of occupation falling under this control is designated as paramedical, by which is meant the healing activities controlled obtrusively or unobtrusively by physicians. Freidson distinguishes such control by the amount or degree of technical knowledge 'released' by physicians, the extent of the assistance of paramedical workers, the subordination of paramedical workers, and finally the degree of prestige assigned to paramedical workers is less than that given to physicians.

Consequently, Freidson argues that paramedical workers are to be distinguished from established professions by their lack of responsibility, autonomy, prestige and authority. Some occupations, such as herbalism, society designates as 'quack' or 'freaky'. It must be remembered that the designation 'paramedical' is a sociological one and not in any way implied as denigrating these occupations. Historically, through the university and the guild, the medical profession has consolidated its predominance in the areas of diagnosis and prescription.

Even the paramedical division of labour is hierarchically stratified, with nurses ranking far higher than medical technicians and attendants. Other factors to be taken into consideration is that many paramedical occupants are *women*, and that prerequisite qualifications such as 'A' levels for university entrance are usually required for the former, that is the medical profession.

The training of personnel appears to be closely associated with the prestige of the occupation, and training geared to a university or in some way connected with one invariably occupies a higher position in the division of labour. Recruitment to medicine and nursing training is not a particular problem in either America or Europe, as the difficulty seems to lie in getting women to *stay* in the job and to reconcile the labour pattern with the competing demands of marriage and family life.

Friedson argues that p: fessional autonomy is more easily developed by occupations that can successfully operate *outside* the confines of organizations. Traditionally the nurse has cared for the sick on the orders of, and in the absence of, a physician. Historically, the separation of secular nurses from the religious orders did not give the former any special claims based on the possession of skills and technical training until the middle of the nineteenth century. Because of the development of the modern nursing system under Florence Nightingale, the roots were firmly established in the subordinate position of the nurses of the Crimea under the military physicians. Even after her initial success at Scutari, the basis of the ideology of nurses was based on their social class and morals.

THE DILEMMAS OF NURSING   While anxious to establish itself as a new and independent division of labour, nursing has had to face the dilemma that its work is not controlled by the occupation itself but stands in direct relation to the orders of the attendant physician. Increasingly, however, it has become recognized that the occupation of nursing possesses many tasks and a body of special knowledge that makes the nurse a surrogate doctor. The traditional model of the bedside attendant has given way to one of supervision, and a concomitant growth of occupations such as *practical nurse* or *nursing assistants* or others with fewer qualifications and training in an essentially subordinate position to fully registered nurses.

Now in a state of change, the occupation of nursing sees a route of social and occupational mobility up the hierarchy through an essentially administrative function. In many respects nursing is moving towards its own autonomy and self regulation, although its real dilemma still resides in its members being subordinate to the authority of the physician.

TEACHING AS AN OCCUPATION

The foregoing analysis of the occupation of nurses brings out the sociological implications of professionalization. Such implications are not confined to nursing but shared by other occupations such as teaching, from which many researchers would wish to withhold the title of 'profession'.

Any conceptions of teaching which a society or community has must involve a consideration of the occupation's status. Some of the important factors to take into considerations are the salary structure; the qualifications necessary both for entry and qualified exit, the general working conditions, the importance attached to education as judged by the amount of money spent on it, and the influence that teachers can wield as an organized body of decision makers. Socio-historical studies of teachers can throw substantial light on their status. For example, they may be accorded more status by a community than they themselves think, as is the case in Germany. One of the complications in an analysis is that the word 'teacher' covers a wide diversity of types within the educational system, involving different orders of *skills*. The status of any one individual teacher depends on the general status of the total occupational group, the status of the teacher's group relative to other occupational groups within the system, and his status within the individual school. Status within the educational system depends to a large degree upon such factors as the age of the pupils taught, their academic level, and the status of the school in which they are taught, as well as other factors such as the social class of pupils, the qualification of the teacher, and the subject which he or she teaches. Undergraduates, when asked to list in order of preference the status of teachers, did so in relation to the type of teaching situation and in the following order: at the high level were grammar-school sixth-form teachers followed by grammar-school teachers generally, then comprehensive, independent, secondary modern, junior and finally infant.

A recent survey comprising social rankings across six different countries showed that the position of teacher was virtually the same in all of them, ranking slightly below such occupations as accountant and army officer, and slightly above skilled craftsmen and farm owners. The editors of the 1953 *Yearbook of Education* concluded that teaching could not be considered a profession, although some have disagreed with this verdict. One drawback is that teaching associations do not exercise 'negative' functions as do professional organizations. That is, it is very difficult to be 'struck off' the teaching list (teachers possess no professional register apart from a Department of Education and Science 'number'). Neither do teachers as an occupation have control over those who enter the work force the training and selection being undertaken by the staff of Colleges of Education and University Departments of Education, and local authority selection by education advisers and education officers. The 1953 *Yearbook* listed several criteria which an occupation had to fulfil before becoming designated as a profession. Firstly, it had to be work which was performed as a major source of livelihood and not 'an amateur's dilettantism'. Secondly, the members of a profession control some kind of esoteric knowledge not generally available to the public. Thirdly, there must be a measurable difference between the gifted amateur and the average professional. Teaching generally satisfies the first criterion but there is disagreement that most teaching involves some 'special' kind of knowledge that the educated laymen is not aware of, and that the work entails any measurable difference between amateurism and professionalism. Unlike medicine and para-medical work which *does* involve both a high degree of special knowledge and esoteric wisdom teaching fails to satisfy this criterion. Two other criteria which are mentioned we have already hinted at, namely the granting of a special licence and the creation of social gains which are clearly demonstrated. Clearly there are discrepancies within teaching itself. For example, the university graduate has always legitimized his professional status by reference to the university, despite many such teachers in the past being without training. Two criteria, despite the apparent weaknesses in the ones we have discussed, stand out above all others in calling teaching a profession. One is the actual level of recruit (in 1968 only 36% had two or more A levels) and the other is the academic level at qualification (a degree on completion of training rather than a certificate).

The brief discussion of teaching as a profession highlights some of the problems that sociologists face in an analysis of the professional role. Clearly nursing fulfils far more acceptable criteria than teaching with its professional register, control over entry, a firm body of special and esoteric knowledge and so on. The one unsatisfied criteria appears to be that of autonomy and the particular relationship of nursing to the physician, although there is some indication that nursing authorities and associations are taking steps to remedy this.

THE NURSING PROFESSION

We turn now to looking at the occupation of nursing by trying to apply some of the perspectives we have discussed above. It is an impossible task to look at the occupation *in vacuo* because we must constantly relate it to the broad structure of occupations within the social structure and market situation of a country.

CHARACTERISTICS OF RECRUITS   Recruits to nursing tend to be predominantly female. Nowadays about 10% of recruits are males who work mainly in mental and mental subnormality hospitals rather than general hospitals. Students nurses are generally drawn from the Registrar General's Classes I, II and II, are unmarried and in the 18–20 years of age range. One in four of nurses in training in this country come from outside Britain; English and Welsh nurses form the largest section and Irish and Scottish nurses comprising a minority. Recruits stem from a wide range of educational levels, with the majority possessing no formal school-leaving certificate but above average in educational attainment and a wide range of IQ according to Jillian Macquire in a fairly recent survey.

The majority of recruits appear to have chosen nursing as a first choice, and in a positive manner, at an early age, and generally to have had some work experience or voluntary experience relevant to their career choice. On the whole those who opt for nursing appear to know more about different kinds of training and career opportunities in nursing than potential recruits. As in many other occupations the choice of career is relevant to encouragement from relatives and information being passed on to them by friends and relations. With most recruits to nursing the over-riding reason for choosing nursing is because it is seen as helping people in a practical way.

CHARACTERISTICS OF INTAKES   Intakes into non-teaching hospitals tend to be based on the immediate geographical locality supplemented by recruits from overseas. Such rely heavily on cadet courses, whereas teaching hospitals have a higher level of education in their recruits while those at the lowest level are in non-teaching hospitals.

NATURE OF ATTRITION   Attrition or 'wastage' or 'withdrawal' is mostly due to voluntary withdrawal from training rather than nursing, and there are differences between types of nursing schools. Such withdrawal is higher in the first year than in the two subsequent years, and particularly high in the Introductory Courses. Male recruits have higher attrition rates, according to Jillian Macquire's survey, but it makes no difference to either male or female recruits what age they were at entry or how near they live to their home. Grammar-school recruits have less attrition than other recruits but those from abroad have the highest rates. Lowest rates of attrition are from sick children, nurses and general nurses. As we might expect, those with positive attitudes are more likely to complete their training than those possessing negative attitudes.

THE ATTITUDES OF THE GENERAL PUBLIC TO NURSING   Nearly 26% of the general public regard nursing as a suitable first choice but rate secretarial and teaching work as higher. This same general public, however, had three out of five members who knew what SRN stood for, and only two out of five who knew what SEN stood for. Nursing was generally agreed upon as being harder than teaching or being a bank clerk, and a much more worthwhile job than these other occupations. Adults in the general population entertained a general image of nursing which included the idea that nurses worked harder than others. The majority thought nurses were underpaid but nevertheless would encourage their daughters to nurse. One third of all women develop an intention to nurse at some time, and this can be as many as 77% in those of school age. One in six develop a strong interest in nursing, and this reaches its peak between the ages of 13 and 16. Jillian Macquire's survey also showed that there was no interest in nursing which could be related to social class. The main deterrent was felt to be the hours worked and the pay, although the better educated tended to be more critical of the general conditions. The main positive factor was that nursing was worthwhile.

THE SELECTION OF RECRUITS   As we might expect those who apply for nursing are a highly self-selected group. The degree and kind of selection varies from hospital to hospital, and the ratio of those accepted to those rejected out of those who apply is greater for RHB hospitals than it is for teaching hospitals. Obviously, prestige of training establishment is as important in the choice of where a recruit chooses to do training as it is in choice of university, that is Oxbridge over Redbrick, large Civic over small Civic, and so on. Many hospitals set academic standards above the preliminary minimum set by the General Nursing Council, and some hospitals use batteries of tests in selection of students.

THE CAREER PATTERN OF THE QUALIFIED NURSE   All but a small minority of those qualified work as staff nurses, half working less than one year in a staff nurse grade. Within two and a half years one third of females are married and two thirds of these are not working. This can be compared with the Plowden Report's comment on young women teachers: 'We can expect that of every hundred women who enter the training colleges, only

47 will be in the schools after three years' service and after six years only 30.' With the changing institutions of society, and the changing role of women, the wastage pattern of women in trained occupations appears somewhat alarmingly high, but if we take the training of nurses in a wider context we can argue that it is not only a training for an *occupation* but also an education for life and motherhood. Two and a half years after qualifying 44% are working in hospitals as compared with 81% of males working. The average staff nurse is single, works full-time, is among the youngest and most recently qualified, and is more mobile than other trained staff. The majority of married staff nurses work part-time, and nearly half of the total number of staff nurses are working in their own training school. Only a small percentage become ward sisters.

Enrolled nurses are usually under twenty-five, but more than a quarter are over-thirty-one. Most married nurses of all kinds have a break in service, either with childbearing or marriage. The longer the break the less likely they are to return. Family commitments, the age of children, and the lack of career prospects for part-time nurses are the main factors determining the pattern of employment.

THE NURSE IN THE HOSPITAL ENVIRONMENT In traditional training programmes there is a constant conflict between the educational requirements or needs of students and the staffing requirements of the ward. As we might expect, and sharing a pattern with teacher training, for example, there is substantial confusion about the desired end product of the training process and about the definition of the 'good nurse'. We would expect the attitudes of nurses to be linked to the training that they have received, but evidence for this view was only established by Jillian Macquire between the attitudes of mental nurses and the therapeutic organization of the institution for which they are working. Discipline in hospitals tends to be externally imposed and authoritarian, which produces conflict and makes adaptation difficult for entrants schooled in a society which is becoming increasingly permissive in relation to authority.

The turnover of qualified staff depends, it appears, not on the characteristics of individuals but on some institutional effects peculiar to a specific hospital, probably the communication system of the hospital. Absence rates were 80% due to sickness for all grades, but were greater for the student nurse than for the trained ones. These sicknesses tended to be for respiratory and non-specific gastro-enteritis, which emerged as the major 'causes', and the absence for non-residential nurses was surprisingly greater than for residents.

STRUCTURE AND IDEOLOGY

We have outlined some of the characteristics of recruits and the qualified nurse. The general features of the occupation present a picture of nurses as composed almost wholly of women employed not only in hospital wards but also in administrative capacities. They are mostly employed in salaried positions in subordination to physicians. The occupation in general has a relatively open recruitment (almost any woman can enter *some form of* nursing) and a spatial transferability of skills (they can move about the country if they so wish). The majority of nurses, both in this country and America, work in hospitals, public health sectors or private homes. The occupation is embedded within a hierarchy of authority which stretches upwards to the physicians and the nursing hierarchy and downwards to student and ancillary nurses. Nurses are found in a number of diffuse occupations such as teaching, administration and bedside nursing. They also specialize within the hierarchical lines of the hospital or agencies and within the clinical specialization of medicine itself. It appears, then, to be predominantly a woman's occupation, with a relatively open recruitment and a high degree of geographical mobility.

The nursing reform movement, which paved the way for the near-professionalization of nurses, led eventually to sweeping changes in both the role of the nurse and her task within the hospital organization. Nurses no longer, in theory, were regarded as a pool of potentially cheap labour to be drawn upon at the discretion of physicians, and neither were they any longer anything approaching a nineteenth century description, which said they were 'Ward-maids . . . in much the same position as housemaids, and require little teaching beyond that of poultice-making.'

PERVASIVE IMAGERY OF BEDSIDE NURSING   The image of the nurse as one whose task is that of providing bedside comfort for the sick and dying is one which still persists despite the increasing pattern, especially in America, of nurses as administrators. The persistence of this imagery has something to do with the sacred character of the occupation stemming both from its religious and secular origins, which Florence Nightingale did little to dispel. The religious significance and influence of the concept of 'vocation', for example, finds its most obvious example in the nursing world. Olesen and Whittaker's account of this world brings out a parallel between the nurse's Hospital Training School and a convent. Both are comparatively total institutions, in Goffman's sense of the term, in which the novices are depersonalized and resocialized. Values and personality attributes are deliberately manipulated to designated ends. 'Inevitably, in this secluded company, notions so much a part of both occupations arise: sisterhood, committed purpose, dedication of one's life to a 'calling', and a sanctity of one's trust.' The image of the administering angel, the Lady with the Lamp, coupled with the *affective* nature of women (so the cultural stereo-type would have it) as sensitive creatures, has in modern times led to the formulation of various socio-psychological approaches such as 'total patient', 'the communicative approach', 'psychological needs', 'the psychodynamic' and that of 'interpersonal relations'.

This has in turn led to certain ambiguities in the nursing administrator. Indirect patient care is believed to be as important as direct patient care, with the consequence that the nurse as supervisor is playing as vital a part in the overall nursing structure as her colleague who acts in a direct relationship. Nevertheless, the hospitals and public health authorities have made administration the route into professional viability and visibility, and also institutional power. Most women enter the profession seeing themselves as bedside nurses and yet the dilemma or ambiguity lies in the fact that promotion and salary beyond a particular level depend on an upward mobility through the administrative route.

ORGANIZATIONAL CONTEXT OF NURSING CARE   Hospitals and the employees of hospitals in theory cannot practise medicine. Only the physician is licensed to do this, with the consequence that this represents an extreme concentration of a given function around a position which, to some extent at least, is part of a complex institutional division of labour.

Because the 'private duty' model of nursing care gave way to the institutionalized (or incorporated into an institution such as a hospital) model, we had the result that there was an increase in categories of nursing staff. 'Functional' nursing as perceived from the perspective of the nurse herself meant that her duties were assigned according to the level of competence of the nurse and the needs and requirements of the situation. The 'system' itself acted as a deterrent to professional nursing because the organization of the hospital was bureaucratic and hierarchically structured.

This has led some, such as Isabel Menzies, writing in 1961, to postulate recently that certain psychological defences are erected by nurses in relation to patient care. She argues that because of the emotional intensity of the nursing act, certain psychological barriers are unconsciously built up, making it difficult for nurses to engage in significant relationships with patients. Her study of some London hospitals concludes that even the social organization of the nursing service has been evolved, largely without conscious awareness, for the express purpose of avoiding any activation of those emotions arising from patient contact. Thus, the organization aims at preventing nurses from having long or intense contact with patients. The often distasteful and frightening tasks that confront a nurse in the hospital setting arouse strong feelings of both a positive and a negative kind. The organization of the modern hospital, in order to shield the nurse, creates socially structured defences. Each nurse is asked to perform only a few of the nursing tasks, thus giving her a comparatively restricted contact. Simultaneously the patients are depersonalized, for example by being called the 'liver case' or by their bed number. It is almost an 'ethic' that patients are to be treated and viewed as alike. The uniform, furthermore, is a symbol of expected behavioural conformity, and of the attempt to establish an operational identity among all nurses in the same category in the hospital. Thus nurses are interchangeable in staff assignments. In this way, Isabel Menzies argues, there is built into the institutional setting of the hospital and the role of the nurse, a 'safety valve' which ensures that no nurse has a contact nor involvement such as to allow her to develop any intensity of emotional commitment to the patient.

From the patient's point of view 'functional' nursing has the effect of increasing his anxiety. On admittance to a hospital he is anxious both about his condition, his new 'communal' situation, and his family whom he has left. From his very admittance he finds himself in an impersonal atmosphere and very often whatever personal treatment he might receive merely seems to accentuate his anxiety. Sometimes he is left for a long time on his own before anyone attends to him. He finds an added anxiety from the multiplicity of staff because he has not had time to recognize the different categories. He suffers, above all, a loss of independence and self-identity which results in a craving for individual identity and attention. Most of the problems of these different perspectives arise from the nurse and the patient viewing the situation within the hospital from two different viewpoints.

The nurse in the modern organizational context has a role which clearly recognizes a set of tasks which may be exactly or almost exactly specified and which involve a specialized and easily defined expertise. Nevertheless, there is a distinct boundary around the nurse's role beyond which she cannot go simply because to do so would involve a knowledge of the skills of the medical technician, the physician, the laboratory technician, and so on. But these are part of her role-set, the web of other roles with which her own interacts within the institutional setting. The old view of the nurse's role as being purely instrumental no longer applies. Her role is also expressive, that is, concerned not simply with a person's sick nature but with the *total* patient over a period of time. The role is affective in the sense that Isabel Menzies is talking about. The nurses cannot help but *feel* for the patient she is caring for but is guarded by the institutionalization of the role from the dangers of extreme affectivity.

The nurse is constantly subjected to some of the conflicting values in industrial society, some of which we have discussed in a previous chapter, such as religious, political and cultural values. Like all other role-incumbents the nurse must resolve, within the framework of role within the modern hospital, the dilemmas of general social interaction designated by the sociologist Talcott Parsons: affectivity versus affective neutrality (the emotional tone or level of a relationship); specificity versus diffuseness (should the nurse act as simply an aid to healing or should she see the role as a wider one incorporating a counselling or 'friendship' type of approach); universalism versus particularism (should she regard one patient just like another or can she 'particularize'); quality versus performance (does the nurse relate to the patient on the basis of the latter's sex or age or colour or on the basis of the latter's progress in health); self-orientation versus collectivity orientation (does the nurse put her own needs first or the requirements of the profession). Obviously we cannot go into these pattern variables, as they are called, in too great a depth here, but the pattern which emerges is that of the nurse's role as one involving a choice between these variables both from her own individual point of view and also from the institutionalization of the role by the hospital organization in which she finds herself.

CONCLUSION

Our discussion has examined the sociological concept of occupation in modern industrial society with particular reference to some of the implications of the concept to others such as status. The profession was regarded as a special category of occupation having special criteria which marked it off from other occupations. Nursing was analysed in order to bring out some of the nuances of the concept of profession, and perhaps the only drawback to nursing being accepted as a fully fledged profession was its lack of autonomy. Teaching appeared to fail several criteria for qualification as a profession. It may appear rather strange that both nursing and teaching, both generally regarded by the layman as professions, failed a sociological 'test' but we must remember that we were engaged in a kind of sociological exercise which was using the word in a strict sense. It is obvious that those criteria used were themselves open to debate, and perhaps there is a happy medium between using profession as loosely as the general public does to refer to virtually any occupation, and as strictly as the sociologist does, which severely limits its use. Nevertheless, an analysis of the concept and its application did throw some interesting light on the role of the nurse in the modern hospital setting and the relationship of her occupation to that of the physician and other medical and paramedical personnel. The sociology of occupations clearly recognizes that many new 'professions' are emerging in keeping with the growth in the complexity of modern industrial and technological society which are termed *qualifying associations*. Nursing is clearly in a very strong position to consolidate its strengths and to achieve either professional autonomy in the near future or at least some form of alternative to the present position. Nursing in the above analysis shares a category similar to that of pharmacist and slightly below that of optician, but only if we use the criterion of being able to prescribe. There are many other criteria we could opt for, such as service orientation, which nursing undeniably shares with physicians. We have tended to adopt the criterion of occupational autonomy in this chapter, following Freidson and others, which was as much intended as an exercise in the sociology of occupations as such as a stand for one particular criterion.

SUGGESTIONS FOR FURTHER READING

ABEL-SMITH, B. (1960). *A History of the Nursing Profession*, Heinemann, London.
DAVIS, F. (ed.) (1966). *The Nursing Profession*, John Wiley, New York.
FRANKENBURG, R. (1966) *Communities in Britain*, Penguin, Harmondsworth.
FREIDSON, E. (1972). *Profession of Medicine*, Dodd, Mead and Company, New York.
GOODE, W. J. (1960). 'Encroachment, Charlatanism, and the Emerging Profession: Psychology, Medicine and Sociology,' *American Sociological Review*, 25, 902–914.

HUGHES, E. C. *et al.* (1958). *Twenty Thousand Nurses Tell Their Story*, J. B. Lippincott, Philadelphia.

MACQUIRE, J. (1969). *Threshold to Nursing*, Bell, London. (Occasional Papers on Social Administration, 30.)

MENZIES, I. E. B. (1961). The Functioning of Social Systems as a Defence against Anxieties. Tavistock pamphlet No. 3, London.

OLESEN, V. L. and WHITTAKER, E. W. (1968) *The Silent Dialogue*, Josey-Bass, San Francisco.

THE SOCIOLOGY OF MEDICINE

It seems astonishing that hysterectomies could ever become fashionable. Yet in nine years, between 1961 and 1970, the number of women undergoing this operation has increased from 43 350 to 61 020. Several reasons can be given for this increase, including the rise in the population and the feeling that operations of this kind are now surgically safer. There is even some evidence that a hysterectomy is becoming a middle-class status symbol. Further evidence from America suggests that one fifth of the operations performed there are unnecessary, including 50% of tonsillectomies, 30% of hysterectomies and 20% of appendectomies, making a total of 2 000 000 unnecessary operations every year. Apart from factors such as incompetence in surgeons, and a greed for money from the fees, there is a strong pressure for such operations from the patients themselves. Another factor appears to lie in the training of doctors in America. That is, if there is an excess number of surgeons then it is possible that they will perform an excess number of operations. The American system also means that an empty hospital bed costs as much, or almost as much, as a full one, and the tendency is to fill these empty beds. The number of appendectomies performed in a given area, for example, does not relate to the number of people in that area that would be liable to have the operation performed but rather to how many surgeons and how many hospital beds there are in the area. People in areas with few surgeons and hospital beds appeared to exist quite happily with their appendices intact, and in areas with more surgeons and beds available produced a concomitant increase in appendectomies. In America hysterectomies are almost automatic for middle-class women over the age of 40, and a study at Columbia University put the figure of unnecessary operations of this sort at 33%.

In this country, although we do not have a system of payment by results, nevertheless there do appear to be unnecessary operations performed. Professor Neville Butler, Co-Director of the National Child Development Study, found that one third of all children who enter hospital in Britain do so to have their tonsils removed. Consequently, by the age of seven 16% of British children are without tonsils. The surprising evidence was the variation of the rates throughout the country. In Wales 14% of children had their tonsils removed, in the North of England 15%, the South 17%, and Scotland 21%. Again, one local area can have fifteen times as many tonsillectomies as an adjoining area. Part of the reason for this regional and local variation lies in the services available, so that in an area where hospitals and surgeons are available then the operation is more in evidence. But there is also a general belief among the population as a whole that the removal of tonsils is conducive to health even if the child has not been ill. The higher up the social scale one goes the more likely the child it so be without tonsils. 15% of unskilled manual workers' children have had their tonsils removed, while among the children of white-collar workers the figure is nearer 22%.

These examples from America and Britain illustrate very clearly the scope and the contribution of sociology to medicine. In its origins sociology was concerned to establish itself as a scientific discipline and it turned readily to social areas and problems such as poverty and anomie, which were conditions highlighted by the industrial revolution. Medicine, for its part, developed in the nineteenth century heavily under the influence of biological germ theories of disease and relied on the laboratory and its techniques to give it respectability. Various factors can be seen as contributing to the convergence of the two subjects, as suggested by Coe.

1. MORBIDITY RATES   The twentieth century has witnessed dramatic drops in the rate of epidemic disease, with the result that many of the population now live to feel the effects of chronic illness. Many of the population are reluctant to benefit from scientific advances such as screening tests. The changing pattern of disease has meant a shift in attention away from a single-cause theory of disease to the view that there are situations in common in the lives of individuals with some form of chronic illness which differ from those for individuals without evidence of such illness. Epidemiological studies have consequently become concerned with the life experiences and habits of individuals in society.

2. THE RISE OF PREVENTIVE MEDICINE AND THE PUBLIC HEALTH SECTOR   The spread of contagious disease in the population has been for the large part replaced by a wider concern for the *ecology* of any disease (how it is distributed in the general population). Many factors such as family background, type of housing, type of water, have now to be taken into account in the field of treatment. It is now clearly recognized that certain actions are bad for an individual's health, and a new area of health education has emerged. Of interest to the sociologist of medicine is the resistance to health measures from certain social strata of the population. This century has experienced the emergence of a total view of medicine with such concepts as community care, and techniques for measuring the level and type of health care that may be required by a particular area or community. Other growth areas include concern for the rehabilitation of individuals into families and communities after particular accidents and the increasing concern that certain occupations, e.g. work with asbestos, may carry with them grave risks.

3. THE IMPACT OF MODERN PSYCHIATRY   Biological theories of the causation of disease broke down with the contribution of psychologists and

psychiatrists that mechanisms other than biological ones could be involved. Such concepts as psychosomatic cause and stress began to play an important part in modern medicine. Mental illness, for example, came to be seen as having important social aetiologies, and the relationship of the patient with the physician was recognized as a very positive aspect of the treatment. In some cases the entire context of medical practice and the total environment of the patient became part of the *milieu* therapy.

4. ADMINISTRATIVE MEDICINE   More attention is now being given to the provision of medical facilities to regions in a way that would ensure a minimum of regional disparities. Hospitals themselves are becoming more humanized and patients given help in adjusting to their environment. The nursing profession has been among the first to employ social scientists in order to enhance the level of patient care, and indeed nursing schools have themselves been innovators of new perspectives.

By 1950 it was clearly seen in America, and to a lesser extent in Britain, that sociology, with its particular areas of study, had much to contribute to medicine. For example, the study of socialization, the family, the beliefs of individuals, social differentiation, the demographic and ecological techniques of social scientists, and the social psychological heritage of studying small groups and communities—all these had an important part to contribute to the field of medicine. Coupled with this the new view of health as not merely the absence of disease but the complete well-being of the individual, physical, mental and social, then it was but a short step to a conception of medicine as a social science.

Sociologists are increasingly employed as research workers, as lecturers in nursing and medical schools, and on psychiatric problems. With the growth of medicine, the contribution of sociology and its techniques will probably become even more relevant. Nevertheless, the four main perspectives of the sociology of medicine will still encompass those mentioned by Rodney Coe in 1970. First, disease in the population is neither random nor uniform but located in social groupings of various kinds. Because social structure imposes different life-styles on people this difference is often seen to provide clues to the origins of illness, an example being the incidence of bronchitis in unskilled labourers. Second, people respond to disease, and define it, in a predictable way from the perspective of their own culture and their own social class within that culture. Third, society erects a whole set of institutions to treat disease, whether it is the medicine man of the Trobriand islands or a modern teaching centre. Fourth, medical institutions for the treatment of the sick are supported in modern industrial societies by a vast array of other institutions, ranging from voluntary organizations to drug companies.

DISEASE AND THE SICK PERSON   The field of epidemiology is concerned with the way disease occurs and is distributed in a population, and it examines this distribution with the aid of different data before going on to construct logical chains of inference which explain the many factors that cause disease. The epidemiologist is concerned with the change in causes of death as well as simply the number of deaths. He has to rely to a great extent on official statistics on death, and although these may be accurate in modern industrialized societies there may still be some inaccuracy in the exact cause of death. In strongly religious countries suicide verdicts, as we have seen, need not necessarily give a reliable or *true* picture of the pattern.

The measurement of *morbidity* (the level of disease in the population) is a difficult task because there is no general agreement as to what constitutes a disease, the disease itself may remain undisclosed, treated disease may present a different picture to actual disease, and diseases tend to be under-reported. An important concept is *life expectancy* (the average number of years as measured from birth that an individual is expected to live measured by characteristics such as race, sex, and age). So, for example, we could compare rural with urban dwellers, and the North of England with the South. The *incidence* of disease is the number of new cases of a disease which arise over a certain period of time, while the *prevalence* is the actual number or cases which exist at any given point in time.

The *rate* of disease is generally measured by epidemiologists in one of three ways. There is the *crude* rate (the number of people for a given unit of the population who possess the characteristics being measured for a particular unit of time), the *age-specific* rate (the number of deaths of people in a particular age-category divided by the number of people alive in that category at the middle of the year), and the *standardized* rate (for which age-specific rates are adjusted to compare age groupings in different populations). The standardized rate ensures that a fair comparison is made.

Epidemiological research methods involve the search for specific *disease agents*, factors in the *environment*, and *human* elements such as life-styles. Often a dramatic element is introduced in the work of the epidemiologist when he traces the source of a particular disease, or in the work which has been done on the correlation between cigarettes and lung cancer.

One of the areas which lends itself to this particular aspect of the sociology of medicine is that of regional differences in the health of the population in Britain, and of concomitant regional responses in the preventive and general-practitioner services provided. By the use of epidemiological methods we can discover the distribution of mortality from all causes in England and Wales. For example, we find that large-population areas are high risk, and that Salford is second only to Berwickshire in its unfavourable mortality for males. Mortality from all causes for females tends to be concentrated in Southern Scotland, North and North-West England, Wales and sections of Northern Ireland. Research such as this can show that the average risk of dying in Burnley, for example, is 60% greater than in Oxford, and that infant mortality rates are in excess in South Lancashire. Generally speaking the British Isles has two broad areas of disparity, one running from North of a line from the Humber to the Bristol Channel, and the other South of that line. Even when we look at mortality from accidents, regional variation is marked sometimes as much as 43% in excess. The same general differentiation can be shown for mental illness rates and suicide, in some areas the latter being 50% above the national average. Bronchitis, tuberculosis, cancer of the trachea, lung and bronchus, morbidity from pernicious anaemia and breast cancer can also be calculated by these methods. If we take the areas with a high excess of breast cancer we must also consider that it tends to be most common in women who are unmarried, married women who are childless, and married women who have children but have not breast-fed them.

When we turn to examine the provision of health services we find that these are relatively better in the South and East, despite the fact that people in the North and West are at a higher risk of mortality. Although the North and West are better off for hospital beds, the South and East have large areas of relatively low provision. To complicate matters there is an over-concentration of teaching hospitals in the London area with a large number of consultants with merit awards. Hospital costs per patient by regional hospital boards tends to have wide variations within each region but no great difference between the large regions to the North and South of the imaginary line from the Humber to the Bristol Channel. Similar research can produce a distribution for residence in mental hospitals and units by regional hospital board, average list size of general practitioner, number of school children per medical officer of country, and general dental services by counties. The picture can be further elaborated by data showing the distribution of overcrowding (over one and a half persons to a room), household facilities (exclusive use of a cold and hot-water tap, a fixed bath and a water closet), those on Income Tax Schedule E, second-year sixth formers, income above the UK mean, the proportion of children for whom free school meals are claimed, children granted university awards, and so on.

MEDICAL PRACTITIONERS

Until the consolidation of medical practice with the formation of the General Medical Council in 1858, many of those practising medicine were unqualified and came from a very heterogeneous background. It was not, perhaps, until the outbreak of the 1914–18 war that medical practitioners became competent enough to ensure a patient more than a 50% chance of benefiting from consultation.

The sociology of medicine includes in its sphere of inquiry surveys and examination of trends in the composition and deployment of doctors. Ann Cartwright's work has shown that of general practitioners 5% are women (based on her sample of 422); 13% qualified either during or after 1955; 25% before 1934; 59% have a university degree and no further qualifications; 20% have licentiate qualifications only; only 4% have an MD.

As many practitioners are employed as junior and senior hospital staff as are engaged in general practice, and a strict hierarchy of office exists from House Officer to Consultant. Some two thirds of Consultants have only a part-time National Health Service appointment, the remainder of their week being in a private capacity. Half of the junior hospital staff in England and Wales are from overseas. Since 1963 both general practitioners and hospital practitioners have not increased to keep pace with the rise in population. There seem to be three reasons why this is so. Firstly, there was a serious error in forecasting future requirements and trends at the end of the 1950s. Second, the forecasters failed to allow for the rate of emigration from Britain to more remunerative nations. Thirdly, the career structure of medical practitioners has not taken into account the rapid technological progress. The Willink Committee, which was responsible for these gross errors, failed to take into account, or even to utilize, any sophisticated data and analysis whatsoever. For example, the increase in the general population is double what they forecast it would be by 1971, that is an increase of 7% and not $4\frac{1}{2}$% between 1955 and 1971. The forecasters also failed to take into account an increased demand for medical staff which would follow more advanced diagnostic and preventive techniques, and they also did not allow for an increased demand for practitioners following an increase in economic prosperity. Although the findings of this committee had disastrous consequences, they also had the effect of increasing the scarcity value of personnel and therefore giving them additional leverage in pay and status negotiations.

Much of the work of researching into medical practice has highlighted serious faults in such areas as the doctor–patient relationship, and displayed extreme apathy on the part of the general public to the work of medical personnel. It is uncertain exactly what sort of work that the role of the family doctor should adopt in the future. The education of medical personnel is often inappropriate for what is expected of them, and some studies have found both general and hospital practitioners ignorant of local authority services available for the patient's after-care, and unwilling to cooperate with health visitors and social workers.

PATTERNS OF DISEASE AND THE MEASUREMENT OF HEALTH

One of the means of measuring the level of a nation's health is by the infant mortality rate of a country. Britain comes sixth in the world table compared with America's sixteenth position. Naturally, infant mortality is not an isolated factor but one which must be viewed in conjunction with housing facilities, industrialization, income and education. We must also consider the effectiveness and availability of local health services.

Post-neonatal mortality shows a marked regional variation, partly because respiratory weaknesses are linked with social and environmental factors. Neonatal mortality is generally the result of natal and prenatal malformations, which again can be linked to regional differentiation due to such factors as urbanization, occupation, income, sex, and so on.

THE DISEASE OF THE URBAN MAN Large conurbations, as we have already mentioned, tend to display the highest rate of mortality, and the lowest levels are generally rural areas. No doubt respiratory disease is the important element which we must associate with city living, in large measure due to the pollution of the atmosphere, but also partly the result of the higher risk involved in being constantly in close proximity to others in crowded places. Pneumonia, cancer, and respiratory tuberculosis are all higher in urban areas than rural, but a great deal of further work needs to be done to determine whether city dwellers are more sophisticated in recognizing a need for treatment and hospitalization, or whether facilities are more available in urban than rural areas.

INCOME AND DISEASE The Registrar General's classification of the population into five groups, as we have seen, is a useful research tool:

Class   I   Higher professional and administrative occupations,
Class   II   Employers in industry and retail trades and the lesser professions,
Class   III Skilled occupations,
Class   IV   Semi-skilled occupations,
Class   V   Unskilled occupations.

The common pattern in nearly all disease is that it tends to be concentrated in Classes III, IV and V, although naturally there are diseases which are peculiar to Classes I and II. For example, infant mortality among unskilled workers in the early 1950s was twice that among professional families. Despite the overall decrease in mortality between the early 1920s and the 1950s the *difference* between Classes I and V remained proportionate. Two reasons for this have been suggested. Firstly, the better educated are more able to make use of existing medical provision (as they are in most things) than the unskilled sector of the population, and secondly, because of the increase in social mobility, those who are in Class V are probably there because of a general ill-health or lack of ability, which is not the case with those who were in the same sector forty-odd years ago. Gastroenteritis and pneumonia are the chief contributors to infant mortality in the unskilled class, both of which, of course, are fully treatable.

In the adult male population Class I has a higher rate of mortality for coronary disease, leukaemia and Hodgkin's disease than Class V, but the reverse is true for carcinoma of the stomach, bronchitis and influenza.

OCCUPATION AND DISEASE Certain occupations appear to be more prone to certain diseases than others. The statistics are to be treated with caution because certain occupations attract individuals who are already disposed to develop certain illnesses. For example, we would expect manual workers to be fitter than those in sedentary occupations. Many who contract a disease due to performing a certain task subsequently change their work at the onset of incapacitating symptoms, and it is the latter occupation that is statistically recorded. Very often an occupational category slides over age differences and obscures them. In data of this type the information gathered from relatives is often false or inaccurate, as McKeown and Lowe indicate.

Occupational mortality can be calculated from all mortality taken together and from specific mortality taken singly. For example, doctors have a low mortality from all causes but a fairly high one from suicide and cirrhosis of the liver. High on the list of mortality from all causes are occupations such as glass blowing, mining and sandblasting, while low on the list are occupations such as teaching and herding sheep. Publicans and innkeepers have a high rate of mortality from all causes and the highest from cirrhosis of the liver.

SEX DIFFERENCES   It is indisputable that death rates for males are constantly higher than for females, mainly due to arteriosclerotic disease of the heart, bronchitis, cancer of the lung and accidents. In other words, the differences can be attributed to the different habits of males to females and to different occupations, rather than to biological origins. Strangely enough, morbidity rates are higher among women than men, which may be due to women being more ready to consult their doctors or having more time available to do so.

INTERNATIONAL VARIATION   The statistics of the World Health Organization, despite difficulty in gathering facts for many countries with inaccurate records, nevertheless demonstrate clear differences in the incidence of disease between countries. Infant mortality rates, for example, vary from 20 per 1000 live births in Holland, Sweden and Norway to over 120 in Egypt and Chile. In Africa and India it is probably over 200. Yet in modern industrialized nations arteriosclerotic diseases are high while in Africa, Asia and India it is infectious diseases which are predominant.

International variations are accounted for by a number of factors. One such factor, instanced by the spread of malarial infection, is the geographical and climatic condition of a country. Trypanosomiasis and yellow fever is dependent to an even larger extent on these conditions. Hot and humid climates provide a setting for the spread of disease by insects much more readily than colder areas. By far the most important factor, however, is the level of social development of a nation, when such elements as housing conditions, income level, and general level of education become significant. Consequently, even in the same country, for example South Africa and the southern part of America, black mortality from all causes is generally very much higher than white mortality.

MEASUREMENT   Many mortality tables measure deaths from all causes for all ages, but obviously in many respects this is a crude measurement which disguises many of the subtleties. In 140 years, causes of death

have grown from 100 to over 1000, and just as the instruments for diagnosis and measurement become finer so the total picture becomes more
detailed. Different measurement produces very different pictures. If we
calculate the number of years lost in a working life, we get a very different
perspective than if we calculate simply the leading causes of deaths from
all causes for all ages.

An interesting study was done by MacQueen in Aberdeen on home
accidents. Contrary to what one might expect, that such events are purely
random, the study unveiled a number of interesting sociological facts.
The highest accident rate was in children, especially pre-school children,
with the elderly next. Non-gas poisoning was a particularly high risk
with pre-school children, followed by burns and scalds. Surprisingly,
but as already noticed when we discussed suicide and suicide attempts,
there were variations in the month, day and hour of the accident. As we
might expect, burns were more frequent during the months of December,
January and February. Monday is the day of greatest risk for women,
old people of both sexes, and pre-school girls, although Saturday is the
day of greatest risk for school children, young men and middle-aged men.
The time of accidents is generally between 10 a.m. and 12 noon for the
elderly, toddlers and women. The picture that emerged was that the time
of greatest danger was at the end of a busy period of household activity.
When we come to look at the social and environmental factors involved
in accidents we discovered that the widowed, divorced and separated of
either sex were more prone to falling than if they were married, but this
factor does not seem to affect other accidents. The old and alone were
more prone, but accidents in children tended to increase with the size
of household. The more rooms in a house the fewer accidents, and scald-
ing occurred mostly in one-roomed households. Children whose fathers
are unemployed were more prone to accidents than those whose fathers
were in Social Class IV or V, but surprisingly children whose mothers
worked were no more prone than those who did not. Work such as this
can throw important light on situations and circumstances conducive to
accidents and perhaps prepare the ground for a local authority home-
safety campaign, and the work itself illustrates very well the use of
measurement.

MORBIDITY MEASUREMENT We have already mentioned some of the ways
of measuring morbidity and some of the problems associated with such
measurement, such as definitions of health and the judgement of individuals. Again, a person may be ill and yet not conscious of the fact, and
be ill from more than one disease at the same time. One of the ways
round these problems is to have an exact definition of the index being
used together with an indication of the *severity* of the disease. McKeown
and Lowe found it useful to distinguish between illness most frequently
complained of, illness which led to a person consulting a doctor, absence
from work caused by illness, and illness requiring hospital admission.
Research both in America and this country has suggested that during

one month, in an average adult population of 1000 patients, 750 were likely to report one or more illnesses, some 250 would consult their GP and 9 would be admitted to hospital. This has been diagrammatically represented by Horder and Horder as shown in Fig. 11.1.

Source: Office of Health Economics (1968). *Without Prescription,* London.

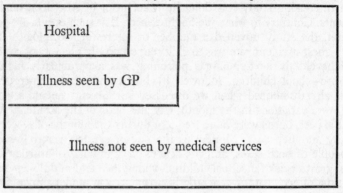

Fig. 11.1

Several tables have been constructed which show that individuals are more likely to consult GPs over some ailments than others. For example, they are more likely to go to a doctor if they are suffering from tuberculosis, anaemia, personality disorders, heart, respiratory and skin disorders, and diseases of the bone, than if they have coughs, chest pains, swollen limbs and joints, refractive errors, and so on. Some studies have been carried out on the extent of self-medication in the general population and this suggests that often as many as two out of three take some form of self-medication without prescription over a four-week period. Such self-medicants can include analgesics, skin medicines, lower respiratory medicines, tonics, vitamins and salts, sedatives, upper respiratory medicines, and ear and eye medicines, and laxatives and purgatives. The implication of this form of self-treatment are enormous. For example, should the pharmacists, so often described as the country's best-qualified shop assistants, play a more substantial role in the preparation and recommendation of non-prescriptive remedies, and perhaps also in giving advice to individuals on whether they should consult their doctors? This would certainly enhance the social status of this occupation and also call into question the legislative monopoly exercised by doctors over certain treatments. The 1968 Medicines Bill was intended to clarify the range of products suitable for self-medication.

The annual morbidity in an average general practice of 2500 persons that a doctor might be expected to see each year would include upper respiratory infections (500), emotional disorders (250), digestive disorders (200), skin disorders (200). These are minor disorders. For more serious disorders he would expect to see pneumonia (50), 'anaemia' (Hb 70% or less) (40), five new and ten old cases of coronary heart disease, new cancers (3), severe depressions (12), acute appendicitis (5), glaucoma (3), killed or injured in road accidents (17). On top of this there is a long list of chronic illness such as chronic arthritis, bronchitis, emotional illness, hypertension and asthma with which he must cope. In addition, there is a substantial caseload of sociomedical problems which the GP is expected to deal with, and for this he is given virtually no training and often is in the position of giving very inadequate advice. Problems such as the following no doubt were dealt with by the family physician some fifty years ago but society today has its own specialists qualified to deal with social pathology in a sophisticated manner. The sorts of problems one would designate as sociomedical are patients on Supplementary Incomes Benefit, the aged, lonely, broken homes, deaf and blind, alcoholics, delinquents, problem families, homosexuals, illegitimate births, and so on. An excellent description of this is given by Dr Fry in *The Consumer and the Health Service*.

More females complain of ill-health than males, and of all people complaining only one in four had consulted a doctor during the preceding month of the complaint. The Central Office of Information survey which highlighted this also showed that only one person in eight had lost time from work. The types of illness complained about were most commonly rheumatism, digestive disorders and colds. The types of illness for which a GP was consulted were acute and chronic bronchitis, acute nasopharyngitis, influenza and acute tonsillitis. Surveys have shown that two thirds of the patients on a doctor's list can be expected to consult him during a given year.

Absence from work is generally due to bronchitis and other respiratory disease, and mental and psychoneurotic illnesses. The data, in this case certificates of incapacity, must be interpreted carefully because not all men, and certainly not women, are employed in a situation which requires a 'sick note'.

Illnesses leading to hospital admission are generally well-documented and reliable, although we must remember that the *sample* of illness is a highly selective one. Some illnesses require an automatic admission but others become treatable in a hospital depending on the socio-economic background of the patient together with the seriousness imputed to the illness by the GP. The general table of causes of admission in England and Wales display a clear bias towards diseases requiring surgery: injuries and accidents, malignant neoplasms, hypertrophy of tonsils and adenoids, diseases of the breast and female genital organs, diseases of bone and organs of movement, appendicitis. McKeown and Lowe make the very interesting point that this is the pattern experienced by medical students during their clinical years, and it is a pattern which bears very little resemblance to either what the general population claims to suffer from or which the GPs record as diagnosing.

STAFF AND PATIENT BARGAINING PROCESSES

It might be apparent so far that the sociology of medicine is concerned solely with epidemiological factors. This is certainly not the case at the present time although it probably was some twenty years ago. Freidson's work, *The Profession of Medicine*, and Goffman's *Stigma* are just two of many examples of the application of theoretical sociology to concrete instances to be found in the medical area. Roth's work examined the treatment of tuberculosis as a bargaining process. He argued that skilled service occupations attempt to control their clients by the utilization of specialized knowledge and vocabulary, and to some extent this is true of non-professional occupations. Most people in work endeavour to surround their practice with a mystique which prevents or tries to prevent others from encroaching on their prerogative. The medical profession is not exempt from this analysis because they, more than perhaps most occupations, have become *the* example of professionalization. Naturally no single occupation in practice stands alone in its autonomy. The doctor's goals never entirely coincide with those of his patient. For example, the doctor may wish his patient to stay in bed but the latter may wish otherwise. In this situation both may appear irrational to the other. Generally, this situation arises because the doctor has a specialized goal in mind (reducing bronchial infection) while the patient has a number of goals other than that of client. Roth found that the dilemma in tuberculosis hospitals was that between educating the patient about his disease to the extent of benefiting from the professional's advice but not to the degree of knowledge which would enable him to assume he knew as much as the doctor treating him. The key to effective decision making and service appears to lie in the control of information, because the client can evaluate the service he is receiving because he is (or thinks he is) in full possession of the facts. In a tuberculosis hospital patients can easily pool their information from respective contact with medical staff, and such information becomes a way of resisting the control of hospital staff. Most professional–client relationships follow a pattern of control and resistance to control, but generally speaking the social interaction takes the form of negotiation, whereby each participant relinquishes some aspect of his territory. Roth describes the treatment relationship as a form of conflict for the control of the patient's behaviour which is usually resolved by bargaining. A form of bargaining goes on in most social situations. Generally, one aspect of the bargaining relationship lies in the relative power of the participants. We are all familiar with the POW camp inmate who manages to 'outdo' his captors, or the Sergeant Bilko who, apparently helpless, manages to gain his desired goals. Unreasonable demands of the client are generally dealt with by the professional's use of subtle means.

If the demands of the clients, opposite to those of the professionals, are centred around fewer restrictions and earlier discharge then the latter can exert control. The client can threaten to leave, but the professional may consequently become alarmed that infection will be carried to others. In the ward Roth found that nurses could control patients by means of diet and medical treatment, but by the pooling of information it became apparent which nurses were 'soft' and which were 'hard'. Surgery is another area in which the bargaining process takes place. Patients may refuse to undergo an operation or may cajole a surgeon into performing an unnecessary operation, sometimes, as we have discussed, from motives of status.

Sometimes a 'deal' is negotiated whereby the staff allow the patient certain privileges in order that the latter will not discharge himself, and at times such privileges will be 'understood' by the patient and the staff member rather than explicitly stated. Roth continues in his analysis of the bargaining process by concluding that naked power and threats are not part of the process but it is rather a matter of A anticipating the reactions of B, who in turn is reacting to A, and so on. All along human behaviour in these social encounters is being anticipated and modified.

THE MYTH OF MENTAL ILLNESS

Szasz, an American psychiatrist, has cogently argued that the term 'mental illness' is a metaphor and that psychiatric intervention is a form of control. All involuntary interventions which involve 'diagnosis', 'hospit-alization' or 'treatment' interfere with the individual. Psychiatric diagnoses are *stigmatas* or derogatory labels that are used as a means for controlling behaviour which annoys or offends other people. Generally speaking, people who complain or suffer in relation to their own behaviour are labelled 'neurotic' while those who make others suffer or about whom others complain are labelled 'psychotic'. The argument he uses is partly sociological and partly philosophical but it remains an example of a systematic application of sociology to psychiatric medicine.

THE DOCTOR–PATIENT RELATIONSHIP

Work done on the doctor–patient relationship distinguishes it from other professional relationships such as social work (but not from law, for example) because the doctor 'accepts' a client or patient while the social worker is 'assigned' one. Freidson and others have shown that very often patients do not do what they are told by physicians. Just as there is ample evidence for a subterranean 'folk-culture' (the unknown gods of the English) existing alongside mainstream religion, so also there is strong evidence that the general population both diagnoses itself and con-sequently treats itself in relation to lay advice. The position is somewhat paradoxical as it is difficult to account for this at a time when the status and prestige of medical science has reached an all-time peak. The answer seems to lie, according to Freidson, in the perpetual conflict of the layman and professional worker's perspectives. He is essentially saying what Roth and others have also said. The practitioner is applying to a *case* a detached knowledge gleaned from his professional training. The client, on the other hand, is personally involved in judging and controlling what the physician is doing to him, with the consequence that while the goals of the respective parties are usually similar the means often differ.

Generally mistakes occur in the diagnosis either from incomplete knowledge or because the categories of diagnosis are inappropriate. He instances the confusion of typhus and typhoid until 1820, and the identification of syphilis with gonorrhea. A second source of error, however, resides in applying knowledge to everyday life. Medical science has only a limited number of categories into which to 'fit' the 'flow of reality'. Quite diverse elements of human experience therefore become both equivalent and ordinary. An example is the category of complaints in general practice designated as upper respiratory. Because they are so common they are considered ordinary, and because they are considered ordinary they become complaints which one is not permitted to display a great amount of fuss or suffering over. To the patient, however, the pains and the suffering are real enough. Furthermore, because a large number of complaints are diagnosed as upper respiratory in origin it becomes a simple clinical diagnostic matter to insert into the same category any single complaint which exhibits roughly the same features. Problems of diagnosis are real for the patient as well as the doctor. If the latter tells the patient not to worry, then when is it legitimate for the former to claim that his own special feelings are acute enough as to warrant special attention? Often the patient is crying wolf, but sometimes medical science is inaccurate.

The role of the professional in society is such as to entitle him to *a priori* trust and confidence, but it is a mistake to assume that *all* who occupy the role of professional automatically have bestowed upon them a special competence. Sometimes the professional prescribes a remedy which the client or patient was not led to expect. This is essentially a clash of culture, the cultural expectations of the client not being those of the physician or medical professional. The introduction of the social sciences into medical and nurse training stems partly from the assumption that something may be taught about 'the patient as a person'. But doctors and nurses and medical professionals in general can only comply with the patient's knowledge to a certain extent because often this knowledge is both bizarre and ignorant. To comply wholly would result in the professional relinquishing the specialized knowledge which marks him off as a professional. At some point, presumably when the doctor or nurse can no longer concede, the patient must change in order to comply with the expectations of the professional. But education of the patient in order to better understand medical knowledge has the unfortunate concomitant of also making the educated layman more critical of professional performance.

Finally, it is well documented that medical professionals do not perform as competently with patients from the equivalent or higher socio-economic bracket. If the professional is from a higher social class, then this is an additional source of leverage to add to his specialized knowledge.

DOCTORS' INTEREST GROUPS

Doctors are a powerful and well-organized group in the National Health Service who function as an interest group in order to negotiate pay and conditions. Often they utilize goals and methods that may be in conflict with those of other employees of the NHS and even with those of the organization for which they work. There has been a tendency in recent years for the Government to negotiate with the BMA and to rely on that body for technical knowledge as though the BMA represented all doctors. However, other bodies and organizations represent different groups of doctors, such as the Royal Colleges, although the BMA is undoubtedly the supreme body in terms of membership, and represents both specialists and GPs. Like many formal organizations, the greatest power lies in the hands of the full-time officials of the BMA.

One of the factors which militates against the effectiveness of the BMA as an interest group is the division that exists between GPs and specialists. Although part of the intention in creating an NHS was to reduce such conflict and to foresee the specialist and GP working together as a team for the good of the patient, nevertheless the GP is uncertain of his future role. For example, is he to be integrated into the hospital setting or excluded from it? And is the occupation to become salaried, thereby becoming open to the effects of a significant change in the status and independence of the GP? The bureaucratic structure of the BMA is dominated by GPs who are successful in their profession, and usually in private practice. This leads to tension with younger and less well-established GPs. Within the hospital sector, junior hospital and public health doctors may be in conflict with each other.

NATIONAL HEALTH SERVICE INTEREST GROUPS Pressure or interest groups possess varying degrees of power which are used as weapons for negotiation. Doctors are not the only interest groups, and others exist with varying degrees of power. Firstly, there are those groups who have some form of skill to offer, for example, nurses, doctors and dentists. Second, there are groups who have administrative machinery to offer, for example, the local authorities. Thirdly, there are groups with some form of property to offer, for example, the GP and his surgery and the chemist with his shop. Fourthly, the patient and potential patient has a form of power which can be described as the choice of opting for private medicine or for competing between two forks of service, for example between domiciliary and hospital maternity services. The last few years has seen the emergence of another group of lower-skilled employees, such as hospital porters and cleaners, who have exhibited considerable force in the bargaining process.

Increasing specialization within the NHS ranks has seen the emergence of some new professions of laboratory and clinical technicians. These are represented by different interest groups from the BMA, and the latter is itself in difficulty because it has to represent quite diverse interests. Specialization in medical occupations has led psychiatrists, who generally enjoy low esteem, to solicit pressure for the district general hospital which brings together psychiatric and physical medicine. Another specialist group, anaesthetists, are pressuring for a ward role. The pressure groups representing specialists merely serves to highlight the plight of the general practitioner and led to the establishment of the Royal College of General Practitioners. Other groups with distinct interests concerned with the scientific areas of medicine (in the laboratory and X-ray departments), and curative areas (therapists, etc.), and community field (health visitors, social workers), are all exercising their concern over status and employment conditions. The growth of specialisms in the paramedical field has entailed both conflict with the medical profession, and the gradual erosion of the area of competence of the medical profession as it becomes increasingly obvious that many social and psychological areas require special qualifications and training.

This outline of the application of sociological theory to pressure or interest groups within the NHS highlights both the complexity of the negotiating machinery and also one of the ways in which sociology can be applied to medical areas. Further discussion on some of these aspects were touched upon when we discussed the sociology of professions and occupations and in particular the role of the nurse. Further subtleties in the division of labour will be discussed when we examine the social structure of the modern hospital.

CONCLUSIONS

Some of the salient features of the sociology of medicine have been touched upon in this chapter. Other areas that the subject concerns itself with are important enough to devote an entire chapter to, for example a sociological approach to the social structure of the modern hospital (Chapter 12), the nursing profession (chapter 10), responses to disease and death (Chapter 7), and so on. The relevance of the other chapters of this book, for example those on the family, social class and social deviance are such an integral part of the sociology of medicine as to leave no doubt that they deserve a separate treatment in order to do them full justice. The sociology of medicine is much more than the epidemiological study of medicine, and even more than the study of social medicine (which limits itself usually to epidemiology and the medical 'needs' of society). It is the application of a subject respectable in its own right to another subject respectable in its own right, in the sure knowledge that each will benefit. Historians of medicine could argue, no doubt, that social consequences in the field of medicine have always been with the best of the practitioners. However, the last few years have heralded an increasing search for social factors in the causation of disease and indisputable evidence that many chronic diseases have their aetiology in socio-psychological factors. More important, perhaps, is the emergence of a sociological body of theory and methodology able to cope with the complexities of the subject.

SUGGESTIONS FOR FURTHER READING

CARTWRIGHT, A. (1967). *Patients and their Doctors*, Routledge and Kegan Paul, London.
COE, R. M. (1970). *Sociology of Medicine*, McGraw-Hill, New York.
FREIDSON, E. (1962). 'Dilemmas in the Doctor–Patient Relationship' in Rose, A. M. pp. 207–224.
FREIDSON, E. (1972). *Profession of Medicine*, Dodd, Mead and Company, New York.
MACQUEEN, I. (1960). *Home Accidents in Aberdeen*, E. and S. Livingstone, Edinburgh.
McKEOWN, T. and LOWE, C. R. (1966). *An Introduction to Social Medicine*, Blackwell, Oxford.
OFFICE OF HEALTH ECONOMICS, (1968). *The Consumer and the Health Service*, edited by McKenzie, J. (see especially pp. 11–13).
OFFICE OF HEALTH ECONOMICS, (1968). *Without Prescription*.
ROSE, A. M. (ed.) (1971). *Human Behaviour and Social Processes*, Routledge and Kegan Paul, London.
ROTH, J. (1962). 'The Treatment of Tuberculosis as a Bargaining Process' in Rose, A. M. pp. 575–588.
SOCIAL SCIENCES COURSE TEAM, Open University (1972). *Health*, Decision Making in Britain, Part V, Open University Press, Bletchley.
SZASZ, T. (1972). *The Myth of Mental Illness*, Paladin, London.

12

THE SOCIAL STRUCTURE
OF THE HOSPITAL

We generally think of the study of organization as something connected with efficient management in industry. Sometimes we are led to think of schools, the army, social clubs, political parties, and so on, as exhibiting a form of social relationships and control which we feel resembles the large corporation or organization. At other times some of us might be led to the view that there are certain characteristics which seem similar to all these which are also to be found in the growth of the modern hospital. Indeed, in a modern hospital we find many of the features which sociologists claim to belong to organizations as such, including bureaucracy, professionals, the existence of rules and control by seemingly impersonal forces.

THE CONCEPT OF BUREAUCRACY

Max Weber regarded modern industrial society as being characterized by bureaucracy and it was he who developed a systematic theory of bureaucracy in organization. Weber conceived of a bureaucracy as having the following characteristics:

1. tasks are specialized;
2. authority is hierarchical;
3. there is a system of rules;
4. employees are technically qualified and career-oriented;
5. the system is impersonal;
6. the system is efficient.

A bureaucratic organization becomes, then, more than a 'rule by officials or office'. In the way that Weber develops the idea it becomes a *model* or *ideal type* to which actual existing organizations might approximate. Weber appears to use 'bureaucracy' in three distinct ways: (a) as a type of organization in which there are fixed and official areas of jurisdiction, a graded system of authority, a system of central files, a set of special skills called office management, full-time personnel, a set of rules for defining procedure; (b) as the ideal type of rationality in organization which possesses clearly conceived goals, and which is also impersonal (office and incumbent are separated) and routinized (activities and relationships are simplified and regularized).

Some sociologists would claim that there is a certain ambiguity in Weber's use of the term 'bureaucracy' to imply a kind of rational organization. If he meant by it an organization that maximized administrative efficiency, then the above list *is* ambiguous. For example, some studies have shown quite clearly that efficiency is often best served by informal personal relations among staff and by unofficial practices. However, Weber is *not* in fact, equating rationality with efficiency. What he is most concerned with is the idea of authority, by which he means charismatic *authority* (based on some sacred or outstanding quality of the individual), *traditional authority* (based on a respect for custom), or *rational legal authority* (based on regulations and a code of legal rules).

GROWTH OF THE MODERN HOSPITAL   The modern hospital is regarded by sociologists as an example of a modern institution exhibiting many of the characteristics of a complex organization. It is not surprising, therefore, that one of the organizational features it exhibits is a form of Weber's bureaucracy. The hospital that we recognize as such today can trace its origins back nearly two thousand years. Medicine was formerly regarded as an ancillary branch of religion, and in its beginnings its activities were defined in terms of a narrow and restricted religious dogmatism. Such a state continued until after the Middle Ages. The very word *hospitalis* (from the Latin noun *hospites* meaning guests) gives a clue to the function of the early hospitals, which were more akin to monasteries providing food and shelter for their guests. These buildings were in the charge of a hospitaller or chaplain who was aided by women, generally from a religious order. Such seemingly remote beginnings have had some considerable influence on the development of the modern hospital and its 'ethic'. For example, the foundation of Christian charity has emerged in modern times as 'working for others', as 'service' and 'welfare', and so on (although this is not to suggest that such considerations are restricted to Christians). Another idea which has survived is that hospitals and their personnel do not discriminate but are 'open' to all.

During the Renaissance period hospitals declined with the fall of the monastic orders and the conditions that consequently prevailed led to the passing of the English Poor Law in 1601. It was not until the development of the scientific outlook that hospitals became measurably better than under the monastic orders—some two hundred years later. One interesting feature of the period is that through their professional association physicians have gained control over the standards practised in the hospital setting.

The modern hospital became established as a remarkable improvement on the institutions of previous years, partly because of medicine becoming established on a scientific basis (for example, the evolvement of bacteriology and physiology) but also with the development of anaesthesia and antisepsis. A third and important development was the establishment of a trained and highly competent nursing staff originating with Florence Nightingale. As a result of the enhanced social status of the medical personnel, more and more of the affluent sectors of society were willing to entrust their prognosis and treatment to the hospitals. Furthermore, hospitals began to be seen as institutions for teaching and research. Today, the location of hospitals is mostly determined by existing buildings, mostly in inner urban areas, and which comprise the most famous of our teaching hospitals. New hospitals, however, must locate themselves in relation to the centres of population, the recruitment of appropriate staff and so on. In order to manage a vast and complex organization such as the modern hospital, staff and techniques are required which maximize efficiency. Consequently, a sociological concern has arisen towards the processes of decision-making which are carried out in hospitals and the way in which social roles are allocated, how they interact with each other and how they change over time.

The increase in the technological efficiency of the modern hospital has also meant an increase in the specialization of the roles within it. For example, at the end of the eighteenth century there were nine basic roles to be found in British hospitals. Gradually, with the increase in human skills and technological 'know-how', many additional categories were attached to hospitals, such as radiologists and cardiologists. Similarly, original categories became subdivided and multiplied. Coe gives the example of the nurse. 'At first, nurses did not only patient care and administrative duties but housekeeping tasks as well. Gradually, they were relieved of these lesser chores by personnel who filled a series of positions of orderlies, attendants, maids, and others. Today, skilled nursing consists mostly of coordinating the activities of many skilled and semiskilled personnel and supervising the execution of physicians' orders for technical care of their patients.'

THE GROWTH OF THE HOSPITAL INDUSTRY AND MEDICAL MANPOWER Between 1946 and 1963 the number of hospitals in America increased by 16·5%. Such hospitals of the 7138 in existence at the latter date as are designated voluntary, non-profit short-term institutions had, in the seventeen years' interval, increased the number of hospital personnel per patient by 56·4% whereas the number of personnel employed had increased by 154·4%. This meant that the number of personnel to every patient in 1963 was 244, as compared with 156 in 1946. The total expense had increased by 574·5% to £5491 million. Similarly, the trends in Great Britain between 1949 and 1964 show a pattern which follows that of the American hospital industry. By 1969 there were approximately 701 280 whole-time employees in the hospital services in this country which included the following:

hospital medical staff   25 657
hospital nursing staff   300 598 (including 80 000 in training)
hospital midwifery staff   19 438
hospital ancillary staff   257 351

approximately a further 50 000 were clerical and administrative staff. These figures give an indication of how complex an organization the modern hospital has become.

THE SOCIAL STRUCTURE OF THE MODERN HOSPITAL   We began by sketching the characteristics of Weber's bureaucratic model, and in the next section we will examine the extent to which it is accurate to claim that hospitals are bureaucracies. Before we do so it will be useful to outline some of the practices which are carried out in this complex medical setting, paying particular attention to the authority system of the modern hospital which many sociologists have highlighted.

The division of labour within a hospital generally comprises seven sections as follows: (1) physicians; (2) paramedical, divided as (a) nursing ward and therapeutic personnel who serve the patient directly; (b) laboratory and technical staff; (3) service workers such as those employed in the laundry and kitchens; (4) clerks; (5) administrators; (6) governing body; (7) patients. These categories, listed by Freidson, interact with one another in a highly complex manner within the organization of the hospital. Such an organization has been described as a prototype of a multi-purpose organization: 'it is a hotel and a school, a laboratory and a stage for treatment'. Because it is an organization a hospital possesses goals or aims which might include the care of the patient. However, such goals may be various and include some which are important and some which are minor, such as saving on laundry costs. Whatever the goals there is a need to create and sustain an organization which can realize them. Apart from the formal goals which might be held by the majority of personnel there exist a number of sub-goals and informal goals which might be entertained by only a minority or specialized category of hospital staff.

Within the bureaucratic framework there exists a *dual* line of authority as mentioned by Coe, which consists of the administrative section and the medical section. Unlike other bureaucratic institutions it is the medical staff who have the control of the authority system (in the former the management would direct the line workers). 'Thus the medical staff usually directs the "line" in its activities while the management's authority is often restricted to matters concerning providing the means by which the doctor's orders may be successfully carried out.' Traditionally, the patients are the physician's. This has the result that the nurse receiving orders from the physician while at the same time being herself an employee of the hospital, and the added peculiarity that the position of the former is that of a 'visitor' or 'guest' stemming from the days when the hospital was completely separate. 'Often the demands of patient care, especially when they are of an emergency nature, cannot be accomplished within the framework of administrative rules; thus the nurse is caught in a conflict between the expectations of the physician that his orders be carried out and the expectations of the administrator that administrative procedures will be complied with.' Two other features of the hospital mentioned by Coe include the extreme division of labour with many specialities and the authoritarian nature of the hospital, which apparently can only survive in a setting in which orders are given and not questioned and where expertise is the keynote for action. Freidson goes so far as to suggest that physicians often intrude into ambiguous areas of hospital life on the grounds that these constitute an emergency 'so as to gain the aid or resources he believes he needs'. Again, such is the charismatic authority of the physician that his line of authority (defined by those to whom he gives orders) often extends to other personnel in the hospital to whom he is not a bureaucratic superior.

The modern hospital is no exception to other organizations which contain conflicting perspectives held by the personnel within it. For example, the patient has a highly personal and emotional involvement in his own illness which he is generally prevented from seeing correctly due to his lack of technical expertise in such areas as diagnosis. The medical staff, on the other hand, cannot *afford* to see the patient as an individual to the extent that they become emotionally involved with him. Hospital ancillaries are another example of a group of non-professionals who cannot be expected to have very much of a share in a professional ideology. Freidson sees the nurse as the 'intense focus of conflicting perspectives' because she provides the professional perspective on the ward and the locus of both administrative and medical authority. In the process of bargaining with the physicians she has the advantage of knowing her patients intimately, and in bargaining with the latter she can make full use of her access to the physician. 'Thus, while she may serve as a troubled focus of conflicting perspectives, she also may very well hold the balance of power in determining the outcome of bargaining among patient and staff.' Finally, the physician can well act as a hierarchical authority within an ostensibly democratic setting. As Freidson puts it, 'There is no court of appeal from superior training, knowledge, and judgement; technical decisions are not made by vote.'

PATTERNS OF WARD CARE AND MODELS OF PATIENT CARE Some hospitals contain more than one pattern of ward care, but generally such patterns can be broken down into three categories, as described by Freidson:

'domestic service pattern' (feeding, clothing, amusing—found in badly staffed institutions, mental and nursing and geriatric institutions)
'medical-intervention pattern' (medically dominated, generally excluding socio-psychological treatments)
'therapeutic interaction' (therapeutic milieu, rehabilitation).

Coe presents these models in table form and under different names. They are still, however, basically the same three which Freidson describes, and arise from the goals entertained by the organizations, certain ideological assumptions about disease, and a set of role expectations (Table 12.1). Obviously there is not a complete overlap in the two sets of terminology but the similarities are sufficient to equate the two.

TABLE 12.1

Dimension	Custodial	Classical	Rehabilitation
	(Domestic Service Pattern)	(Medical intervention pattern)	(Therapeutic intervention)
1. Stated goals	Comfort	Cure	Restoration
2. Assumptions about the disease process			
(a) Therapy	Sporadic	Central	Supplementary
(b) Sick role	Permanent	Temporary	Intermittent
3. Patient motivation	Obedience to institutional rules	Obedience to 'doctor's orders'	Achieve mastery
4. Resulting institutional model	Total institution	Acute general hospital	Rehabilitation centre

(Adapted from Coe (1970), p. 283)

HOSPITALS AS BUREAUCRACIES Weber's model of a bureaucracy was based more on the way work was organized (the administration) than the actual performance of tasks. Moreover, his model was heavily influenced by the Prussian government of his day and the almost complete absence of client-serving organizations in his time. Nevertheless, his model has influenced sociological studies of hospitals on the basis of its main features which we outlined at the beginning of this chapter, namely a hierarchy of authority which is official rather than personal, a series of impersonal relationships, a career which is clearly guaranteed, and an equally clear area of authority. Several reasons spring to mind as to why Weber's model is illuminating but not *exactly* appropriate. For example, the physician in the hospital often gives orders to those to whom he is not a bureaucratic superior. This has the affect of breaking the 'line of authority' which Weber conceives of as unilinear and necessary for efficient and organized performance in the day-to-day running of the hospital. Rosengren and Lefton suggest other reasons. Weber, for example, talks about authority residing in the 'hierarchy of offices *and* in demonstrated expertise', although in practice the more complex the organization the more likely it is that expertise is held by individuals who come from *outside* the administrative line. This is what has been termed the dual-authority system of the hospital. Again, hospitals may approximate more to the bureaucratic model depending on the type of hospital. Thus many hospitals are *total institutions* in Goffman's terms in which control of the patient is improved by bureaucratic organization, for example mental hospitals. It is true to some extent, also, that wards within hospitals differ from each other to the extent that they approximate to the bureaucratic model. One study suggested that medical wards in hospitals 'conformed more closely to the bureaucratic model with a clearly demonstrated hierarchy of authority from the residents to the internes. Autonomy in decision making at the nursing level was minimal. Specific "orders" and "commands" stemmed from routinised and standardised channels. On the surgical side, however, the authority system was considerably more flattened.' Consequently, the nurses were able to, and indeed expected to, exercise more authority, autonomy and inventiveness than medical nurses. One of the reasons given for the differences between the two types of wards is that surgical wards have patients whose illnesses are more specifically defined, and where diagnosis is not so ambiguous. Other studies of surgical wards have suggested that it is they that are more highly bureaucratized.

BUREAUCRACIES AND THE PSYCHIATRIC MILIEU   Some studies have suggested that bureaucratic features are dysfunctional to the goals of psychiatric hospitals because they create stresses and tensions and are not fitting to the flexibility required by the treatment. Further, the traditional lines of hospital bureaucracies based on a hierarchy of authority aggravate psychiatric patients.

AUTHORITY AND INFLUENCE STRUCTURE   Several factors can affect the power structure as it exists within the hospital organization. Mechanic cites such factors as expertise, effort and interest, attractiveness (personality), location and position, coalitions and rules. The larger and more complex the organization the more inevitable it becomes that responsibility is delegated with the consequence that lower-ranking personnel often assume power in areas that the planners and the experts have opted out of due to other priorities. The lower-ranking personnel 'must see to it that the daily and more mundane activities progress. In taking this responsibility they assume considerable power which may appear trivial in the light of long-term organisational policy.'

DECISION MAKING AND ORGANIZATIONAL STRUCTURE IN THE BRITISH HEALTH SERVICE   Kogan and Balle have listed some fourteen organizational activities which might be carried out in a hospital as follows: (1) board and housing; (2) general nursing services; (3) medical diagnosis; (4) in some hospitals the provision of treatment prescribed by a GP; (5) paramedical services; (6) training facilities; (7) development; (8) research facilities; (9) in psychiatric hospitals the provision of facilities for compulsory detention; (10) pre-registration facilities or training for doctors; (11) post-registration training facilities for doctors; (12) pre-registration training for nurses; (13) medical laboratory facilities; (14) public health education. They reiterate a point made before that out of the 20–30 professions that constitute a hospital the doctor occupies a dominant place because he is the only one able to prescribe within a legal framework. The group officers include the HMC, the Group Secretary and the Chief Nursing Officer. The last two work in a collateral relationship because in theory neither can instruct the other. Kogan and Balle present each hospital as possessing two (at least) executive hierachies, that of the hospital secretary and the senior nursing officer, both built upon superior–subordinate relationships.

The registrars and housemen are accountable to consultants, but consultants themselves are 'not accountable to any role within the hospital or within the group. They are employed and deployed by the RHBs'. Relationships between medical and paramedical staff (chiropodists, medical laboratory technicians, occupational therapists, physiotherapists, radiographers and remedial gymnasts) can take a variety of forms as follows: (1) paramedical workers subordinate to an administrator; (2) paramedical workers subordinate to a consultant; (3) paramedical workers subordinate to heads of department who are also paramedical but not clearly subordinate to anyone; (4) when the paramedical department does not have a medical head a lot of the work is prescribed by a doctor although he leaves a great deal of discretion to the paramedical worker; (5) when the paramedical department does not have a medical head the doctor and the paramedical worker may work collaterally. The dual-authority system of the medical and administrative personnel means that there are a limited number of criss-cross points which consist of a common manager 'with authority to determine issues between subordinates', for example the first criss-cross point in a dispute between a ward sister and a catering manager would be the Hospital Management Committee.

HOSPITALIZATION   When an individual becomes ill he or she will undergo a number of changes both in the bodily state and in a psychological sense. For example, there may be actual pain or bodily discomfort due to the physical nature of the illness and, in addition, a perceived change in how others regard the patient, which results in loss of status, feelings of inferiority, uselessness, and so on. Admittance to hospital entails entry to an institution that is very different from the world outside. Not only are routines, attitudes, dress and so on abnormal, but a previously active individual is now reduced to a state in which physical movements are extremely limited. In addition, the admitted individual carries with him anxiety about the family he has left behind, certain tasks which have to be completed by others, and, in the case of admission to a mental hospital, some stigma. As Coe points out, however, certain cases of admission may actually reduce the strain on the remaining family who had found it almost impossible to cope.

Most institutions of this nature have the characteristic of totality in the sense that 'all aspects of life are conducted in the same place and under the same single authority'. Goffman's analysis of such a total institution is more applicable to mental hospitals, which allow the inmates to be treated in 'batches'. General hospitals are not quite the same. For example, patients are not as 'long-stay' as in mental hospitals and the 'batch' approach is carried out only in a few activities such as 'feeding, administering medication, bathing, assessing vital signs (blood pressure, temperature, pulse), arising and retiring . . .' Both medical establishments are socially stratified with the administration and the medical branches separated. As Coe says, 'The main points of convergence are the significant distinction between those who give care and those who receive it and the kinds of occupational groups found in the organization and the ways in which these groups are stratified.'

When an individual enters a hospital he brings with him what Goffman has termed a 'presenting culture' of the whole way of life that he had before his entry. In order for the hospital to function effectively, however, and to obtain its goals, it is necessary for the patients to be assimilated into the organizational processes of the hospital. These are described by Coe as stripping, control of resources, and the restriction of mobility. The stripping procedure results in 'every distinctly personalising symbol, material or otherwise . . . (being) . . . taken away, thus reducing the patient to the status of just one of many'. The second organizational process, the control or resources, 'is concentrated in the hands of the staff. This enables them to manipulate the physical environment (including patients, regardless of the desires or expectations of the patients) for the purpose of regulating the patient behaviour . . . ' Such control is not only over physical items but extends to severe limitations being placed upon knowledge. '. . . more often it is the patient who is deprived of information about events in the hospital and particularly information concerning himself.' Lastly, the patient is severely restricted as to where he can or cannot go within a hospital. More often than not a patient is confined to a small physical space such as his bed or his ward.

There are four ways of adjustment to the process of hospitalization which are mentioned by Coe. The first way is by physical or psychological withdrawal. Secondly, the patient can contravene the hospital and staff's rules by overt aggression. Thirdly, the patient may integrate himself into group and institutional activities. Lastly, patients may acquiesce by complying with the institutional way of life. The degree and combination of these modes of adjustment vary according to age, sex, race, degree of illness, and so on.

PATIENT CARE AND THE INFLUENCE OF ORGANIZATIONAL FACTORS   The type of organization in which a patient is 'housed' can have a varying affect on the care he receives. One simple example is that a mental patient in a large custodial and bureaucratic nineteenth-century institution receives a totally different course of treatment (if any) than someone perhaps in a small 'open' psychiatric hospital. Several studies have shown considerable variation between mental hospitals in the treatment of patients, for example in the degree of physical freedom allowed to ward inmates, the amount of locker space, personal effects. Another factor influencing patient care is the attitude of relatives. When there is no one at home to care for him a patient may be retained in hospital even when his symptoms have disappeared. It has also been found that frequency of visitors was correlated with a shorter stay in hospital, a patient with fewer visits being more likely to stay in hospital for a longer period. New trends in community care have meant that it is now easier to relocate patients in the community.

One study, by Emerson, deals with how definitions of reality are sustained in gynaecological examinations by the elaborate medical ritual and organization. 'The medical definition grants the staff the right to carry out their task. If not for the medical definition the staff's routine activities could be defined as unconscionable assaults on the dignity of individuals.' Such examinations are carried out in 'medical space' (hospital or doctor's office). 'The staff wear medical uniforms, don medical gloves, use medical instruments. The exclusion of lay persons, particularly visitors of the patient who may be accustomed to the patient's nudity at home, helps to preclude confusion between the contact of medicine and the contact of intimacy . . . The patient's body is draped so as to expose only the part which is to receive the technical attention of the doctor. The presence of a nurse acting as "chaperon" cancels any residual suggestiveness of male and female alone in a room.' Any threat to the medical detachment is counteracted by appropriate responses by the gynaecologist and his team nurse.

HOSPITALS AND PATIENTS AND ENVIRONMENTS   Hospitals sometimes pursue goals which are in conflict with one another, such as trying to provide a service while at the same time attempting to maintain the system. While the organization attempts to depersonalize the patient, the latter combats such moves by various strategies available to him. Sometimes the patient has to acquiesce to the demands of the institution even though they are presented as an aid to the maintenance of the social system rather than to any improvement in his health.

Relationships between staff and between staff and patients differ according to the medical setting in which they occur. Rosengren and Lefton suggest that 'special' cases such as a metabolic unit, a tuberculosis unit, a children's hospital, a rehabilitation unit, and a terminal ward or hospital all present changes in relationships because the patients or clients are specially selected for care or treatment.

Finally, hospitals exist within communities and are to be regarded as to some extent the product of various ecological, demographic and economic characteristics of the area which they serve. The *community morphology* approach tends to view them as micro-structures of the community they serve.

THE FUTURE   The 1974 Green Paper on the Health Services has proposed a united structure for a varied number of health services under Area Health Authorities. The idea is to make it unnecessary for individuals to spread their inquiries over a number of agencies but rather to have a number of basic services in the health field, such as maternity, geriatric, mental health and physical medicine, concentrated under one heading and a unitary decision-making body.

Such changes may also bring with them changes in hospital organization which will be in keeping with numerous recommendations by research committees and the contribution of the social sciences over the last twenty-five years. One of the hopes is that there will be a combination of improved scientific practice with a genuine humanistic concern based on empirical data, with the result that more and more patients are receiving the benefit of personalized care.

The patient, also, may in the future be credited with having rather more say over the interpretation of his particular symptoms and over his own particular preferences, which too often have been sublimated to the bureaucratic functioning of the hospitals. As Rosengren and Lefton state, 'he is increasingly coming to be regarded as the co-author of the outcome of any treatment program. More than ever before, the patient is being solicited as an active participant in the pursuit of positive health. And a galaxy of changes in medical care are in the making once the patient is no longer regarded as a passive recipient of medicines, manipulations, and prescriptions.' Similarly, the training of future doctors may well consider the antiquity and irrelevance of much of their training programmes. The need here, just as we require it in the training of nurses, is for a training tailored to the late twentieth century and to the provision of a knowledge adequate to cope with many of the problems which accompany, and often precipitate, physical illness.

SUGGESTIONS FOR FURTHER READING

ABEL-SMITH, B. (1964). *The Hospitals: 1800–1948*, Heinemann, London.

COE, R. M. (1970). *Sociology of Medicine*, McGraw-Hill, New York.

EMERSON, J. P. (1970). 'Behaviour in Public Places: Sustaining Definitions of Reality in Gynecological Examinations,' in Dreitzel, H. P. (ed.) *Recent Sociology*, No. 2. Collier Macmillan, New York.

FREIDSON, E. (ed.) (1963). *The Hospital in Modern Society*, Free Press, New York.

FREIDSON, E. (1970). *Profession of Medicine*, Dodd, Mead and Company, New York.

GOFFMAN, E. (1968). *Stigma*, Penguin Books, Harmondsworth.

GOFFMAN, E. (1961). *Asylums*, Anchor Books, New York.

KOGAN, M. and BALLE, J. (1972). Decision Making and Organisational Structure in the British Health Service,' in *Health*, Social Sciences Course Team, Open University. Open University Press, Bletchley.

MECHANIC, D. (1968). *Medical Sociology*, Free Press, New York.

ROSENGREN, W. R. and LEFTON, M. (1968). *Hospitals and Patients*, Atherton Press, New York.

SILVERMAN, D. (1970). *The Theory of Organisations*, Heinemann, London.

13

SOCIOLOGY AND THE CARE
OF THE SICK

We have so far attempted to give a general picture of the way that sociologists study certain areas of human behaviour and interaction, and have paid particular attention to areas which may be relevant to medical and paramedical work. Some of these areas, such as an examination of the nursing profession or the sociology of medicine, have a more obvious bearing than such areas as social differences, although an astute reader will be readily aware of the relevance of most of sociology. This section is an attempt to put into more direct focus the way in which sociology can help those who are hospitalized.

HOSPITALS It is an undeniable fact that hospitals and the 'drama' enacted within their walls stirs the popular imagination in a way that very few other institutions manage to do. The evidence for this is found in popular TV 'soap operas' such as Emergency Ward Ten and General Hospital, which are, or were, with us. Books and television programmes about doctors and medical matters in general are still churned out regularly.

More seriously, social scientists, especially in America, have for many years now been examining the way in which hospitals function in the hope that their disciplines might enlighten some of the practices. There is, however, still a considerable gulf between the average GP, nurse or houseman, and the theoretical output of many social scientists, just as there is between advanced medical research and the actual practice of medicine on the 'shop floor'. The problem exists in trying to demonstrate the practical use of sociology to the care of the sick.

CULTURE One of the important contributions of sociology is that it has demonstrated quite clearly that culture is transmitted and learned and that innate characteristics of individuals and groups have been relegated to obscurity. Let us simply take the example of hospital food: once we are aware of how culture is acquired through the process of socialization, we may be less inclined to label a patient as 'fussy' or 'awkward' simply because he or she has been accustomed to different food prior to hospitalization.

In the section on illness and death, and throughout, we have stressed that disease has a social meaning. This has implications both for the degree to which people seek medical advice and also how they interpret the

189

dialogue which they have with the medical staff. Both the patient and the staff have paradigms or models of 'sickness' and 'health' with which they interpret what the other says. The dominant model of most industrialized nations is that 'good health is a desirable end in itself, and this has significant implications for the 'health' consciousness' of the general population, and especially of certain social strata. Preventative procedures such as cervical smear tests are taken advantage of by the general population more than ever before—but again only by certain social classes. Similarly, patients more than ever *expect* adequate and successful medical and nursing care. Nearly three times as many patients are admitted to hospitals for assistance or diagnosis today than 40 years ago, and those who become in-patients tend to stay for a shorter time.

The beliefs that people hold about treatment and illness, although part of their culture, nevertheless is an important determining factor in exactly who they go to seek medical advice. Certain sections of the population may more frequently seek the help of 'health quacks'—herbalists or itinerant healers—than of medical practitioners, and some with distinctive religious beliefs, such as Christian Scientists with their abhorrence of conventional medicine and Jehovah's Witnesses with their blood taboos, may actually militate against medical services.

SOCIAL STRUCTURE   Some hospitals are undeniably better to work in than others. This is because the administration may be different, staff relationships better, and so on. The concept 'social structure' is a convenient way of stating that individuals occupy positions which are structured and patterned. A nurse who is new to a particular hospital is able to function because she is aware of the roles of all the personnel involved from her previous experience. Admittedly there are some aspects that are peculiar to that particular hospital, but on the whole most of the features are generally recognizable, the hospital itself giving certain clues, for example, in the different types of uniform. As we have seen, for a patient to be 'sick' not only bestows a number of privileges upon him but also several obligations such as 'wanting to get well'.

OBSERVATION   Medical and paramedical staff are trained to observe and interpret certain organic behaviour, and perhaps nurses, because of their prolonged contact with in-patients, can often do this better than doctors. A patient always has certain clues which can aid the nurse in her observation, such as occupation, education, marital status, and so on, and it is now more and more realized that often some of these can give valuable insights into the origin and nature of a patient's illness. There are, however, certain mechanisms of selective perception that ensure that what a nurse 'sees' fits in to her stereotypes. If she conceives a patient as unco-operative, she may behave towards him in a certain way which makes him actually so, although he wasn't initially. One of the complaints usually levelled against medical staff is that they treat everyone uniformly. In terms of treatment, attention, and so forth this may be admirable. But people do differ in a great number of ways that require one to modify one's behaviour, so that a university teacher is not chatted to in the same way as a building labourer, or a mother of three children in the same way as a grumpy old bachelor.

COMMUNICATION Not only do we spend a considerable amount of time communicating to one another, but in particular locations such as hospitals it could be very important that there is no failure of the process. One of the reasons why communication can sometimes break down is because we use words which represent different categories of object (like 'good'), we differ in the emotional meanings attached to words, and the words we use may be embedded in different intellectual frameworks. Similarly, communication may be verbal or non-verbal, at the cognitive or affective level, and direct and indirect. Patients are very quick to seize upon facial expressions, for example, or over-endow a seemingly innocent statement with meaning. Communication, or lack of it, in hospitals is the largest source of discontent. Lack of effective communication in the hospital setting is usually due to lack of time on the part of personnel, lack of effective structure for communication, the existence of social distance between patients and nurses and doctors, and so forth. Often, of course, there are real social and educational barriers to effective communication, even given that the medical and paramedical personnel feel a desire to communicate.

PROBLEMS There is no doubt that the nurse offers real comfort to the terminal patient, and it is a situation in which real tact and understanding are required. Difficult patients who do not behave according to the requirements of the institution and do not cooperate with the other patients also present additional worries to the nurse. One of the ways in which an ostensibly theoretical sociology can help is in the concept of 'taking the role of the other'. Here the nurse can utilize a particular social skill, namely identifying with the other's standpoint or taking account of his role. A beneficial exercise for the nurse to undertake would be to ask herself exactly *why* the patient is difficult. Often the patient is described as 'difficult' if he upsets the nurse in some way and as 'good' if he makes the nurse feel that she is doing her job well. When we share the feelings of another an empathetic relationship develops. This is particularly facilitated when we ourselves have experienced what the other is going through.

The study of sociology, as we stated as the beginning of this book, is not specifically *for* anything. Nevertheless, perhaps more than nearly any other subject, it has been utilized in a variety of ways, including the training of personnel in a variety of occupations. It forms an important part, for example, in the training of teachers, not only as an academic subject for 'intellectual enlightenment' but also as part of their professional training. The reason for this is that it is felt a knowledge of society, how it works, and the formation and social interaction of individuals and groups, considerably enhance a teacher's understanding of the children he or she teaches. Even policemen now incorporate some elementary sociology in their training. And more schoolchildren sit Advanced Level Sociology than nearly any other subject.

Many of these patterns new to Britain have had a considerable vogue in America and Canada for some years and were introduced shortly after the Second World War. It is only very recently, in this country, that sociology as a discipline in its own right has been considered as being of some use in the professional training of doctors, nurses, health visitors, social workers, probation and welfare officers, and other 'caring' programmes. It is hoped that in the very near future those responsible for such training programmes will make substantial efforts to incorporate a fully considered sociology scheme.

SUGGESTIONS FOR FURTHER READING

BIRD, B. (1955). *Talking with Patients*, Lippincott, Philadelphia.

BROWN, E. L. (1964). *Newer Dimensions of Patient Care*, Parts I, II, and III, Russell Sage Foundation, New York.

CARTWRIGHT, A. (1964). *Human Relationships and Hospital Care*, Routledge and Kegan Paul, London.

FREEMAN, H. E., LEVINE, S. and REEDER, L. G. (eds.) (1963). *Handbook of Medical Sociology*, Prentice-Hall, Englewood Cliffs, New Jersey.

HALL, E. (1965). *The Silent Language*, Premier Books, Fawcett, Greenwich, Conn.

HUGHES, E. C., HUGHES, H. M. and DEUTSCHER, I. (1958). *Twenty Thousand Nurses Tell their Story*, Lippincott, Philadelphia.

JACO, E. G. (ed.) (1958). *Patients, Physicians and Illness*, Free Press, Glencoe, Illinois.

KING, S. H. (1962). *Perceptions of Illness and Medical Practice*, Russell Sage Foundation, New York.

MAUKSCH, H. and TAGLIACOZZO, D. (1963). *The Patient's View of the Patient's Role*, 2nd ed. Illinois Institute of Technology, Health Research Centre, Chicago.

MACGREGOR, F. C. (1960). *Social Science in Nursing*, Russell Sage Foundation, New York.

MUMFORD, E. and SKIPPER, J. K. (1967). *Sociology in Hospital Care*, Harper and Row, New York.

SKIPPER, J. K. and LEONARD, R. C. (eds.) (1965). *Social Interaction and Patient Care*, Lippincott, Philadelphia.

UJHELY, G. B. (1963). *The Nurse and Her Problem Patients*, Part II, Springer, New York.

14

SOME WELL-KNOWN SOCIOLOGISTS
AND THEIR THEORIES

There are two basic ways in which we can approach sociological theory, namely through the individual *theorists* or through the *schools*. Neither way is entirely satisfactory, but by having a brief look at the two ways we can, perhaps, hope to cover all the important areas.

ECOLOGISM

This is basically the view that our environment, especially the non-human part of it, determines our responses, and that we are organisms that adapt to the habitat. Thus man adjusts to the habitat as part of the process of community development. Although in its modern form it lays some stress on a part of social development other than that dependent on the ecosystem such as man's psychological, spiritual and symbolic nature, this is very much a secondary consideration. Sociologists who may be affiliated with this school include Hawley, Duncan, Schnore and Park.

DEMOGRAPHISM

This encompasses both demographic analysis and population studies. Basically, it holds that social phenomena are influenced (and consequently explained) by the number of participants in them and to the extent to which participants lost, either through death or emigration, are replaced. Thus the density of population along the Nile is said by demographists to have given rise to the emergence of geometrical and mathematical techniques which were necessary to predict the tide levels. Malthus was a well-known demographist because he was concerned that the number of social participants should not rise faster than the available food supply. Simmel argued that a triad (three members of a group) significantly affected each other in a way that a diad (two members of a group) did not. Members of this school include Ryder and Moore.

MATERIALISM

The economic structure of a given society is primary because it first of all satisfies man's physiological needs for food, drink, etc., and secondly creates new physiological and non-physiological needs which are satisfied by the emergence of a legal and political superstructure. Thus the religious ideas of men are seen as cushioning them against social and economic deprivation, and the emergence of Calvinism is seen as a vehicle for the capitalist economic system. A modern version focuses on the external system as the means by which the group survives its environment. Those inclined to this view include Marx, Engels and Homans.

PSYCHOLOGISM

Forms of social behaviour are imposed on culture rather than generated by it, the imposition stemming from the psychological characteristics of participants themselves. A well-known proponent of this is Homans.

TECHNOLOGISM

Material culture or technology accumulates and forces changes in other parts of the culture in such areas as social organization and custom. Another variation is that technology determines the available energy for man which in turn imposes limits on what man can and will do. Ogburn stressed *cultural lag*. More precisely, Ogburn notes that the development of 'adaptive culture' (i.e. nontechnological social phenomena) lags behind technology and can therefore produce 'social maladjustment'. Cottrell stresses technological lead and holds that 'the development of technology precedes the development of other social phenomena and thus facilitates the latter'.

FUNCTIONAL STRUCTURALISM

Social life is carried forward in time, irrespective of the fact that the social content (i.e. humans) are virtually completely renewed every hundred years. How is this possible? As Parsons and others would argue: 'Social life persists because societies find means (structures) whereby they fulfil the needs (functions) which are either pre-conditions or consequences of organised social life.' Talcott Parsons, Radcliffe-Brown, Merton and Davis are all of this school.

EXCHANGE STRUCTURALISM

This tries to explain the social structure as basically an exchange of behaviour between two or more participants. The theory talks in terms such as reward, reciprocity, benefit and costs. Proponents of this view include Blau, Gouldner, Goode, Thibaut and Kelley.

CONFLICT STRUCTURALISM

This is related to exchange structuralism and views the social structure as an exchange of behaviour between two or more participants which involves some injurious behaviour. Supporters of this view include Dahrendorf, Berghe and Coser.

SYMBOLIC INTERACTIONISM

The development of the self in relation to the social process with particular reference to the significant other is the keynote of this view. Human interaction is the process which entails interpretation and understanding and it is an ongoing process. It uses such terms as actor, career, situation and encounter. Includes among its adherents Mead and Blumer.

ETHNOMETHODOLOGY

This is a sub-section of symbolic interactionism. It is concerned with the way in which social order is possible and believes that it is made possible by tacit understandings (usually unutterable and not talked about or noticed) of rules and knowledge. Concerned with the analysis of social order, this school attempts to lay bare the 'deep structures' of social interactions. Its main activators are Garfinkel, Sachs and Sudnow.

SOCIAL ACTIONISM AND FUNCTIONAL IMPERATIVISM

Basically, these stem from a different emphasis on the theories of Talcott Parsons. The first regards the social in terms of subjective behaviour relations. Both the environment and the participants generate social phenomena. The second stressed the imposition of conditions.

CLASSIFICATION OF SOCIOLOGISTS

Very often, according to who is doing the classifying, an important theorist may be placed in more than one category or school both by the same person and by different persons. As an example, we list in Table 14.1 three separate schema which differ from each other.

It can be seen that the same name appears in more than one category and that Inkeles, Wallace and Martindale have nowhere near the same categories.

TABLE 14.1

Inkeles	Wallace	Martindale
(1) *Evolutionary*. Sumner, Durkheim, White, Redfield, Ogburn Sorokin	*Ecologism*. Hawley, Park, Duncan, Schnore	*Positivist organicism*. Ward, Tonnies, Durkheim, Redfield, Pareto, Sorokin, Lundberg
(2) *Organismic structural functionalism*. Radcliffe-Brown, Merton, Malinowski, Parsons	*Functional structuralism*. Parsons, Merton, Davis, Radcliffe-Brown	*Sociological functionalism*. Malinowski, Radcliffe-Brown, Pareto, Merton, Parsons, Homans, Znaniecki
(3) *Equilibrium versus conflict*. Galtung, Coser, Mills, Dahrendorf	*Conflict structuralism*. Dahrendorf, Coser, Berghe	*Conflict theory*. Hobbes, Malthus, Marx, Sumner, Small
(4) *Physical science model*. Lundberg, Dodd Stouffer	*Materialism*. Marx, Engels, Homans	*Formal school*. Simmel, Park, Burgess, Gurvitch
(5) *Statistical–Mathematical*. Bales, Simon	*Psychologism*. Homans	*Social behaviourism*. (a) Social action: Weber, Veblen, Mannheim, Parsons, Merton, Mills;
(6)	*Symbolic interactionism*. Mead, Blumer	(b) Symbolic interactionism: Giddings, Ogburn, Nimkoff, Cooley, Thomas, Mead
(7)	*Demographism*. Ryder, Moore	
(8)	*Technologism*. Ogburn, Cottrell	
(9)	*Exchange structuralism*. Blau, Gouldner, Goode, Thibaut, Kelley	
(10)	*Ethnomethodology*. Garfinkel, Sachs, Sudnow	
(11)	*Social actionism and functional imperativism*. Parsons	

SOME INDIVIDUAL THEORISTS

Adam Ferguson (1723–1816) was one of the first to formulate general propositions about social phenomena.

Saint Simon (1760–1825) was the Father of French Socialism and proposed the scientific reorganization of society.

Auguste Comte (1798–1857) at first Simon's secretary but later a propounder of the Law of the Three Stages. The Father of Positivism (which he later came to dislike) and a social reformer.

Frederic Le Play (1806–82) is chiefly known for his theories on the family and laid the foundations of a sociology of law.

Karl Marx (1818–1883) and *Friedrich Engels* (1820–1903) laid the groundwork for a theory of the development of consciousness for human interaction tempered by economic and industrial forces.

Herbert Spencer (1820–1895) demonstrated the way in which institutional forms of one kind co-existed from society to society while others were seemingly incompatible. Not only are societies systems but their structural variations are patterned and limited.

Charles Booth (1840–1916) and Rowntree prepared the way for a long English tradition of survey work into aspects of poverty.

Vilfredo Pareto (1848–1923) was a positivist who regarded society as a system of forces in equilibrium. Established a theory of residues and derivations which were features of logical and non-logical action.

Emile Durkheim (1858–1917) was instrumental, through his work on suicide and primitive religion, in shaping the whole field of sociological investigation.

Max Weber (1864–1920) was a man of great theoretical and historical study. He developed conceptual tools for the analysis of society.

Arthur Radcliffe-Brown (1881–1955) was basically a social anthropologist but very influential both as a teacher and as a scholar.

Bronislaw Malinowski (1884–1942) was a significant field worker and produced important studies on Trobriand systems of marriage, the family and economics.

Talcott Parsons (1902–   ) is a contemporary structural functionalist and social actionist. He has produced important work on the social system and has been very influential.

A CLOSER LOOK AT SOME CONTEMPORARY SOCIOLOGISTS The very fact that we are human implies, to Erving Goffman, that we use and in turn are used by language. In a sense, he sees man in his day-to-day social interaction as operating very much on the same sort of lines as the con man. Thus we are constantly engaged in a process of managing the social impressions which are given to us by others, impressions such as language, clothes and gestures.

Language is seen as comprising two elements, that of *content* (what we say) and that of *style* (how we say it), and the latter is a vital part of the process of human communication. Another phrase that Goffman gives to the style of language is *symptomatic behaviour*, which serves to validate a performance. Cuzzort presents the argument as shown in Table 14.2.

In this table, the first case is a person who not only knows what he is doing but does it extremely effectively. The second instance is someone who may be very able in knowing about something but ineffective in actually trying to convey this. The third example is that of a phoney, who gives the impression of knowing something but is void of content. The last instance is of someone who neither knows what he is doing nor gives the impression that he does.

TABLE 14.2

Content	Symptomatic behaviour	Audience reaction
(1) positive	positive	A person possessing control over both levels of expression will be highly effective.
(2) positive	negative	Despite content mastery, such a person may lose his audience because of incongruities in his performance.
(3) negative	positive	This person may prove acceptable so long as he can conceal the existing incongruity.
(4) negative	negative	This person will be highly ineffective.

Discussing instances when the dramatization of one's work constitutes a problem, Goffman concludes that medical nursing staff have a problem that surgical staff do not. The surgical nurse is engaged in purposeful activities such as bandaging. No less skilled, the medical nurse often appears to be engaged upon activities, such as stopping to talk to patients, which appear to the patients to be 'wasting time'. That such activities are part of the context of medical nursing and observation cuts no ice with the patients who desire above all some visible and concrete activity.

Goffman is offering a *dramaturgical* model of society which is basically democratic because everyone is manipulated by everyone else. Criminals con and manipulate the police and patients manipulate the hospital staff. Some sociologists such as Alvin Gouldner have accused Goffman of avoiding the problem of social stratification. 'It is a social theory that dwells upon the episodic and sees life only as it is lived in a narrow interpersonal circumference, ahistorical and noninstitutional, an existence beyond history and society, and one which comes alive only in the fluid, transient "encounter".' Nevertheless, Goffman offers very readable accounts of social interaction processes that give us not only the glossy image of the play and the players but also take us behind the scenes on which the play is set.

The traditional view of sociological theorists that man is born into a society which traps him, with the result that man is a victim who is socially constrained or controlled, is elaborated by Peter Berger as follows. Man is contained by the threat of violence, controlled by belief, ridicule, trickery, the threat of ostracism, control of the occupation in which he finds himself, the influence of one's group, and a system of mutual obligation. Man's identity is 'socially bestowed, socially sustained and socially transformed'. He is born into a world which already exists in concrete phenomena and institutions and which is *objective*, but man also interprets and understands these objectifications in a *subjective* manner. There are very strong pressures which exist in society for the purpose of making man conform, presumably because not to conform is socially disruptive. Man consequently believes that he has no alternative other than to conform to institutional directives. Berger describes this in existentialist terms as 'bad faith'. He says that '"bad faith" is to pretend something is necessary that in fact is voluntary. "Bad faith" is thus a flight from freedom, a dishonest evasion of the "agony of choice" . . . The waiter shuffling through his appointed rounds in a café is in "bad faith" insofar as he pretends to himself that the waiter role constitutes his real existence . . .' Freedom, to Berger, is when we play social roles knowingly rather than blindly. And it is bound up with such concepts as social consciousness and choice. He sees sociology as a humanistic discipline which is an antidote to 'bad faith'. 'We see the puppets dancing on their miniature stage, moving up and down as the strings pull them around, following the prescribed course of their various little parts. We learn to understand the logic of this theatre and we find ourselves in its motions. We locate ourselves in society and thus recognise our own position as we hang from its subtle strings. For a moment we see ourselves as puppets indeed. But then we grasp a decisive difference between the puppet theatre and our own drama. Unlike the puppets, we have the possibility of stopping in our movements, looking up and perceiving the machinery by which we have been moved. In this act lies the first step towards freedom.'

SUGGESTIONS FOR FURTHER READING

BERGER, P. (1963). *Invitation to Sociology*, Penguin Books, Harmondsworth.

COHEN, P. (1968). *Modern Social Theory*, Heinemann, London.

CUZZORT, R. P. (1969). *Humanity and Modern Sociological Thought*, Holt, Rinehart and Winston, New York.

GOFFMAN, E. (1969). *The Presentation of the Self in Everyday Life*, Allen Lane, The Penguin Press, London.

GOULDNER, A. W. (1971). *The Coming Crisis of Western Sociology*, Heinemann, London.

MARTINDALE, D. (1967). *The Nature and Types of Sociological Theory*, Routledge and Kegan Paul, London.

RAISON, T. (ed.) (1969). *The Founding Fathers of Social Science*, Penguin Books, Harmondsworth.

WALLACE, W. L. (ed.) (1969). *Sociological Theory*, Heinemann, London.

APPENDIX

It will give you some idea of the broad scope of the subject matter of sociology if you study the table below, which is found on p. 12 of Inkeles, A. (© 1964), *What is Sociology*, Reprinted by permission of Prentice-Hall, Inc. Englewood Cliffs, New Jersey.

A GENERAL OUTLINE OF THE SUBJECT MATTER OF SOCIOLOGY

I. Sociological analysis
    Human culture and society
    Sociological perspective
    Scientific method in social science

II. Primary units of social life
    Social acts and social relationships
    The individual personality
    Groups (including ethnic and class)
    Communities: urban and rural
    Associations and organizations
    Populations
    Society

III. Basic social institutions
    The family and kinship
    Economic
    Political and legal
    Religious
    Educational and scientific
    Recreational and welfare
    Aesthetic and expressive

IV. Fundamental social processes
    Differentiation and stratification
    Cooperation, accommodation, assimilation
    Social conflict (including revolution and war)
    Communication (including opinion formation, expression, and change)
    Socialization and indoctrination
    Social evaluation (the study of values)

Social control
Social deviance (crime, suicide, etc.)
Social integration
Social change

II APPENDIX

The following journals contain articles which would be of interest to those concerned with the use and application of sociology in medicine:

American Journal of Sociology
American Sociological Review
Human Relations
Journal of Health and Social Behaviour
British Journal of Sociology
Sociology
Sociological Review

New Society

BIBLIOGRAPHY

ABEL-SMITH, B. (1964). *The Hospitals: 1890–1948*, Heinemann, London.
ABEL-SMITH, B. (1960). *A History of the Nursing Profession*, Heinemann, London.
ARGYLE, M. (1969). *Social Interaction*, Methuen, London.

BALINT, M. (1957). *The Doctor, His Patient and the Illness*, Pitman Medical Publishing Company, London.
BERGER, P. (1966). *Invitation to Sociology*, Penguin Books, Harmondsworth.
BERNSTEIN, B. (1970). A Sociolinguistic Approach to Socialisation, Gumpertz, J., Hymes, D. Eds. *Directions in Psycholinguistic*, Holt, Rinehart and Winston, New York.
BERTRAND, A. L. (1967). *Basic Sociology*, Appleton Century Crofts, New York.
BIRD, B. (1955). *Talking with Patients*, Lippincott, Philadelphia.
BOTTOMORE, T. B. (1965). *Classes in Modern Society*, George Allen and Unwin, London.
BOWLBY, T. (1957). *Child Care and the Growth of Love*, Penguin Books, Harmondsworth.
BREIDEMEIR, H. C. and STEPHENSON, R. M. (1962). *The Analysis of Social Systems*, Holt, Rinehart and Winston, New York.
BROWN, E. L. (1964). *Newer Dimensions of Patient Care*, Parts I, II and III, Russell Sage Foundation, New York.

CARTWRIGHT, A. (1964). *Human Relationships and Hospital Care*, Routledge and Kegan Paul, London.
CARTWRIGHT, A. (1967). *Patients and their Doctors*, Routledge and Kegan Paul, London.
CHINOY, E. (1967). *Society* (2nd ed.), Random House, New York.
COE, R. M. (1970). *Sociology of Medicine*, McGraw-Hill, New York.
COHEN, P. (1968). *Modern Social Theory*, Heinemann, London.
COHEN, S. (ed.) (1971). *Images of Deviance*, Penguin Books, Harmondsworth.
COHN, N. (1961). *The Pursuit of the Millennium* (2nd ed.), Harper and Row, New York.

203

COSER, L. A. (1963). *Sociology through Literature*, Prentice-Hall, Englewood Cliffs, New Jersey.

COTGROVE, S. (1972). *The Science of Society*, George Allen and Unwin, London.

CUZZORT, R. P. (1969). *Humanity and Modern Sociological Thought*, Holt, Rinehart and Winston, New York.

DAVIS, F. (ed.) (1966). *The Nursing Profession*, John Wiley, New York.

DOMINIAN, J. (1968). *Marital Breakdown*, Penguin Books, Harmondsworth.

EARICKSON, R. (1970). *The Spatial Behaviour of Hospital Patients*, University of Chicago, Department of Geography, Chicago.

EMERSON, J. P. (1970). 'Behaviour in Public Places: Sustaining Definitions of Reality, in Gynecological Examinations, Dreitzel, H. P. (ed.), *Recent Sociology No. 2*, Collier Macmillan, New York.

FLETCHER, R. (1966). *The Family and Marriage in Britain*, Penguin Books, Harmondsworth.

FRANKENBURG, R. (1966). *Communities in Britain*, Penguin Books, Harmondsworth.

FREEMAN, H. E., LEVINE, S. and REEDER, L. G. (eds.) (1963). *Handbook of Medical Sociology*, Prentice-Hall, Englewood Cliffs, New Jersey.

FREIDSON. E. (ed) (1963). *The Hospital in Modern Society*, Free Press, New York.

FREIDSON, E. (1970). *Profession of Medicine*, Dodd, Mead and Company, New York.

GAGNON, J. H. (ed.) (1967). *Sexual Deviance*, Harper and Row, New York.

GLASER, B. G. and STRAUSS, A. L. (1965). *Awareness of Dying*, Aldine Publishing Co., Chicago.

GLASER, B. G. and STRAUSS, A. L. (1968). *Time for Dying*, Aldine Publishing Co., Chicago.

GLASER, W. A. (1970). *Social Settings and Medical Organisation*, Atherton Press, New York.

GOFFMAN, E. (1969). *The Presentation of the Self in Everyday Life*, Allen Lane, The Penguin Press, London.

GOFFMAN, E. (1968). *Stigma*, Penguin Books, Harmondsworth.

GOFFMAN, E. (1961). *Asylums*, Anchor Books, New York.

GOODE, W. J. (1964). *The Family*, Prentice-Hall, Englewood Cliffs, New Jersey.

GOODE, W. J. (1960). 'Encroachment, Charlatanism, and the Emerging Profession: Psychology, Medicine and Sociology', *American Sociological Review*, 25, 902–914.

GOULDNER, A. W. (1971). *The Coming Crisis of Western Sociology*, Heinemann, London.

GREEN, R. W. (ed.) (1959). *Protestantism and Capitalism*, D. C. Heath and Company, Boston.

GUSTAFSON, E. (1972). 'Dying: the Career of the Nursing Home Patient', *Journal of Health and Social Behaviour*, 13, 226–235.

HALL, E. (1965). *The Silent Language*, Premier Books, Fawcett, Greenwich, Conn.

HILL, M. (1973). *A Sociology of Religion*, Heinemann, London.

HUDSON, L. (ed.) (1970). *The Ecology of Human Intelligence*, Penguin Books, Harmondsworth.

HUGHES, E. C., HUGHES, H. M. and DEUTSCHER, I. (1958). *Twenty Thousand Nurses Tell Their Story*, Lippincott, Philadelphia.

HUGHES, H. M. (ed.) (1970). *Delinquents and Criminals: their Social World*, Allyn and Bacon, Boston.

INKELES, A. (1964). *What is Sociology?* Prentice-Hall, Englewood Cliffs, New Jersey.

JACO, E. G. (ed.) (1958). *Patients, Physicians and Illness*, Free Press, New York.

JAHODA, M. and WARREN, N. (eds.) (1966). *Attitudes*, Penguin Books, Harmondsworth.

KELSALL, R. K. (1967). *Population*, Longmans, London.

KELVIN, P. (1970). *The Bases of Social Behaviour*, Holt, Rinehart and Winston, London.

KESSELL, N., WALTON, H. (1967). *Alcoholism*, Penguin Books, Harmondsworth.

KING, S. H. (1962). *Perceptions of Illness and Medical Practice*, Russell Sage Foundation, New York.

KLEIN, J. (1965). *Samples from English Cultures*, Routledge and Kegan Paul, London.

KLEIN, J. (1967). *The Study of Groups*, Routledge and Kegan Paul, London.

KOGAN, M. and BALLE, J. (1972). 'Decision Making and Organisational Structure in the British Health Service', in *Health*, Open University Press, Bletchley.

LAING, R. D. and ESTERSON, A. (1964). *Sanity, Madness and the Family*, Tavistock, London.

LASLETT, P. (1965). *The World We Have Lost*, Methuen, London.

LAURIE, P. (1967). *Drugs: Medical, Psychological and Social Facts*, Penguin Books, Harmondsworth.

LEFTON, M., SKIPPER, J. K. and McCAGHY, C. H. (eds.) (1968). *Approaches to Deviance*, Appleton Century Crofts, New York.
LUNDBERG, G. A., SCHRAG, C. C. and LARSEN, O. N. (1963). *Sociology* (3rd ed.), Harper and Row, New York.

McDAVID, J. W. and HARARI, H. (1968). *Social Psychology*, Harper and Row, New York.
MACGREGOR, F. C. (1960). *Social Science in Nursing*, Russell Sage Foundation, New York.
McKEOWN, T. and LOWE, C. R. (1966). *Introduction to Social Medicine*, Blackwell, Oxford.
MACQUEEN, I. (1960). *Home Accidents in Aberdeen*, E. and S. Livingstone, Edinburgh.
MACQUIRE, J. (1969). *Threshold to Nursing*, Bell and Sons, London.
MARTINDALE, D. (1967). *The Nature and Types of Sociological Theory*, Routledge and Kegan Paul, London.
MAUKSCH, H. and TAGLIACOZZE, D. (1963). *The Patient's View of the Patient's Role* (2nd ed.), Illinois Institute of Technology, Health Research Centre, Chicago.
MEAD, M. (1935). *Sex and Temperament in Three Primitive Societies*, Routledge, London.
MECHANIC, D. (1968). *Medical Sociology*, Free Press, New York.
MENZIES, I. E. B. (1961). 'The Functioning of Social Systems as a Defence *Against Anxieties*, Tavistock Pamphlet No. 3, London.
MILLS, C. W. (1970). *The Sociological Imagination*, Penguin Books, Harmondsworth.
MUMFORD, E. and SKIPPER, J. K. (1967). *Sociology in Hospital Care*, Harper and Row, New York.

NEWSOM, J. and NEWSOM, E. (1965). *Patterns of Infant Care in an Urban Community*, Penguin Books, Harmondsworth.

O'DEA, T. (1966). *The Sociology of Religion*, Prentice-Hall, Englewood Cliffs, New Jersey.
OFFICE OF HEALTH ECONOMICS (1967). No. 25, *Drug Addiction*, London.
OFFICE OF HEALTH ECONOMICS, ed. McKenzie, J. (1968). *The Consumer and the Health Service*, London.
OFFICE OF HEALTH ECONOMICS (1968). No. 27, *Without Prescription*, London.
OFFICE OF HEALTH ECONOMICS (1970). No. 34, *Alcohol Abuse*, London.
OLESON, V. L. and WHITTAKER, E. W. (1968). *The Silent Dialogue*, Josey-Bass, San Francisco.

PARSONS, T. (1951). *The Social System*, Free Press, New York.
PITTMAN, D. (ed.) (1967). *Alcoholism*, Harper and Row, New York.

QUINT, J. (1967). *The Nurse and the Dying Patient*, Macmillan, New York.

ROSE, A. M. (ed.) (1962). *Human Behaviour and Social Processes*, Routledge and Kegan Paul, London.

ROTH, J. A. (1963). *Timetables*, Bobbs-Merrill, Indianapolis.

RUBINGTON, E. and WEINBERG, M. S. (1968). *Deviance: the Interactionist Perspective*, Macmillan, New York.

RUBINGTON, E. and WEINBERG, M. S. (1971). *The Study of Social Problems*, Oxford University Press, New York.

RUNCIMAN, S. (1966). *Relative Deprivation and Social Justice*, Routledge and Kegan Paul, London.

SAINSBURY, P. (1955). *Suicide in London*, Maudsley Monographs, Institute of Psychiatry, London.

SCHEFF, T. J. (1967). *Mental Illnesses and Social Processes*, Harper and Row, New York.

SILMAN, R. (1962). 'Teaching the Medical Student to Become a Doctor', in Pateman, T. (ed.), Counter Course, Penguin Books, Harmondsworth.

SILVERMAN, D. (1970). *The Theory of Organisations*, Heinemann, London.

SKIPPER, J. K., LEONARD, R. C. (eds.) (1965). *Social Interaction and Patient Care*, Lippincott, Philadelphia.

SPITZER, S. P., DENZIN, N. K. (eds.) (1968). *The Mental Patient*, Harper and Row, New York.

STENGEL, E. (1964). *Suicide and Attempted Suicide*, Penguin Books, Harmondsworth.

STORR, A. (1964). *Sexual Deviation*, Penguin Books, Harmondsworth.

SUDNOW, D. (1967). *Passing On: The Social Organisation of Dying*, Prentice-Hall, Englewood Cliffs, New Jersey.

SWIFT, D. F. (1969). *The Sociology of Education*, Routledge and Kegan Paul, London.

SZASZ, T. (1972). *The Myth of Mental Illness*, Paladin, London.

TAYLOR, I., WALTON, P. and YOUNG, J. (1972). *The New Criminology*, Routledge and Kegan Paul, London.

TAYLOR, L. (1973). *Deviance and Society*, Nelson, London.

THOMPSON, K. and JONES, R. K. (1972). 'Religion, Stratification and Deprivation', *Beliefs and Religion*, Open University Press, Bletchley.

VAZ, E. (ed.) (1967). *Middle Class Juvenile Delinquency*, Harper and Row, New York.

WALLACE, W. L. (ed.) (1969). *Sociological Theory*, Heinemann, London.

WALLIS, R. (ed.) (1975). *Sectarianism: Analyses of Religious and Non-Religious Sects*, Peter Owen, London.

WILSON, B. R. (1966). *Religion in Secular Society*, C. A. Watts, London.

WILSON, B. R. (1970). *Religious Sects*, Weidenfeld and Nicolson, London.

WORSLEY, P. (1968). *The Trumpet Shall Sound*, MacGibbon and Kee, London.

WORSLEY, P. (ed.) (1970). *Introducing Sociology*, Penguin Books, Harmondsworth.

WORSLEY, P. (ed.) (1970). *Modern Sociology*, Penguin Books, Harmondsworth.

YOUNG, M. and WILMOTT, P. (1957). *Family and Kinship in East London*, Routledge and Kegan Paul, London.

GLOSSARY

ACCULTURATION The process of acquiring another's cultural characteristics.

ACHIEVED STATUS A social position obtained by effort rather than birthright.

ALIENATION Estrangement from certain social conditions.

ANOMIE (ANOMY). A lack of clear, unambiguous and integrated norms.

AREA SAMPLING Collecting of information from an area.

ASCRIBED STATUS A social position obtained by birthright rather than effort.

ATTITUDE A learned disposition or propensity to a person or object or group.

AUTHORITY The legitimate power to alter the actions of others in some way, on rational, traditional or charismatic grounds.

AUTOKINETIC Movement or shift in judgement affected by external stimuli.

BILATERAL The transmission of property or descent through male *and* female.

BILOCAL Living near the residence of either spouse's parents.

BUREAUCRACY (a) red tape; (b) an ideal type of administrative organization; (c) Weber's set of structural characteristics.

CAREER Any strand of any person's course through life, either shared or individual.

CASTE A closed social-mobility system based on religious dogmas.

CHARACTER (TRAIT) The specific and predictable reaction to something.

CHURCH A dominant, inherited and universal community.

CLASS See *social stratification*.

CLASS CONSCIOUSNESS Originally a stage in capitalism in which the workers become aware of their class position in relation to the bourgeoisie, loosely used as self-awareness.

COGNITIVE DISSONANCE The intellectual rationalization of what might be unpleasant, e.g. 'cancer statistics can prove anything'.

COMMUNITY A shared way of life located in a defined geographical area carried out by a population.

CONCENTRIC ZONE   Distinct area emanating from a city centre to the suburbs.

CONCEPT   A notion or idea at a lower abstract level than a theory.

CONFLICT (SOCIAL)   A relationship which is intended to damage in some way, usually between individuals, groups or nations.

CONJUGAL   Of the family form that emphasizes the spouses and their mutual obligations.

CONSANGUINE   Of the family structure that emphasizes the kin.

CORRELATION   A relationship between two or more variables.

CULTURE   Socially acquired and transmitted beliefs and conduct, tastes and values.

CULTURE CONFLICT   A state of antagonism between two or more cultural fields.

CULTURE LAG   The different rates of cultural change of various elements, and the subsequent lack of total integration.

CULTURE SHOCK   The exposure of an inferior culture to a superior or vitally different one.

DEFINITION OF THE SITUATION   The persception, interpretation or meaning given by an actor to a social situation in which he finds h:mself.

DELINQUENCY   Minor criminal activity.

DEMOGRAPHY   The scientific study of human populations in relation to size, structure and development.

DEVIATION   Behaviour falling outside the tolerated limits established by social custom, the legal system, or other social proscriptions.

DIVISION OF LABOUR   The division of a work process into a number of parts, each part of which is done by a separate individual or group.

ECOLOGY   A study of the spatial distributions of human populations, their behaviour and their physical habitat.

EMBOURGOISEMENT   The theory that all social classes are in the process of levelling out.

EMPIRICAL   Information about the world gained through the physical senses and not necessarily true.

ENDOGAMY   Marrying within a defined group.

EXOGAMY. Marrying outside a defined group.

EXTENDED FAMILY   A married pair and their children and in addition one or more persons related by direct descent.

FALSE CONSCIOUSNESS   The assumption that a state exists which does not.

FUNCTION   A consequence, anticipated or necessary, or an integral aspect of something.

GEMEINSCHAFT(LICHTEN)   An ideal type system of close, community-like social relationship.

GENERALIZED OTHER The set of conceptions held by an individual relating to the socially significant attitudes, expectations and beliefs of those with whom he interacts.

GESELLSCHAFT(LICHTEN) An ideal type of system rational, association-like social relationships.

GROUP Two or more persons linked by some affective characteristic forms a social group, compared with a category or aggregate, who are linked by some common feature such as 'red hair'.

GROUP (PRIMARY) A small, face-to-face association which is unspecialized.

GROUP (SECONDARY) A large collection of individuals with weak ties on the affective level.

HOMOSEXUALITY Sexual behaviour to the point of orgasm between members of the same sex.

HORIZONTAL MOBILITY A change of status and role, particularly in occupation, without a change in social class position.

IDEAL TYPE An abstraction not found in any particular example but to which particular instances refer.

IDENTITY The emotional merging of a person with others, with social roles and with social groups.

IDEOLOGY A pattern of concepts and beliefs which are total explanations of complex social phenomena although not necessarily true.

IMITATION A conscious or unconscious attempt to reproduce the same state as found in another.

INSTITUTION (SOCIAL) Distinctive modes of interaction centred on large and important areas of social concern such as education and the family.

INTERNALIZATION Unconscious learning of symbols and roles.

LABELLING The process by which individuals and groups classify and categorize social behaviour and other individuals.

LEVIRATE The custom of marrying the widow of the elder brother.

LIFE CHANCES Access to the supply of goods, external living conditions and personal life experiences.

LIFE STYLE Generally economic commodities, but sometimes a way of behaving, that accompanies a vertical mobility in the social stratification process.

MATERNAL DEPRIVATION Lack of access to a mother or mother surrogate.

MATRILINEAL The tracing of descent from a common ancestor through women only.

MATRILOCAL Residence near the female spouse's family.

MEANING The significance of an event or action sustained or interpreted.

MOBILITY (SOCIAL) Movement up or down or across the stratification system.

MODEL   A simpler system or conceptual framework capable of being applied to a more complex area.

MONOGAMY   The exclusive union of one man to one woman at one time.

MORBIDITY   The incidence of illness or disability in a population.

NATIVISTIC   A reaffirmation of native tribal culture in reaction to the stress of acculturation.

NEIGHBOURHOOD.   The inhabitants of a small inhabited area exhibiting friendly relations.

NEOLOCAL   Residence independent of the families of either spouse.

NON-VERBAL COMMUNICATION   Communication by shrugs, nods, winks, smiles, eye movements, etc. which often accompany but can be independent of verbal interaction.

NUCLEAR   A small family unit consisting of husband and wife and children under one residence.

OCCUPATION   Employment, business or calling.

OPINION   A view or belief held by an individual on some issue.

ORGANIZATION (SOCIAL)   The interdependence of parts (or sometimes the whole unit under study) such as the social organization of the modern hospital.

PATRILINEAL   The tracing of the lineage through the male.

PATRILOCAL   Residence near the male spouse's family.

PATTERN-VARIABLES   Dichotomies or polar extremes used to identify similarities and differences in cultures.

PEER GROUP   A group or association comprised of members of one's own age.

POLYANDRY   The marriage of one woman to two or more men.

POLYGAMY   Marriage between a member of one sex and two or more members of the opposite sex.

POLYGYNY   The marriage of one man to two or more women.

POWER   The ability to alter a course of action or influence an outcome.

PRESSURE GROUP   A pressure or interest group is a group of persons sharing attitudes or goals who intend to obtain certain decisions.

PRESTIGE   The high or low influence exercised by groups or individuals or institutions and the comparative high or low standing enjoyed by them.

PRIMARY SOCIALIZATION   The initial learning process within a culture and a family.

PROFESSION   Occupations demanding highly specialized knowledge and skills and exercising autonomy.

RATIONALIZATION   Making something intelligible in accordance with certain procedures and in relation to certain goals, and the results of such activity.

REFERENCE GROUP   A group with which an individual aspires and to which he identifies and from which he derives his norms and attitudes and values.

REIFICATION   The process of endowing inanimate objects with life, for example 'the worship of money'.

REINFORCEMENT   The increase in the strength of a state by repetition of the original stimulus which brought that state about.

RELATIVE DEPRIVATION   Deprivation, either material or spiritual, measured against that of other individuals or groups occupying a near similar position.

RELIGION   Systems of beliefs, practices and organizations generally directed at some supernatural power.

ROLE-SET   Complimentary roles that generally cluster together.

SECONDARY SOCIALIZATION   Learning by contact with individuals or groups which takes place after early childhood. Sometimes called Adult Socialization.

SECT   Small and exclusive voluntary organization that stands in contrast to a church.

SECULARIZATION   The process in which religious influence and considerations retreat from the major areas of activity.

SELF   The factor which integrates the various states of the individual and which is predominantly social.

SELF-FULFILLING PROPHECIES   A consistent attitude and behaviour towards some individual or group which creates what was felt to be there but in fact was absent.

SIGNIFICANT OTHER   A group, but generally a person, taken as a significant reference in the formation of attitudes, beliefs and policies of social action.

SOCIAL ACTION   An action based on a social attitude which is conscious or intentional.

SOCIAL FACT   Ways of acting and thinking external to the individual.

SOCIAL INTERACTION   Reciprocal action between persons and groups, usually through communication.

SOCIAL NORMS   A standard shared by members of a social group to which individuals conform.

SOCIAL ROLE   A named social position which is a dynamic aspect of status.

SOCIAL STRUCTURE   Social regularity or pattern.

SOCIAL SYSTEM   The system arising from the interaction of a number of actors who behave to each other according to a shared set of structured definitions.

SOCIALIZATION   The process by which a culture is learned.

SOCIETY   The totality of social relationships between people.

SOCIOLOGY   The scientific study of social behaviour.

SOCIOMETRY   A way of measuring preferences and dislikes in the choice of companions.

STATUS (PASSAGE) A social position or a collection of rights and duties, and the moves in and out of one social position to another during the course of a career.

STRATIFICATION The position occupied by a family, person or kinship group in a social system relative to others in a system of stratified ranking according to prestige, power and property.

SUB-CULTURE A sub-division of a national culture reflecting a regional, class or religious characteristic.

THEORY A statement or proposition which is true or false and which directs attention towards a set of relationships which may exist between phenomena. Thereby facilitating an empirical explanation.

TOTAL INSTITUTION A setting such as a mental hospital or army in which most of the daily lives of individuals takes place.

TYPOLOGY A classification usually related to a hypothesis which it tests.

UNILINEAL Descent through either the mother or father's family.

VALUE-FREE The value commitments of the social scientist should not intrude on the social data.

VALUE-ORIENTATION A typology or schema of basic approaches to major problems such as 'mastery over nature'.

VERSTEHEN The understanding of human behaviour by direct observation of the subjective meaning of a given action.

VERTICAL MOBILITY Movement upwards or downwards involving a change in social class position.

SUGGESTIONS FOR FURTHER REFERENCE

GOULD, J. and KOLB, W. L. (eds.) (1964). *A Dictionary of the Social Sciences*, Tavistock Press, London.

MITCHELL, G. D. (ed.) (1968). *A Dictionary of Sociology*, Routledge and Kegan Paul, London.

WEEKS, D. R. (1972). *A Glossary of Sociological Concepts*, Open University Press, Bletchley.

INDEX OF SUBJECTS

INDEX OF NAMES AND PLACES